W9-BAU-031

THE UNDERGROUND RAILROAD IN CONNECTICUT

The Underground Railroad in Connecticut

By HORATIO T. STROTHER

Wesleyan University Press: MIDDLETOWN, CONNECTICUT

LIBRARY OF CONGRESS CATALOG CARD NUMBER: 62–15122
MANUFACTURED IN THE UNITED STATES OF AMERICA
FIRST EDITION

TO THE MEMORY OF

David Louis

MY SON

CONTENTS

ILLUSTRATIONS

PREFACE

It has been said that we shall never know the events of the past as they actually occurred. And it is true that the historian, writing from a position more or less distant in time and viewpoint from the happenings that concern him, can hardly know his materials as his more or less distant forebears knew them. Nonetheless he must do his best, bearing in mind a maxim of Ralph Waldo Emerson: "Speak your latent conviction, and it shall be the universal sense." Such is the task of the historian in resurrecting and presenting the missing links of the Underground Railroad.

Even at the height of its operations, the work of this "railroad" in Connecticut was shrouded in obscurity; and so it has remained. Detailed contemporary records have not survived; indeed they can hardly have existed, for the entire movement arose, flourished, and came to its end as an extralegal and even a downright illegal enterprise. A few of its passengers and operators wrote some of what they remembered, then or later, in the form of memoirs, diaries, or letters that are still in existence. Contemporary newspapers and periodicals supply some data, often less explicit than one could wish. Family and local legend, passed verbally down through the generations since the era before the Civil War, add a modicum of information and an understanding of contemporary viewpoints.

For leads of these sorts, for many facts and recollections, the writer is indebted to a great number of kind people, who labored conscientiously to help him gather information. It would be impossible to name them all here. But a special word of thanks must be tendered to Wilbur H. Siebert, of Ohio State University; the material he furnished has given this book its heart. To Cedric L. Robinson, Roderick B. Jones, Mrs. Mabel A. Newell, Mrs. Stowell Rounds, Beaufort R. L. Newsom, Mrs. Alfred H. Terry, Mrs. Charles Perkins, Mrs. Harold S. Burr, Mrs. Warren N. Drum, Miss Felicie Terry, Mrs. Lillian L. Clarke, Mrs. Alice Weaver, Henry Sill Baldwin, Benjamin L. Douglas, Mrs. Louise Kingsley, Miss Fedora Ferraresso, Mrs. Madeline Edgerton, and Miss Virginia Skinner, who helped the writer gather the fruits of research, goes his deepest gratitude.

He is indebted, too, to many hard workers at the Yale University Library, the Connecticut State Library, the Springfield City Library, and the Schomburg Library in New York City—and especially to Miss Gertrude M. McKenna of the Olin Library, Wesleyan University. Their generous cooperation has made his researches much easier and more profitable. The staff of Wesleyan University Press, by their encouragement and detailed cooperation, did much to bring this work to its final shape. The Connecticut Historical Society was a fruitful source of illustrations.

For their wise encouragement and valued suggestions, the writer is most thankful to Peter Schroeder and to Albert E. Van Dusen, of the University of Connecticut. And finally, to his wife Joanne, without whose constant support this work could not have been completed, goes his highest regard.

—Horatio T. Strother

Higganum, Connecticut
January 1962

THE UNDERGROUND RAILROAD IN CONNECTICUT

INTRODUCTION

News traveled slowly in 1831, but few newspapers in the United States failed to report with all possible speed that a bloody slave insurrection, led by Nat Turner, had broken out in Southampton County, Virginia. This dramatic attack against the South's "peculiar institution" proved in the end to be fruitless. The uprising was put down by armed force, Turner was captured and executed, and scores of Negroes—many of whom had taken no part in the revolt—were murdered in savage retaliation. But "nearly sixty whites" had died in the initial outbreak, and a wave of terror swept through every slave-holding state. Months earlier, in Boston, the first appearance of William Lloyd Garrison's antislavery newspaper *The Liberator* had made the South—and the nation—aware that the entire institution of slavery was coming under unremitting attack from zealous abolitionists in the North, although how effective that attack would be was as yet unclear. Turner's rebellion was an attack of a different and more terrifying kind. It was too close to home, too immediate a threat to the prosperity of King Cotton and Prince Sugar, too dangerous to life itself, to be forgotten when it was over.

The Southern master knew that he could not rest content with the capture of Turner and his accomplices, and that merely "a harsher and more vigilant discipline" over the slaves could not assure the continued acceptance of slavery as an institution. Something more was needed, some moral principle that would justify slavery forever, in the eyes of all men. That something Professor Thomas Dew attempted to supply in a declaration before the Virginia legislature in that same crucial year: slavery was "not only God's commanded order, not only the most humane order, but also the most natural order." This idea, it has been said, "proceeded to envisage the South as on its way to becoming a rigid caste society." [1]

Whether slavery was a civilizing influence or a cause of degradation to masters and chattels alike is not a question today. But in the middle decades of the nineteenth century there were violent partisans on both sides, and no meeting of minds was possible between them. It would have been sheer folly for extreme abolitionists like Garrison or Wendell Phillips to argue the point with such convinced advocates of slavery as John C. Calhoun or Robert B. Rhett. It is safe to say, at the outset, that men like these embittered the sectional conflict that culminated in the Civil War.

For by 1831 the ideological struggle over slavery was well under way; and at the same time, in all the states from the Midwest to New England, abolitionists and humanitarians were developing a chain of escape routes and hiding places for runaway slaves fleeing the South. Only a few ordinary citizens had even a glimpse of this activity; those engaged in it, in the main, knew little more than the stations and byways in their own vicinity; even the fugitives who escaped through these clandestine channels became familiar with only the pathways and the resting places through which they themselves moved. Yet most people, North and South, were aware that, despite the heavy legal and social penalties for assisting runaway slaves, there existed a widespread, loosely knit network of hideouts and secret routes of escape; and that these were known collectively as the Underground Railroad.[2]

That name, it is said, was first applied to the system in 1831, the year of Turner's death and *The Liberator's* birth. A slave named Tice Davids escaped from his owner in Ripley, Ohio, and immediately disappeared. The master searched the vicinity as thoroughly as he could but found no trace of his runaway bondsman. At length he concluded ruefully, "He must have gotten away by an underground road." From "road" to "railroad" was a simple transition, especially in that time when the newly established steam railroads were a nine days' wonder. Besides, the terminology of railroading afforded easy names with which to mask a range of activities that lay outside the law. So the Underground Railroad—more the "name of a mode of operation than the name of a corporation"—had its "conductors" and "passengers," its "stations" and "station-keepers"; but they, like its "tracks" and "trains," were concealed from public view. They had to be; it was the only way to be safe.[3]

The system, of course, had had its origins long before 1831. There had been bondsmen in the colonies since the earliest days; and where there were bondsmen, there were those who sought freedom in escape. Colonial laws dating from the 1640's are witness to this fact, and the records for the next 150 years are dotted with instances that substantiate it. To what extent these fugitives received outside help in their flight to freedom is unknown, but it appears that by the 1780's sentiment in favor of the runaways had become fairly widespread, and that there were people prepared to help them. In two letters written in 1786, George Washington spoke of a runaway slave who had reached Philadelphia, "whom a society of Quakers in the city, formed for such purposes, have attempted to liberate";

and again, of the "numbers who would rather facilitate the escape of slaves than apprehend them when runaways." By that time the subject of escaped bondsmen was sufficiently important to engage the attention of Congress, which passed the first Fugitive Slave Law in 1793. And it is known that underground activities of a more or less planned sort were taking place in Philadelphia and its vicinity by the first decade of the nineteenth century, where Isaac T. Hopper was a leader in the work.[4]

It is not the purpose of this study to treat the Underground Railroad as a whole. But it may be said in general terms that the Railroad had no formal, over-all organization at any time. It consisted rather of a loosely knit plexus of individual centers, where a man or a family or a small group stood ready to receive such fugitives as might be sent them, to feed them and hide them as long as necessary, and then to send or conduct them along a line of escape. Each stationkeeper, as a rule, knew no more of the over-all pattern than fell within his immediate range of activities. He knew that he might receive passengers from any one of several stations below his on the road from slavery; he knew that he might forward them to any one of several other stations farther along the road to freedom. How long he entertained a passenger at his own station, and which one he selected as the passenger's next stop, depended on local circumstances of the moment—the state of the roads and the weather, the known or suspected presence of slave-hunters in the area, and so on. The decision was the Undergrounder's own.

In carrying out his work, he made use of all the courage and discretion he possessed and all the means he commanded or could invent. As stationkeeper, he might hide his charges in a secret place in his house, a barn, or even a cave in the woods or a hole in the ground. He might act further as a forwarding agent, letting his passengers travel by themselves according to his directions or turning them over to a conductor. He might himself be the conductor, taking the runaways with him to the next stop—on foot, in a carriage in the guise of servants, or under the cargo in a wagon. Hay wagons were widely used for this purpose, and travel over highways was generally done under cover of darkness; but there was no one universal procedure. Indeed there were places and times when the Underground Railroad was quite literally a railroad. Many a fugitive was simply put aboard the steam cars, with money to pay the fare, where under the eye of a sympathetic trainman he might travel for many miles by the most rapid means then available. Many others made at least part of their journey by water, on ocean-going vessels, river steamers, or humble canal boats. Any form of transport that went north and was reasonably safe could be used; and all were used, here or there, as circumstances made possible or expedient.

The men and women who engaged in this demanding and hazardous work came from all walks of life—farmers, shopkeepers, artisans, teachers, physicians and lawyers, businessmen of every sort. Many were ministers; many more were escaped slaves who had found precarious refuge in the North. Some, perhaps a majority, were convinced and active abolitionists; others seem to have been impelled to the cause in the first instance by more purely religious or humanitarian motives. Their total number, in any given year or over a span of decades, remains unknown, but they were certainly to be counted in the thousands. Few of them had any knowledge of the system beyond their own circumscribed orbits, but here and there a man or woman emerged whose activities spanned the country.

Such a one was Levi Coffin of Ohio, who was reputed to

have helped more than three thousand fugitives and who in time came to be known as "president of the Underground Railroad." Another was the Reverend Samuel J. May, whose range of activity at different times included eastern Connecticut, Boston, and Central New York. Two others of national prominence, both in the Underground Railroad and in the abolitionist cause, were the escaped slaves Frederick Douglass and the famous Harriet Tubman.

But these were the exceptions. The average Undergrounder performed his unpaid and demanding task in secrecy, in danger, and—except for the handful of neighboring co-workers with whom he was in contact—in solitude.

The system these dedicated people constructed was a slow growth, but by the 1850's it had reached virtually nation-wide proportions. Its stations and routes extended through all the free states from the cornfields of Kansas to the rocky harbors of New England, with tenuous fingers stretching into the stronghold of slavery itself—the South. Its terminals lay scattered along the line of the Great Lakes and the country's northern border, beyond which lay the one real refuge, the one region that put an end to all fear of re-enslavement—Canada.

For runaways who sought permanent freedom, it had always been Canada. As early as 1705, when the French flag flew beyond the St. Lawrence, escaped slaves had fled there from Albany. Under English law, which came to Canada in 1763, slavery was permitted. But the American Revolution soon followed; in Canadian eyes the United States became an enemy country, and enemy property would not readily be returned. Within twenty years thereafter slavery was ended in Canada by a series of court decisions, holding that the air of this British land was "too pure for a slave to breathe." [5]

This made Canada more than ever the refugees' goal, and before the War of 1812 reached its inconclusive end, the words "Canada" and "freedom" were used interchangeably by slaves in all the shanties and quarters in the South. Men who knew what it was to be flogged by merciless masters, women who lived in fear of having their chastity stolen by lecherous overseers, mothers and fathers who dreaded the day when they would be torn from their families and "sold down the river" to the rich new cotton lands of the Mississippi Delta and East Texas, came to know that the way north was the way to freedom. Follow the Drinking Gourd, they said, follow the North Star; up there were people who would see you got safely across the border. Every month the number who made a break for freedom grew larger, until by the time of the Civil War it has been estimated that anywhere from 25,000 to 100,000 fugitive slaves had escaped from bondage.[6] The whole story of those who safely crossed the Mason-Dixon line will not be told here—perhaps it will never be fully known—but in this study it is proposed to examine in detail what happened in a single Northeastern state.

CHAPTER 1

BLAZING THE TRAIL

THERE had always been runaway bondsmen in Connecticut. In 1643, just four years after the first slave set foot on the colony's soil, the Articles of Confederation between the United Colonies of New England—Massachusetts, New Plymouth, Connecticut, and New Haven—provided that "if any servant run away from his master into any of these confederated jurisdictions, that, in such case, upon certificate of one magistrate in the jurisdiction of which the said servant fled, or upon other due proof, the said servant shall be delivered, either to his master or any other, that pursues and brings such certificate of proof." [1] Such was Connecticut's first fugitive slave law—although the runaways to whom it referred were likely to be white indentured servants or apprentices rather than Negro slaves, who in 1643 were a mere handful.

In 1680 the number of slaves was still only thirty. And in the very next year, one of these became Connecticut's first known runaway Negro. This was a certain Jack, property of Sam Wolcott of Wethersfield. He was said to be a shiftless slave, his master a merciless man. One day in June, 1681, this unpleasant relationship ended; Jack ran off and set out on a journey northward. Along the way he managed to steal a gun, but it had no flint and he abandoned it in a woodland. Eventually he reached Springfield,

Massachusetts, where his journey ended on the first of July:

> Anthony Dorcester saith that today about noone this Negroe came to his house & after asking for a pipe of Tobacco, I told him there was some on the table, he tooke my knife & cut some & then put it in his pocket & after he tooke down a cutlass & offered to draw it but it coming out I closed in upon him & so Bound him with the help of my wife & daughter when he scrambling in his Pocket I suspected he might have a knife & searching found my knife naked in his Pocket which he would faine have got out but I prevented him & tooke it away. . . . I committed the Negroe to Prison there to remain & be safely secured till discharged by Authority.[2]

Jack apparently set an example that others were ready to follow, for a law of 1690 provided that no Negro servant was to be ferried across any stream unless he had a certificate.[3] It is obvious that even at this early date fugitives were becoming a problem; and at least some of them were finding friends among Connecticut's respectable citizens. In 1702 a mulatto slave named Abda fled from his owner, Captain Thomas Richards of Hartford, and was secreted by Captain Joseph Wadsworth of the same place. Some time later, when the town constable approached him with a writ to reclaim the fugitive, Wadsworth resisted, and the case was brought before the governor and council for decision. As a man of partly Caucasian descent, Abda filed a countersuit against Captain Richards, asking damages of twenty pounds sterling "for his unjust holding and detaining the said Abda in his service as his bondman." But Governor Saltonstall made short work of Abda's case and of similar cases that might arise later. In one breath, he consigned "all persons born of Negro bondwomen" to slavery. Abda was returned to his owner.[4]

Others who went farther were likely to fare better, for Massachusetts soon proved to be a fairly safe refuge for Connecticut runaways. In Pittsfield, it was reported, many became house servants for respectable families. Springfield, where "sympathy for the slave, fleeing from bondage, was often manifested . . . years before the odious fugitive slave law," was a special magnet.[5]

It must not be supposed, however, that the runaway was automatically safe as soon as he reached Massachusetts. Harboring a fugitive slave, even at that period, could be a dangerous business. In the town of Wilbraham, for example, an elderly and honored magistrate of Hampden County "suffered a serious injury in his own house, in an ineffectual attempt to protect a colored man in his employ from being seized and dragged back to slavery in Connecticut." [6] The state legislature, too, evinced little friendship for Negroes in general and fugitives in particular when, in 1788, it adopted a measure providing that "Africans not subjects of Morocco or citizens of one of the United States are to be sent out of the State." Of the persons expelled under this law, twenty-one were from Connecticut.[7] Some of these were undoubtedly freemen, since during this period one frequently finds on record in Connecticut applications to selectmen to "free the master from responsibility in case of emancipated slaves." [8]

An emancipation movement struggling to be born; a restless urge for freedom among those enslaved—these were the twin sources from which the Underground Railroad arose, and both were evident in Connecticut in the early 1770's. It was a time of ferment; new ideas of liberty and the rights of man were in the air. Antislavery pamphlets and books were beginning to appear from the pens of such writers as John Woolman, Anthony Benezet, and Thomas Paine.[9] Very soon Thomas Jefferson was to draft a document stating, among other things, that "all men are created equal"; and already there were those who, in general agreement with such views, were prepared to speak for complete freedom and equality for Connecticut's 6500 slaves. One such was Aaron Cleveland of Norwich, hatter, poet, legislator, "minister of the gospel and tribune of the people," who in 1775 published an antislavery poem, and who has been recognized as the first writer in Connecticut "to call in question the lawfulness of slavery and to argue against it." [10] This position was too advanced for the time, but in the previous year the General Assembly had taken a first halting step toward abolition in a measure providing that "no Indian, negro, or mulatto slave shall at any time hereafter be brought or imported into this State, by sea or land." Thereafter, the courts were "inclined towards the support of liberal interpretations of the antislavery laws." [11]

After the Revolution, that basic lesson in freedom, the General Assembly moved further toward universal emancipation. A law of 1784 provided that no Negro or mulatto born in Connecticut after March 1 of that year was to be held as a slave after reaching the age of twenty-five. This law was soon followed by further measures in the same direction. An enactment of May, 1792, gave teeth to the 1784 law by defining penalties for its violation; anyone who removed from Connecticut a slave who was entitled to freedom at twenty-five would be punished by "a fine of $334, half of which should go to the plaintiff and half to the State." The same session of the Assembly also enacted that all slaves between the ages of twenty-five and forty-five were entitled to freedom. A measure of 1797 took an additional step, decreeing that no Negro or mulatto born after August of that year should remain a slave after reaching the age of twenty-one. But complete and final emancipation did not come to Connecticut until 1848.

Meanwhile, the state's slaves had been busy emancipating themselves by direct action, sometimes through their sole effort, sometimes with the help of their friends—or their country's enemies. The British were perfectly aware that some damage could be done the American cause by encouraging slaves to escape. Indeed, as early as 1768, a New London citizen of "probity" heard three English officers agree that "if the Negroes were made freemen, they should be sufficient to subdue those damn'd Rascals." [12] In the general unrest and the near presence of British troops, slaves saw a handy avenue to freedom. One is known to have escaped from his owner in Colchester to the enemy lines in 1776, and in the same year three other runaways found refuge on a British vessel in New Haven harbor.[13]

Of those who made the break for freedom alone, many—unlike their Southern counterparts of later decades—seem to have helped themselves to their masters' wardrobes or other valuable articles. Thus a fugitive from Stamford ran off with a felt hat, a gray cut wig, a lapelled vest, several pairs of stockings, two pairs of shoes, a small hatchet, and a violin.[14] A Hartford runaway of 1777 also took his master's violin, presumably for his entertainment along the way; while the owner of another violin-stealing fugitive shrugged off his loss with the remark that the thief was a "miserable performer." [15]

Not all the runaways in Connecticut at this time were friendless, however. A classic example was set by citizens of Hebron and the vicinity, when seven or eight men from South Carolina attempted to kidnap a slave there in 1788. There was hardly a man in the neighborhood, it is reported, who failed to resist the abduction; and after a council of war among residents of Hebron, East Haddam, and East Hampton, the Negro was rescued and set free.[16]

Ten years later, in the northwest corner of the state, citizens of Norfolk rallied with equal wholeheartedness to the support of another runaway. This was James Mars, who in 1798 was only eight years of age. He lived in Canaan, and by the provisions of the law of 1784 his legal freedom was just seventeen years away. However, his owner—a Mr. Thompson, a minister and a strong proslavery spokesman—planned to take James and his family to Virginia, where he would sell them to a planter. In what was to have been his last sermon to the people of Canaan, Thompson said that his chattels were fine slaves and would bring him at least two thousand dollars in the Southern market.

James' father, however, had other ideas. Though he was only "a slave without education," yet he was a vigilant man; and as a father, he was naturally greatly concerned for the welfare of his wife, his daughter, and his two sons. He saw and heard much, kept it to himself—and planned his family's escape. He knew there was some ill feeling between Canaan and Norfolk, so to Norfolk they would go. Accordingly, he hitched up the parson's team in the dark of night, put his few possessions and his family aboard the wagon, and set out. The trip was not without incident—among other things, they ran afoul of someone's woodpile in the darkness—but they reached Norfolk well before daylight. There they found refuge in Pettibone's tavern, whose owner, like his descendants, was a friend of fugitive slaves. He welcomed the Mars family, helped them unload, and gave them a resting place for the balance of the night. But the tavern obviously could not be a permanent refuge. Of what happened next, James wrote many years later:

> It was soon known in the morning that we were in Norfolk; the first enquiry was where will they be safe. The place was soon found. There was a man by the name of Phelps that had a house that was not occupied; it was out of the way and out of sight. After breakfast, we

> went to the house; it was well located; it needed some cleaning and that my mother could do as well as the next woman. . . . Days and weeks passed on and we began to feel quite happy, hoping that the parson had gone South.

But Thompson had not gone, and after some time the word spread that he was planning to recapture his slaves—particularly James and his brother Joseph. Therefore a Mr. Cady, who lived next door to Phelps, volunteered to take the boys to a place where they would be safe. At twilight he led them over hills and through woods, over rocks and fallen logs. At one point they came out on top of Burr Mountain, in the northwest corner of the township. "We could look down in low grounds," said James, "and see logs that were laid for the road across the meadow; at every flash they could be seen, but when it did not lighten, we could not see any thing; we kept on, our pilot knew the way." He led them down from the hills toward the center of town, and so to the Tibbals house.

Here the boys were welcomed by "an old man, a middle aged man and his wife and four children. . . . We had not been there long," James continued, "before it was thought best that my brother should be still more out of the way, as he was about six years older than I, which made him an object of greater search, and they were at a loss where to send him, as he was then about fourteen years of age." Fortunately for Joseph, a young man named Butler, who was visiting in the neighborhood, agreed to take him to Massachusetts.

James, meanwhile, remained with the Tibbals for "a few days," after which he rejoined his parents and sister at the Phelps house. But before he arrived there, Thompson had come and gone; he had left James' mother with this proposition: "If she would go to Canaan and see to his things and pack them up for him, then if she did not want to go [to Virginia], she need not." Since this was a bargain, James and his sister were obliged to return to Canaan with their parents. Still the parson, mindful of the profits from the Virginia auction block, was not satisfied—he wanted Joseph. Hence he demanded that James' father search for him and bring him back. Now was the time for the elder Mars to act, and again he plotted to rescue his family. With Thompson's team of horses, he slipped his family away along the familiar route to Norfolk. Reaching Captain Lawrence's tavern there about two in the morning, they were given lodging for the night; then, to make their recovery more difficult, the Captain advised them to disperse and hide in different houses in the neighborhood.

James, at the outset, was passed to the home of an old woman nearby. "I stopped with her a few days, with instructions to keep still. You may wonder why I was sent to such a place; most likely it was thought that she had so little room that she would not be suspected of harboring a fugitive." A man named Walter frequently stopped by "to see how his boy did"; he told James that, if anyone else came to the house, he "must get under the bed." After several days of this hole-and-corner life, James was moved again, spirited from house to house through a chain of hiding places. "I was sent to Mr. Pease, well nigh Canaan, and kept rather dark. I was there for a time, and then I went to stay with a man by the name of Akins, and stayed with him a few days, and went to a man by the name of Foot, and was with him a few days." Finally, he said, "I went to another man by the name of Akins, and was there some time."

While James was being whisked about in this fashion, Thompson decided to sell him and Joseph on the spot; and to encourage the boys to appear on the scene, he allowed their parents to select the persons to whom they might be sold. Thus, when they came home in September of 1798, their new owners had been decided upon. Mr. Munger of Norfolk agreed to pay Thompson $100 for James, while Mr. Bingham of Salisbury undertook to pay the same for Joseph. Had there been a well-organized underground system in the community, this transaction might never have materialized. At any rate, James' parents and sister were set free, while Joseph, it is supposed, remained a slave until he reached the age of twenty-five. James, on the other hand—after the death of Mr. Munger—became a freeman at twenty-one, married, and settled down in Norfolk for the balance of his fruitful life.[17]

The help that the Mars boys received from so many individuals bespeaks a widespread sympathy for the fugitive in the northwestern part of the state, as well as some embryonic sort of organization on a local scale. Even so prominent a citizen as Judge Tapping Reeve, the eminent jurist and Federalist leader, was involved to some extent. He acquired a reputation for helping runaways, and it is said that several of them sought him out at his famous law school in Litchfield "simply from hearing about him." [18]

But there were still slaveowners in Connecticut; and others of them than Parson Thompson were minded to dispose of their chattels in the South. Some tried persuasion, telling their slaves of the soft climate that awaited them, in contrast to the severity of New England winters. Some were more blunt. On the Hanchet estate, near Suffield, a rumor spread that Master would take his Negroes South and sell them; and when Hanchet told them to pack their clothes and get ready to go to Maryland, "there was a great outburst of excitement and tears" among his eleven slaves. As might have been expected, the day set for departure found only the oldest and the youngest on the farm. The rest had taken flight. Hanchet was furious, and he "spent some weeks in a most energetic effort" to recover them. As a last resort, he hired two slave-hunters from Maryland to find them for him.

The fugitives meanwhile had split into several groups. One, consisting of Titus and Phill, took shelter in "a sort of cave in the side of a mountain." Another group hid in an old dugout above Enfield Falls; here they were found by another colored slave named Ned, who provided them with food and kept them informed of developments. The two girls who made up the third group, Lize and Betty, wandered in the woods until they became thoroughly bewildered and finally separated.

Lize, somehow, struggled on through a notch "near the Rising Corners," where next morning members of the Eldad Loomis family found her nearly exhausted. They comforted the weary girl and took her to their home. During the day they concealed her in an attic; in the evenings, they discreetly kept her out of view of any neighbors who might come visiting.

Betty, left alone, strayed farther north over the Massachusetts border, where she encountered the Indians of Agawam. These people had themselves been slaves; they immediately sensed Betty's situation and made her feel at home. Subsequently, however, the Maryland slave-hunters picked up Betty's tracks, and at length they reached the Indian village. One of them addressed the chief:

> "Who were those colored girls that came here the other day?" "Who say colored gal come?" "But you know they did, and now if you will give them to us we will give you what you ask." "How much that?" "Will ten dollars be enough?" "No!" "How much then?" "White man listen. Injun hunt. Injun fish. Injun fight, but no Injun hunt blachies. White man better go home."

The slave-hunters were beaten, and they knew it; they went back to Suffield. Hanchet was beaten too; he set out for Maryland, leaving his quondam slaves to enjoy the freedom they had won by taking it.[19]

How many runaways made good their escape in the decades from 1790 to 1820 is not known, but flights were common enough. Such advertisements as the following were a frequent sight in many Connecticut newspapers of the period:

> Run away from me the subscriber about the 28th of February last, a Negro Man named London, about 50 years of age, had on when he went away a strait bodied blue coat and leather breeches, as to his other cloathing I am not certain; he is a middling sized fellow, speake faint and slow, but tolerable good English, is a crafty subtle sly fellow, and has and can pretend sickness when well. Whoever will apprehend said Negro and bring him to me in Hartford, or secure him in any gaol in this or the neighbouring States and send me word so that I may have him again, shall have 50 dollars reward and all necessary charges paid. I also forewarn all persons from either harboring, secreting or employing said Negro, as they will answer the same at the peril of the law. (1790)

> Ranaway, from the Subscriber [in Greenwich] on the ninth inst., a negro man named James, nearly 18 years of age and about 5 feet 10 in. high: took with him at the time a brown cloth coatee & pantaloons a light figured cotton vest and tow cloth frock and trousers. He is marked by a scar obliquely across the ridge of his nose and others on his feet, particularly a large one on his left foot just back of the small toe, occasioned by the cut of an axe, which causes it to be stiffened. All persons are hereby cautioned not to harbor said runaway: and whoever will give information of him so that he can be obtained by the subscriber (to whom he is bound until he is 21 years of age) shall be liberally rewarded. (1813)

One of the last notices of this sort appeared in the *Connecticut Courant* of August 5, 1823. In it Elijah Billings of Somers announced that a mulatto boy named William Lewis had run away from him. Billings apparently had little use for the lad, however, for the last words of the advertisement were: "Any person who will return said boy shall receive one cent reward and no charges paid." [20]

Meanwhile, sentiment not merely in favor of runaway slaves but against the entire institution of slavery was becoming manifest among Connecticut's citizens. In Glastonbury, Hancy Z. Smith and her five daughters originated the first antislavery petition in the United States, circulated it among their neighbors, and forwarded it to Congress with forty signatures. They held frequent antislavery meetings in their dooryard, where a large door mounted on a sturdy tree stump made a platform for the speaker. They lectured in the cause themselves and distributed abolitionist literature. As acknowledged independents, they had little to lose by their activities.[21]

Abolitionist sentiment was sufficiently widespread by 1790 to result in the formation of a Connecticut antislavery society in that year—its resounding title was "The Society for the Promotion of Freedom, and for the Relief of Persons Holden in Bondage." Its president was Ezra Stiles, the theologian who had been president of Yale College since 1778; Judge Simeon Baldwin was secretary. Under vigorous leadership, the Society "speedily showed great activity." On January 7, 1791, it sent off a petition to Congress, setting forth its position and demanding action. This document stated that, although the Society was of recent origin, its work had "become generally extensive through the State" and reflected the sentiments of a large majority of citizens. "From a sober conviction of the unrighteousness of slavery," it went on, "your petitioners have long beheld with grief a considerable number of our fellow-men doomed to perpetual bondage. . . . The whole system of African slavery is unjust in its nature, impolitic in its principles, and in its consequences ruinous to the industry and enterprise of the citizens of these States." In conclusion, it requested that Congress should use all constitutional means to prevent "the horrors of the slave-trade . . . prohibit the citizens of the United States from carrying on the trade . . . prohibit foreigners from fitting out vessels in the United States for transporting persons from Africa . . . and alleviate the sufferings of those who are now in slavery, and check the further progress of this inhuman commerce." The petition met a cool reception in Congress. It was referred to a special committee, where it quietly died.[22]

Before this same society, later in the year, Jonathan Edwards Jr. unequivocally stated the moral necessity of immediate emancipation. "To hold a man in a state of slavery who has a right to his liberty," he said, "is to be every day guilty of robbing him of his liberty, or of man-stealing, and is greater sin in the sight of God than concubinage or fornication. . . . Every man who cannot show that his negro hath by his voluntary conduct forfeited his liberty, is obliged immediately to manumit him."[23] Edwards thus foreshadowed the opinion of Judge Theophilus Harrington of Vermont, who would accept nothing less than "a bill of sale from God Almighty" as valid proof of one man's ownership of another.[24]

The next two decades produced other influential spokesmen in the antislavery cause—men like Alexander McLeod, George Bourne, and Thomas Branagan, who saw in the South's "peculiar institution" nothing but immorality, barbarism, and degradation for master and slave alike. No one of these, it is true, wrote or published in Connecticut, but their works were circulated widely and in some cases for many years.[25]

However, the time had not yet come when a majority of Connecticut's ordinary citizens shared such views. Side by side with sympathy for the escaping slave, and overshadowing it in the minds of many, was the feeling that the free Negro was a problem. The number of slaves in the "Land of Steady Habits" had shrunk to insignificance by 1820, but the number of free persons of color had risen to 7844—nearly 3 per cent of the total population—and not a few people were disturbed by the effects this increase might have on the state's settled ways.[26] To some of these, the idea of establishing a colony for free Negroes in western Africa appealed as a practical and not inhumane solution to a perplexing question.

The plan of colonization arose in Washington, D. C., where men from North and South assembled in 1816 to discuss the "growing evil" of the free Negro population. From this meeting came the simple solution: send them back to Africa; and the American Colonization Society was forthwith formed for that purpose.[27] In the next year the Society sent two representatives to the west coast of Africa to investigate the possibility of establishing a Negro colony there. Both these emissaries were ministers, the Reverend Samuel J. Mills of Connecticut and the Reverend Ebenezer Burgess of Massachusetts; and both had the honest belief that colonization would encourage emancipation. They completed their mission and recommended a site. It was not, as things turned out, the place where the first American asylum for free Negroes was established, yet Mills and Burgess may be called the pioneers of the Liberian settlement.[28]

The colonization movement gained ground apace. Beginning in 1820, the Connecticut Colonization Society met annually at Hartford, and auxiliaries of this group sprang up in many sections of the state—among them, a juvenile association formed in Middletown in 1828.[29] From the very beginning, however, the genuine friends of colored people saw the colonization scheme as a sort of "gentleman's agreement" between free and slave states. It was nicely calculated to drain off the insurrectionary free Negroes of the South and to strengthen the bonds of the slave system, thus serving an economic purpose. In the North, however, colonization would reduce the number of Negroes and work against the amalgamation or equalization of races—effects that would be primarily social.[30]

However good or evil the intentions of the colonizationists, one outcome of their activity was certainly to dampen the growing ardor for abolition. At least partly as a result of their work, the decade 1820–1830 was "a period of general apathy and indifference on the subject of slavery and the wrongs and needs of the colored race." [31] The colonizationists were concerned only with the free Negroes, and by focusing a spotlight in that direction, they distracted attention from the larger matter of slavery itself and from the increasingly unbearable plight of the slaves. Antislavery writings became less frequent and generally milder in tone than they had been in preceding decades.[32] The country as a whole—and Connecticut with it—was lulled into a false sense of complacency by the Missouri Compromise and by colonizationist propaganda. As a leading abolitionist said later, it began to take on the appearance of a nation "slumbering in the lap of moral death." [33]

CHAPTER 2

THORNY IS THE PATHWAY

In Boston, on the first day of the year 1831, that same abolitionist issued a forthright call to action in the anti-slavery cause. His name was William Lloyd Garrison; and in the initial number of his newspaper *The Liberator* he stated his position in words that no man could fail to understand:[1]

> I am aware, that many object to the severity of my language; but is there not cause for severity? I will be as harsh as truth, and as uncompromising as justice. On this subject, I do not wish to think, or speak, or write with moderation. No! No! Tell a man whose house is on fire to give a moderate alarm; tell him to moderately rescue his wife from the hands of the ravisher; tell the mother to gradually extricate her babe from the fire into which it has fallen;—but urge me not to use moderation in a cause like the present. I am in earnest—I will not equivocate—I will not excuse—I will not retreat a single inch—and I WILL BE HEARD!

Garrison was as good as his word. For three decades, in the face of opposition at first nearly overwhelming and always formidable, he led the fight for emancipation—not partial, not gradual, not linked to such disguised forms of discrimination as colonization, but immediate, unconditional, and complete. The band of reformers who gathered about his standard were idealists all, stirred by the same zeal for human betterment that inspired the contemporary movements for temperance and for universal popular education. Among themselves, abolitionists might—and sometimes did—differ over strategy and tactics, but never over the ultimate goal. To these standard-bearers, with their crusading spirit and selfless deeds, the Underground Railroad owed more of its organization and effectiveness than to any other group.

An early result of Garrison's challenge was the formation of the New England Anti-Slavery Society, established at Boston in 1832. Within a year it had become the American Anti-Slavery Society and had spread over the North, carrying Garrison's principles wherever it went. Its purpose was dual: "To endeavor, by all means sanctioned by law, to effect the abolition of slavery; and to improve the character and condition of the free people of color." Its program included the following points:

1. To organize in every city, town, and village.
2. To send forth agents to preach the gospel.
3. To circularize antislavery tracts and periodicals.
4. To encourage the employment of free laborers, rather than of slaves, by giving market preference to their products.[2]

A fifth purpose, not explicitly stated but evident in the acts of many Society members, was to encourage and assist the escape of fugitives from slavery—the passengers of the Underground Railroad.

Among the earliest antislavery societies in New England was that of New Haven, established in 1833. Two of its leading spirits were clergymen, the Reverend Samuel J. May of Brooklyn, Connecticut, and the Reverend Simeon S. Jocelyn. Their reasons for enlisting in the cause of immediate, complete emancipation were well phrased by May:

> Often it was roughly demanded of us Abolitionists "Why we espoused so zealously the cause of the enslaved? Why we meddled so with the civil and domestic institutions of the Southern States?" Our first answer always was, in the memorable words of old Terence, "Because we are men, and therefore, cannot be indifferent to anything that concerns humanity!" Liberty cannot be enjoyed nor long preserved at the North, if slavery be tolerated at the South.[3]

In the South, indeed, slavery was not merely tolerated; it was encouraged and was growing apace. The cotton gin, invented as far back as 1793, was by now in widespread use; and with it, cotton production became increasingly profitable, so that more and more land was brought under cultivation and more and more slaves were demanded to work it. Moreover, the trans-Appalachian region of Alabama and the Mississippi Delta had become safe for full-scale settlement and exploitation only comparatively recently, with Andrew Jackson's victory over the Creeks in 1814. After that came a rush of settlers to the newly opened areas—hard-driving men, intent on carving a cotton empire out of the forests and canebrakes, and more than willing to burn up any amount of slave labor in the process. Where once the buckskin-clad hunter had roamed, it was now the overseer and the slave coffle, the endless rows of cotton growing through the long hot season, the back-breaking tasks of chopping and picking, and the human beasts, ill fed, ill clothed, and ill treated, on whose driven labors the master might wax fat. Even the planters of the upper South, whose eighteenth-century forebears may in fact have treated their slaves with a certain patriarchal concern, could not fail to realize that the auction block now offered them high profits in human flesh sold down the river—especially since the importation of slaves from overseas had been banned in 1807. Everywhere, the lot of the slaves grew steadily worse, while the Southern slaveowners—never more than a small percentage of the white population in the slave states themselves—grew steadily more powerful and more arrogant.[4]

As reports of these conditions filtered back to the North, more and more persons of conscience came to see that slavery could no longer be regarded as a local matter but was becoming a national concern. This conviction fed the rolls of the antislavery societies, which by 1837 numbered twenty-nine in Connecticut, with memberships ranging from twelve to three hundred.[5] They set about their work with resolute purpose, often against determined opposition.

Part of that work had to do with providing better conditions for free Negroes. Two cases in Connecticut, both arising in 1831, showed how difficult was the fight that lay ahead.

In June of that year, at a United States convention of colored people in Philadelphia, the Reverend Simeon S. Jocelyn proposed the establishment, at New Haven, of "a Collegiate school on the manual labor system" where Negro students would "cultivate habits of industry" and "obtain a useful *Mechanical* or *agricultural* profession." The school would be "established on the self supporting system," but preliminary backing was essential to its founding. The proposal was ratified by the convention, and a committee with the Reverend S. E. Cornish as "agent" was appointed to solicit funds. Forthwith there was issued an "appeal to the benevolent," setting forth the difficulties met by colored youths in gaining admission to ordinary institutions, their need for adequate preparation, and the purpose of the proposed school to supply it.

Opposition to the plan among citizens of New Haven was immediate. The mayor, as soon as he heard of the idea, summoned first his Council, then a town meeting. Here, it is reported, the "air ran hot and foul" as the plan was heatedly discussed. Despite all the proponents could do, the town meeting adopted resolutions fatal to the reformers' hopes:

> 1. That it is expedient that the sentiments of our Citizens should be expressed on these subjects, and that the calling of this Meeting by the Mayor and Aldermen is warmly approved by the citizens of this place.
> 2. That inasmuch as slavery does not exist in Connecticut, and whenever permitted in other States depends on the Municipal Laws of the State which allows it, and over which, neither any other State, nor the Congress of the United States has any control, that the propagation of sentiments favorable to the immediate emancipation of slaves, in disregard of the civil institutions of the States in which they belong, and as auxiliary thereto, the contemporaneous founding of Colleges for educating Colored People, is an unwarrantable and dangerous interference with the internal concerns of other States and ought to be discouraged.
> 3. And Whereas in the opinion of this Meeting, Yale College, the institutions for the education of females, and the other schools, already existing in this City, are important to the community and the general interests of science, and as such have been deservedly patronized by the public, and the establishment of a College in the same place to educate the Colored population is incompatible with the prosperity, if not the existence of the present institutions of learning, and will be destructive of the best interests of the City: and believing as we do, that if the establishment of such a College in any part of the Coun-

> try were deemed expedient, it should never be imposed on any community without their consent,—Therefore; Resolved—by the Mayor, Aldermen, Common Council, and Freemen of the City of New Haven in City meeting assembled, that we will resist the establishment of the proposed College in this place, by every lawful means.

In face of this attitude, Jocelyn's plan was dropped. The citizens of New Haven had plainly recorded their indifference to the slavery issue; their awareness that Negro education must lead, however slowly and indirectly, to emancipation and racial equality; and their wish to avoid any offense to Southern slaveholders whose sons attended Yale or with whom, as merchants, they had had business dealings.[6]

Starting in that same year, the people of the little village of Canterbury became involved in a somewhat similar case that grew to command nation-wide attention. It began in an atmosphere of general approval when Prudence Crandall, a Quaker from nearby Plainfield, opened a "young ladies boarding school" whose pupils included an impressive number of daughters of "the best families in town." [7] Everyone admired Miss Crandall; she was a lady of all the classical virtues, her pupils became devoted to her, parents recognized her as a teacher of great ability, and ministers and public officials in surrounding towns recommended her school to public patronage. All was going smoothly when Sarah Harris applied for admission to the school.

Sarah was a pious girl of seventeen, daughter of "a respectable man who owned a small farm" in the vicinity, and she was sincerely anxious to "get a little more learning." Everything was in Sarah's favor—except the fact that she was a Negress.

Miss Crandall was perfectly aware of the problem she

thus had to face, and for a time she hesitated. But she had all the sense of justice and the moral courage of her Quaker persuasion. Her sympathies, she said later, "were greatly aroused"; she admitted Sarah as a day scholar. As soon as her action was known, protests arose on every side—mutterings, threats of withdrawal from her pupils' parents, the direct warning from a prominent minister's wife that, if she did not dismiss Sarah, her school would fail. Let it fail then, returned Miss Crandall, "for I should not turn her out." She went further than that; she resolved to remake her school into one exclusively for colored girls.

Local reaction was immediate. The citizens of Canterbury swung into action, under the leadership of Andrew T. Judson, state senator, proslavery spokesman, and advocate of colonization. First a town meeting was called to "avert the impending calamity"—for, as Judson and his followers saw it, "should the school go into operation, their sons and daughters would be forever ruined, and property no longer safe." Most of those present accepted this specious view, and when Arnold Buffum and Samuel J. May attempted to speak in Miss Crandall's behalf, they were shouted down before they could deliver their message—which was, essentially, that Miss Crandall was prepared to move her school elsewhere if given time to do so and a fair price for her property. But the citizens never heard that proposal; they were too busy resolving that "the obvious tendency of this school would be to collect within the town of Canterbury, large numbers of persons from other States, whose characters and habits might be various and unknown to us, there-by rendering insecure the persons, property, and reputation of our citizens," and that they would oppose the school "at all hazards."

These resolutions were conveyed to Miss Crandall. They produced no effect whatsoever. She remained peaceful and kind at all times, but her purpose never wavered. She dismissed her white pupils and reopened the school to colored girls only, with a small group of students from relatively prosperous families in Boston, New York, Providence, and Philadelphia.

Thereupon she and her pupils became the targets for the strongest sort of opposition. First, the selectmen submitted an appeal for help to the American Colonization Society, in which they castigated the members of the Anti-Slavery Society who, they said, "wished to admit the Negroes into the bosom of our society" and to justify "intermarriages with the white people." Then the citizens, at another town meeting, resolved that "the establishment of the rendezvous falsely denominated a school was designed by its projectors as the theatre, as the place to promulgate their disgusting doctrines of amalgamation, and their pernicious sentiments of subverting the Union."

Meanwhile the school was subjected to all kinds of meannesses and harassments. The well was filled with stable refuse. Stones and rotten eggs were thrown through the windows. The village store refused to sell groceries for the school's use. Miss Crandall's father was threatened with mob violence and legal action when he brought her food. She and her pupils were stoned on the streets. Doctors refused to treat her when she was ill. The local authorities dusted off an old vagrancy law and invoked it against one of the girls, Ann Eliza Hammond. Under the terms of this enactment, Miss Hammond had "forfeited to the town $1.62 for each day she had remained in it, since she was ordered to depart; and that in default of payment, she WAS TO BE WHIPPED ON THE NAKED BODY NOT EXCEEDING TEN STRIPES, unless she departed within ten days after conviction." This brutality was avoided only when abolitionists of the vicinity managed to raise $10,000 to meet the financial demands of the obsolete law.

Meanwhile, Andrew Judson introduced a so-called "Black Law" into the General Assembly, which enacted it in the spring of 1833. Its preamble read as follows: "Attempts have been made to establish literacy institutions in this State for the instruction of colored persons belonging to other States and countries, which would tend to the great increase of the colored population of this State, and thereby to the injury of the people." The act went on to provide that "every person, who shall set up or establish any school, academy, or literary institution, for the instruction or education of colored persons who are not inhabitants of Connecticut; or who shall teach in such school, or who shall board any colored pupil of such school, *not an inhabitant of the State,* shall forfeit one hundred dollars for the first offence, two hundred dollars for the second, and so on, doubling for each succeeding offence, unless the consent of the civil authority, and selectmen of the town, be previously obtained."

With the passage of this measure, Canterbury was triumphant. Miss Crandall was arrested at once, imprisoned overnight while May and others collected the necessary bail, and eventually brought to trial before Judge Joseph Eaton and a jury at Brooklyn on August 23, 1833. Judson, appearing as prosecutor for the state, attacked Miss Crandall's school as "a scheme, cunningly devised, to destroy the rich inheritance left by your fathers. The *professed object* is to educate the blacks, but the real object is to make the people yield their assent by degrees, to this universal amalgamation of the two races, and have the African race placed on a footing of perfect equality with the Americans." He further contended that Negroes were not citizens of the United States within the meaning of the Constitution, and that therefore they could not enjoy the "privileges and immunities of white citizens." W. W. Ellsworth, for the defense, maintained the precise opposite: that citizenship was a matter of birth or naturalization, not of color; that Negroes born in this country were therefore citizens; and that as such they were entitled to all the privileges of citizenship, including education, "the first and fundamental pillar on which our free institutions rest." The jury, divided between these two points of view, could not agree. The case then went before Judge David Daggett of the State Supreme Court for retrial.

Daggett, a sometime professor of law at New Haven, had been among the more active opponents of Jocelyn's proposed Negro school there. Now, in his charge to the jury, he categorically denied the citizenship of colored persons: "God forbid that I should add to the degradation of this race of men; but I am bound to say, by my duty, that they are not citizens." Miss Crandall was convicted. On appeal to the Court of Errors, the verdict was set aside on technical grounds and she went free. The constitutionality of Connecticut's Black Law was not called into question.

Having thus failed to stop Miss Crandall by legal means, the opponents of her school now had recourse to violence. First an attempt was made to set the building on fire. Then a mob came by night and broke out every window and window frame in the place. Miss Crandall had just been married, to the Reverend Calvin Philleo; at his insistence, she now closed the Canterbury school permanently, yielding the battle to her enemies. The battle, but not the war; for with her husband she removed to northern Illinois, where she was engaged in the education of Negroes for the rest of her active life.

The pattern of anti-Negro, anti-abolitionist violence set in the Crandall affair was repeated on a lesser scale in many parts of the state during the next years. In 1834 a mob raided an abolitionist meeting at the First Presbyterian Church in Norwich, drummed the parson out of town, and threatened him with tar and feathers if he returned. The following year saw a serious riot in Hartford, when a group of white roughs attacked Negroes on their way home from church.[8] In Middletown, Cross Street was reported to be "crowded with those worse than southern bloodhounds." [9] In Meriden, when Reverend Henry Ludlow came to the Congregational church to deliver an abolitionist lecture, an infuriated crowd stoned the building, battered down the locked door, and pelted the congregation with rotten eggs and trash. Even in the birthplace of John Brown, Torrington, in 1837 the organization meeting of a new county abolition society was attacked by a proslavery mob, whose members had "elevated their courage with New England rum"; blowing horns, yelling, and beating on tin pans and kettles, they surrounded the unheated barn where the meeting was held and broke up the gathering "by brute force." [10] Outbreaks of similar nature were reported during the 1830's in other towns as well—New Haven, New Canaan, and Norwalk among them.[11]

Most of these outrages appear to have been of more or less spontaneous nature—a matter of a few ringleaders surrounding themselves with a hastily gathered group of roughs who perhaps cared little about slavery one way or the other but who, warmed by liquor and hot words, were easy prey to the mob spirit and not at all averse to throwing eggs, destroying property, and pushing people around. The Danbury riots, however, bespoke greater purpose and more careful organization. Danbury was already a center for hat manufacturing, and the Southern trade had been important to it at least since 1800; indeed it was said to have "gained its growth largely by developing the Southern market." Many of its citizens, therefore, sympathized with Southern views and had no patience with abolitionists. To this town, in 1837, came an itinerant antislavery lecturer, the Reverend Nathaniel Colver, who was scheduled to speak at the Baptist church. When the hour arrived for him to do so, a blast of trumpets was heard from near the courthouse; then immediately men charged into the streets from every direction, arranged themselves in military formation, and marched like an infantry regiment to the church. The congregation scattered at once; some of its members, along with two constables, hurried Colver to a private house. The rabble churned around outside for a while but finally dispersed. Colver was not easily scared off, however. He returned to the church, determined to deliver his message. Now the mob's action was decisive; masked men blew up the building with gunpowder.[12]

Behind all these rowdy demonstrations, perhaps not condoning their violence and lawlessness but certainly sharing the same attitude toward abolitionists, there was a large segment of Connecticut's most respectable citizens. One abolitionist paper went so far as to say that the troubles around Norwalk were sparked by "ministers, magistrates, lawyers, doctors, merchants and hatters." [13] Undoubtedly there were many ordinary persons who agreed with Mrs. Frances Breckenridge of Meriden: "Some of the sympathy for the slave might as well be given to the owner. Let any Northern housekeeper select the most idle, insolent, thievish and exasperating servant she ever knew or heard of and multiply by a dozen or two and she will have a faint idea of one of the trials of the Southern housekeeper." [14] Or with the two men who, having worked on a Southern plantation where there were slaves, came back to report that they "didn't think niggers wuz fit fer ennythin but ter be made ter wuk fer white folks." [15]

All during the decade, indeed, the Connecticut Colonization Society continued to preach its gospel of salvation-through-separation. One of its leading spokesmen was Willbur Fisk, president of the newly established Wesleyan University in Middletown, who declared in 1835:

> African Colonization is predicated on the principle that there is an utter aversion in the public mind, to an amalgamation and equalization of the two races; and that any attempt to press such equalization is not only fruitless, but injurious. . . . Hence this society lifts up the man of color, at once from his connections and disabilities; and places him beyond the influence of the shackles of prejudice.[16]

Other colonizationists set forth the view that no good would befall the escaped slave in Canada, that Africa was his only hope. As one of them phrased it:

> A few months since I was traveling near to Canada, and desiring to see the result of freedom, as they found it in their northern flight, with their eyes fixed on the pole star . . . I inquired about them, and I found that when they first came there they were docile and full of hope, but soon their appearances changed, they lost their buoyancy of spirits,—became indolent, unwilling to submit to the restraints of society which the whites submit to, and as a necessary consequence, a large number of them were in the penitentiary, and others are in the greatest state of want and wretchedness. . . . There is no advantage gained by going to Canada. Go and sit with the colored man, and ask him where do you find your best friends? And he will tell you among the colonizationists.[17]

But the free Negroes of Connecticut were saying no such thing. Hartford's colored inhabitants adopted a resolution that the Colonization Society was "actuated by the same motives which influenced the Pharaoh when he demanded that the male children of Israel be destroyed." Those of New Haven declared that they would "resist all attempts made for their removal to the torrid shores of Africa, and would sooner suffer every drop of blood to be taken from their veins than submit to such unrighteous treatment by colonizationists." [18] From the free Negroes of Lyme came "the sincere opinion that the Colonization Society was one of the wildest projects ever patronized by enlightened men." From Middletown, where Joseph Gilbert and Jehiel Beman were among Negro leaders, came the question: "Why should we leave this land, so dearly bought by the blood, groans and tears of our fathers? Truly this is our home, here let us live and here let us die." [19]

That most Connecticut Negroes shared such views is evident. In twenty years, from 1830 to 1850, only ten Negroes altogether sailed from Connecticut ports to Liberia —approximately one per eight hundred of population. It is possible that others sailed from ports in other states, but the total cannot have been great, for the number of emigrants sent to Africa by the Colonization Society from the entire country amounted to less than ten thousand in all the years from 1820 to 1857.[20] In Negro eyes, the answer to the slavery problem remained what it had been: in the long run, abolition and equality; in the immediate moment, escape to free soil, preferably to Canada.

Despite all the violence and the legal penalties, there were citizens willing to help runaway slaves in any way they could. The Underground Railroad was now taking definite shape, and not even Connecticut's own fugitive slave law of 1835 could stop it. This measure, supplementing the federal law of 1793, provided that "no person held to service or labor in one state, under the laws thereof, caping into another, shall, in consequence of any law or regulation therein, be discharged from such service or labor; but shall be delivered up, on the claim of the party to whom such service or labor may be due." The fugitives who succeeded in reaching the Nutmeg State could look for no official help in their quest for freedom.[21]

But they could look for direct and immediate aid from dedicated abolitionists like Samuel J. May, who later stated that he had begun receiving fugitives "addressed to my care" at Brooklyn as early as 1834; and that he "helped them on to that excellent man, Effingham L. Capron, in Uxbridge, afterwards in Worcester, and he forwarded them to secure retreats." [22] They could look, too, to a climate of opinion that was slowly shifting in their favor. Under the impetus of William Lloyd Garrison and his *Liberator*, antislavery speakers were increasingly active, and abolitionist publications were growing in numbers, circulation, and influence. Books like Theodore Weld's anthology *American Slavery As It Is* had nationwide impact.[23] Connecticut had its own antislavery periodicals, too—the *Christian Freeman*, published in Hartford from 1836 onward, and the *Charter Oak*, founded in 1838. There was also one issued at New London, the *Slave's Cry*. Their circulations were limited, yet the *Charter Oak's* 3000 subscribers in 1839 compared favorably with the approximately 5500 readers enjoyed by the *Connecticut Courant*, a leading general newspaper, in the same era.[24] It was estimated that by this time "the number of antislavery publications reached a total of over a million." [25] Much of the abolitionist writing was in the form of tracts, issued by the New England Anti-Slavery Society, which played up the barbarous treatment of slaves by quoting advertisements from Southern newspapers:

> Ranaway, a negro woman and two children; a few days before she went off, I burnt her face, I tried to make the letter M.
>
> Ranaway a negro man named Henry, his left eye out, some scars from a dirk on and under his left arm, and much scarred with the whip.
>
> Ranaway a negro named Arthur, has a considerable scar across his breast and each arm, made by a knife; loves to talk much of the goodness of God.
>
> Ranaway a negro girl called Mary, has a small scar over her eye, a good many teeth missing, the letter A. is branded on her cheek and forehead.
>
> Fifty dollars reward, for my fellow Edward, he has a scar in the corner of his mouth, two cuts on and under his arm, and the letter E. on his arm.[26]

Just how much influence such publications had in arousing public sympathy for the slave it would be impossible to determine, but it was sufficient to stir the ire of the Southern slavocracy. A meeting in Charleston, South Carolina, adopted resolutions against the "incendiary literature" of Northern abolitionists and mailed copies to "each incorporated city and town in the United States." [27] In Hartford and in New Haven, these Charleston resolutions were supported by mass meetings of proslavery citizens, who further resolved that abolitionists in Connecticut and elsewhere had "no authority to interfere in the emancipation of slaves, or in the treatment of them in different states." [28]

None the less, the abolitionist propaganda made itself felt in many groups, not least the General Assembly. In 1838, that body repealed the notorious Black Law that had struck down Prudence Crandall's school; and it did so at the insistence of one of the measure's original backers,

Phillip Pearl, who had been converted to the antislavery cause by Theodore Weld. "I could weep tears of blood for the part I took in that matter," Pearl said. "I now regard the law as utterly abominable." [29]

In that same year the Assembly took an even more important step in the direction of freedom by enacting one of the most detailed personal liberty laws in the union. This measure, while not extending automatic emancipation to runaways who reached Connecticut, severely limited the activities of slave-hunters by providing that "no officer, or other person can remove out of the State any fugitive slave under the laws of any other state in the Union" except in accordance with the following:

1. The claimant must fill out an affidavit, setting forth minutely the grounds for claiming the fugitive, "the time of his or her escape, and where he or she then is, or is believed to be."
2. The claimant must obtain a writ of habeas corpus or a writ to bring the alleged fugitive to court, where the fugitive would be tried by a jury of twelve men, none of whom would be an abolitionist.
3. The claimant must pay in advance all fees and expenses of the proceeding; and if the alleged fugitive were acquitted, the claimant must pay to him "all damages and costs" determined by court or jury.
4. If the alleged fugitive were found to be in fact the claimant's legal property, then the claimant must remove him from the state with all due haste by "direct route to the place of residence of such claimant." [30]

Not everyone in the state was pleased by this enactment. The influential *Columbian Register* of New Haven, for instance, inveighed against it:

> If we put severe penalties upon those who attempt to enforce the laws of the Union, which secured to them

> their labor, they can put as severe or severer penalties on those who attempt to enforce within their limits the tariff laws, which secure to us our labor. Are the northern manufacturers ready for this? . . . Why then has the negro Act been selected in preference to the others, for this special legislation? But one answer can be given. The New England Anti-Slavery Society recently voted that southern slave holders are thieves and robbers.[31]

The law nevertheless reflected a growing concern for justice to the Negro who might or might not be a runaway slave; it demanded legal proof of his status, and it called for a fair trial of the accused fugitive before a jury. It thus helped to focus public attention on the victims of slavery.

By this time, the victims themselves had been escaping to and through Connecticut for four decades in a constantly increasing stream.

CHAPTER 3

FUGITIVES IN FLIGHT

Among the first runaways from the South to reach Connecticut was William Grimes. He came into the state on his own two feet, with little guidance from others, for at this early date—just after 1800—the Underground Railroad as even a quasi-organized entity was still years in the future. Yet he had started on his journey north to freedom with the complicity of some Yankee sailors and even a couple of men in positions of authority. According to the account of his life that he wrote in later years, it happened in this fashion: [1]

Grimes was a mulatto slave in Savannah when his owner decided to go to Bermuda, leaving the bondsman behind "to work for what he could get." The brig *Casket*, out of Boston, lay in the harbor taking on a cargo of cotton for New York; Grimes saw a chance to make "a few dollars" by helping with the loading. While engaged in this work, he became friendly with some of the seamen. As they laid up the bales on deck, they left space between where a man might lie hidden. "Whether they then had any idea of my coming away with them or not, I cannot say," wrote Grimes, "but this I can say safely, a place was left." He slipped ashore in the evening with a colored seaman to buy some "bread and dried beef" for the journey; then he lay low among the cotton bales while the brig edged slowly out of the harbor. As it passed the lighthouse, "the sailors gave three hearty cheers" and Grimes realized he was on the way to being a free man.

The voyage itself was uneventful:

> During my passage, I lay concealed as much as possible; some evenings, I would crawl out and go and lie down with the sailors on deck; the night being dark, the captain could not distinguish me from the hands, having a number on board of different complexions. . . . When there was something to be done some one would come on deck and call forward, "there, boys!" "Aye, aye, sir," was the reply; then they would be immediately at their posts, I remaining on the floor not perceived by them.

There was a tense moment for Grimes, however, as the brig neared the quarantine station in New York Harbor. Standing in the forecastle, he felt hopeful as he saw the dark outline of the city becoming clearer through the sea mist. But when the captain approached and questioned him about his status aboard, he just stood there, wordless and tense. "Poor fellow, he stole aboard," said the captain with a knowing stare. And he gave orders that Grimes was to be put ashore safely.

Another tense moment awaited him as, accompanied by a Negro sailor, he was herded toward a line of seamen who were being examined by a doctor on the wharf. Then, he confessed, "I felt as if my heart were in my mouth, or in other words, very much afraid that I should be compelled to give my name, together with an account of where I came from, and where I was going and in what manner I came there." But his guide stepped up and spoke quietly to the doctor, who simply gave the order "Push off." Grimes "rejoiced heartily," thanking his companion a number of times before they parted.

Now he was on his own in a crowded, friendless city.

New York was dangerous too for men in Grimes' position, for among its colored population were some who "for a few dollars" would betray fugitives to Southern slave-catchers.[2] Not knowing of this peril, he approached a colored girl and asked her to "walk with him a little ways, in order to see the town," explaining that he was "a stranger there, and was afraid of being lost." So they walked "for some time," after which he found a lodging for the night.

Grimes did not feel comfortable in New York, however. Early the next morning he bought "a loaf of bread and a small piece of meat" and set out on foot toward the northeast, with no particular destination in mind. Trudging mile after mile over dirt roads, he crossed the Connecticut line at Greenwich. At first he fancied he was pursued by every "carriage or person" behind him; often he ducked off the road to lie down until those in the rear had passed. But soon he realized that his money would not carry him far, and he resolved to be more temperate, more prudent, and more courageous. Thus he persuaded a teamster to give him a ride for a short distance, and he bought some apples from a couple of boys he met on the road. At length, with just seventy-five cents in his pocket, he reached New Haven, where he paid for one night's lodging in a boarding house "kept by a certain Mrs. W."

Now he needed work, and he found it the very next day with Abel Lanson, who kept a livery stable. "He set me to work in a ledge of rocks," wrote Grimes, "getting out stone for buildings. This I found to be the hardest work I had ever done, and began to repent that I had ever come away from Savannah to this hard cold country. After I had worked at this for about three months, I got employment taking care of a sick person, who called his name Carr, who had been a servant to Judge Clay, of Kentucky; he was then driving for Mr. Lanson."

This job ended suddenly when Grimes was recognized by a friend of his master, who was apparently visiting in New Haven. The fugitive's first thought was to "inform his friends"; his second, to leave town. He went to Southington, where he stayed a few weeks picking apples on Captain Potter's farm; then back to New Haven; to Norwich, where he worked as a barber for Christopher Starr; to New London; and to Stonington, where he had been told that a barber might do well.

But Grimes found it difficult to make a living in eastern Connecticut, so he returned to New Haven. There he found work at Yale College, shaving, barbering, "waiting on the scholars in their rooms," and doing odd jobs for other employers on the side. Six or eight months later he heard that a barber was needed at the Litchfield Law School—Tapping Reeve's famous establishment—and there he went in the year 1808. He became a general servant to the students and was also active as a barber, earning fifty or sixty dollars per month. "For some time," he said, "I made money very fast; but at length, trading horses a number of times, the horse jockies would cheat me, and to get restitution, I was compelled to sue them; I would sometimes win the case; but the lawyers alone would reap the benefit of it. At other times, I lost my case, fiddle and all, besides paying my attorney. . . . Let it not be imagined that the poor and friendless are entirely free from oppression where slavery does not exist; this would be fully illustrated if I should give all the particulars of my life, since I have been in Connecticut."

Back in New Haven in the year 1812 or 1813, Grimes met and soon married Clarissa Caesar, a colored girl whom he called "the lovely and all accomplished." She was also a "lady of education," teaching him all the reading and writing he ever knew. Because his situation was not entirely safe—he was still a runaway slave and still, before the law, his master's property—Grimes and his bride returned to "the back country" of Litchfield, where they bought a house and settled down. And just as he had feared, his owner eventually learned of his whereabouts and sent an emissary, a brisk and rude fellow called Thompson, to reclaim him. This man confronted the fugitive with a plain choice: he could buy his freedom, or Thompson would "put him in irons and send him down to New York, and then on to Savannah." Grimes described his state of mind and his subsequent actions as follows:

> To be put in irons and dragged back to a state of slavery, and either leave my wife and children in the street, or take them into servitude, was a situation in which my soul now shudders at the thought of having been placed. . . . I may give my life for the good or the safety of others, but no law, no consequences, not the lives of millions, can authorize them to take my life or liberty from me while innocent of any crime. I have to thank my master, however, that he took what I had, and freed me. I gave a deed of my house to a gentleman in Litchfield. He paid the money for it to Mr. Thompson, who then gave me my free papers. Oh! how my heart did rejoice and thank God.

Thus William Grimes became a free man, to live out the rest of his long life as his own man in a free state. Yet, as he came to set down his memoirs in later years, he viewed the condition of slavery and the condition of freedom in a somewhat ambivalent light:

> To say that a man is better fed, and has less care [in slavery] than in the other, is false. It is true, if you regard him as a brute, as destitute of the feelings of human nature. But I will not speak on the subject more. Those slaves who have kind masters are perhaps as happy as the

generality of mankind. They are not aware what their condition can be except by their own exertions. I would advise no slave to leave his master. If he runs away, he is most sure to be taken. If he is not, he will ever be in the apprehension of it; and I do think there is no inducement for a slave to leave his master and be set free in the Northern States. I have had to work hard; I have often been cheated, insulted, abused and injured; yet a black man, if he will be industrious and honest, can get along here as well as any one who is poor and in a situation to be imposed on. I have been very fortunate in life in this respect. Notwithstanding all my struggles and sufferings and injuries, I have been an honest man.

William Grimes, escaping in the first decade of the nineteenth century, found only chance friends to help him. A quarter-century later, when Daniel Fisher came out of Virginia and took the name Billy Winters, the Underground Railroad was already partially organized, as his own story shows: [3]

I was born in Westmoreland County, Virgina, about the year of 1808. I had five brothers and two sisters and was known as Daniel Fisher. Our master's name was Henry Cox. When I was about twenty years of age my master was obliged, on account of heavy losses, to sell me, and I was sent to Richmond to be sold on the block to the highest bidder. The sale took place and the price paid for me was $550. I was taken by my new master to South Carolina. This was in the month of March. I remained there until October when, in company with another slave, we stole a horse and started to make our escape. In order not to tire the animal, we traveled from 10 o'clock at night until daybreak the next morning when we ran the horse into the woods and left him, for we knew what would happen to us if two slaves were seen having a horse in their possession. We kept on our way on foot, hiding by day and walking by night. We were without knowledge of the country, and with nothing to guide us other than the north star, which was oftentimes obscured by clouds, we would unwittingly retrace our steps and find ourselves back at the starting point. Finally, after days of tedious walking and privations, fearing to ask for food and getting but little from the slaves we met, we reached Petersburg. From Petersburg we easily found our way to Richmond and thence, after wandering in the woods for three days and nights, we came to my old home at Westmoreland Court House.

One of the greatest obstacles we had to contend with was the crossing of rivers, as slaves were not allowed to cross bridges without a pass from their masters. For that reason, when we came to the Rappahannock we had to wait our chance and steal a fisherman's boat in order to cross. Upon my arrival at my old plantation, I called upon my young master and begged him to buy me back. He said he would gladly do it, but he was poorer than when he sold me. He advised me to stow myself away on some vessel going north, and as the north meant freedom I decided to act upon his advice. While awaiting the opportunity to do so, we (the same slave who had accompanied me from South Carolina being with me) secured shovels and dug us three dens in different localities in the neighboring woods. In these dens we lived during the day, and foraged for food in the night time, staying there about three months. At the end of that time we managed to stow ourselves away on a vessel loaded with wood bound for Washington. We were four days without food and suffered much. When we reached Washington the captain of the vessel put on a coat of a certain color, and started out for the public market, telling us to follow and keep him in sight. At the market he fed us and told us in what direction to go, starting us on our journey, giving us two loaves of bread each for food. We took the railroad track and started for Baltimore. We had gone scarcely a mile before we met an Irishman, who decided that we were runaways, and was determined to give us to the authorities. However, by telling him a smooth story that we were sent for by our masters to come to a certain house just ahead, he let us by. Thinking our bundles of bread were endangering our safety by raising suspicion, we threw them away. After that we went several days without food, traveling day and night until we reached the Delaware river. We walked along the bank of the river for some five miles in search of a bridge. We finally came to one, but on attempting to cross were stopped, as we had no passes. It was a toll bridge, and there was a woman in charge of it, who upon our payment of a penny for each and the promise to come back immediately, allowed us to go by. By this time we were very hungry, but had no food. At the other end of the bridge we were stopped again, as the gates were opened only for teams. However, by exercising our ingenuity and pretending to look around, we finally managed to slip by in the shadow of a team, and then, glorious thought! we were at last on the free soil of Pennsylvania.

We again took to the woods, knowing that we were liable to be apprehended at any time. We made a fire, which attracted attention, and we were soon run out of our hiding place. We sought another place and built another fire, and again we were chased away. We made no more fires. In the course of our further wanderings we were chased by men and hounds, but managed to escape capture, and finally arrived in Philadelphia, being three days on the road. In Philadelphia we found friends who gave us the choice of liquor or food. I took the food, my companion the liquor.

As kidnappers were plenty, it was thought best for our safety that we separate, and we parted. I saw no more of my companion. The only weapon for defense which I had was a razor, one which I had carried all through my wanderings. In company with some Philadelphia colored people, I was taken to New York, and it was there I first met members of the Abolition party. At New York I was put on board a steamboat for New Haven. Arrived in that city, a colored man took me to the Tontine Hotel, where a woman gave me a part of a suit of clothes. I was fed and made comfortable, and then directed to Deep River, with instructions that upon arriving there I was to inquire for George Read or Judge Warner. I walked all the way from New Haven to Deep River, begging food by the way from the women of the farm houses, as I was afraid to apply to the men, not knowing but what they would detain me and give me up. I traveled the Old Stage Road from New Haven to Deep River and in going through Killingworth I stopped at the tavern kept by Landlord Redfield but was driven away. Upon reaching the "Plains" this side of Winthrop, I could not read the signs on the post at the forks of the road, and asked the way of Mrs. Griffing. She drove me away, but called out, "Take that road," and pointed to it. Further on I met Harrison Smith, who had a load of wood which he said was for Deacon Read, the man I was looking for.

I reached Deep River at last, weary and frightened. I called at Deacon Read's, told him my circumstances and gave him my name as Daniel Fisher. All this was in secret. The good deacon immediately told me that I must nevermore be known as Daniel Fisher, but must take the name of "William Winters," the name which I have borne to this day. He furthermore told me that I must thereafter wear a wig at all times and in all places. After that I worked at different times for Ambrose Webb and Judge Warner in Chester, and for Deacon Stevens in Deep River, getting along very nicely, though always afraid of being taken by day or by night and carried again to the South.

In spite of Winters' anxiety, he was relatively secure in Deep River. In those years it was "a sort of out-of-the-way location and all Abolitionist," which made it "a pretty safe refuge for runaway slaves." [4] It was largely self-contained and self-supporting; there was no Valley Railroad, no Shore Line; even the steamers, recently introduced on the river, ran at inconvenient hours. "The first colored man there," a native wrote in later years, "was Billy Winters, a real Christian man, a runaway slave. . . . We boys flocked to see him carry up from the brook a large tub of water on his head without spilling any. Deacon Read took Billy to his home, and he always sat at meals with the family." [5]

This domestic arrangement was quite in line with Deacon Read's reputation as a "very generous and public spirited" man who had a significant role in the growth of a "thoroughly democratic village," [6] where the word "servant" was never used. Read, in fact, was for years an active stationmaster on the Underground Railroad, like Judge Ely Warner and his son Jonathan in Chester. In such an atmosphere, Uncle Billy Winters lived a life that was apparently happy enough. He was a great favorite among the village's children, and with their help taught himself to read, going about among them with a spelling book and asking them what was this word or that.[7] The street on which he lived is known to this day as Winters Avenue.

If the Underground Railroad operated adequately for William Winters in 1828, it ran even more smoothly ten years later when James Lindsey Smith journeyed over its tracks from Philadelphia north. But he had many fears and difficulties before he reached that entry port of freedom. Smith was born in Virginia, where he passed his early years as a slave. In boyhood he suffered a serious injury when a timber was dropped on his knee; through his master's indifference he did not receive proper treatment, with the result that he was lamed for life.[8]

In spite of this handicap, Smith made a break for freedom in 1838, along with two other slaves, Lorenzo and Zip. At their suggestion, he joined them in commandeering a boat on the Cone River, by which they meant to escape to Maryland and beyond. It was quite calm as they started on a Sunday, but once out in the bay they found a good wind. With sails set, they made brisk time as they headed up Chesapeake Bay, and on the Tuesday night they landed near Frenchtown, Maryland. "We there hauled the boat up as best we could, and fastened her," wrote James in after years, "then took our bundles and started on foot. Zip, who had been a sailor from a boy, knew the country and understood where to go. He was afraid to go through Frenchtown, so we took a circuitous route, until we came to the road that leads from Frenchtown to New Castle. Here I became so exhausted that I was obliged to rest; we went into the woods, which were near-by, and laid down on the ground and slept for an hour or so, then we started for New Castle."

As they walked on, however, James found it difficult to keep up with his companions, who occasionally had to stop and wait until he caught up with them. Finally Zip said, "Lindsey, we shall have to leave you for our enemies are after us, and if we wait for you we shall all be taken; so it would be better for one to be taken than all three." Then, telling James the roads he should follow, they went off and left him behind. James was in despair:

> When I lost sight of them, I sat down by the road-side and wept, prayed, and wished myself back where I first started. I thought it was all over with me forever; I thought one while I would turn back as far as Frenchtown, and give myself up to be captured; then I thought that would not do; a voice spoke to me, "not to make a fool of myself, you have got so far from home (about two

> hundred and fifty miles), keep on towards freedom, and if you are taken, let it be headed towards freedom." I then took fresh courage and pressed my way onward towards the north with anxious heart.

Going on in the darkness, James toward morning was following a railroad track through a cut in a high hill. Here he had a terrifying experience:

> I heard a rumbling sound that seemed to me like thunder; it was very dark, and I was afraid that we were to have a storm; but this rumbling kept on and did not cease as thunder does, until at last my hair on my head began to rise; I thought the world was coming to an end. I flew around and asked myself, "What is it?" At last it came so near to me it seemed as if I could feel the earth shake from under me, till at last the engine came around the curve. I got sight of the fire and the smoke; said I, "It's the devil, it's the devil!" It was the first engine I had ever seen or heard of; I did not know there was anything of the kind in the world, and being in the night, made it seem a great deal worse than it was; I thought my last days had come; I shook from head to foot as the monster came rushing on towards me. The bank was very steep near where I was standing; a voice says to me, "Fly up the bank"; I made a desperate effort, and by the aid of the bushes and trees which I grasped, I reached the top of the bank, where there was a fence; I rolled over the fence and fell to the ground, and the last words I remember saying were, that "the devil is about to burn me up, farewell! farewell!"

How long he lay there James did not know, but when he came to himself the "devil" had vanished. Despite his fright, he resumed his journey, shaking and trembling. Soon after sunrise he heard the rumbling sound again, and the "devil" came rushing toward him once more. As the infernal machine charged by, James could see through the coach windows the souls whom the fiend was carrying to hell. They were all white; not a colored face among them. As the train thundered out of sight, James pressed on in relief, for it was obvious that the devil was not interested in him even though in his former home he had been "a great hand to abuse the old gentleman."

By this time he was famished, and despite a close search of the ground he could find nothing fit to eat. At length he came to a farmhouse, where he screwed up his courage to ask for food despite his fear that he might well be turned over to slave-catchers. However, the farm people accepted without question his statement that he was going to visit friends in Philadelphia. For twenty-five cents they gave him a hearty breakfast, and he went on, feeling like a new man.

By noon he reached New Castle, where he ran into Lorenzo and Zip once more. Together, they went to the waterfront, where they learned that a boat made the short run to Philadelphia twice daily. When the afternoon sailing was ready to leave, all three went aboard. James said:

> How we ever passed through New Castle as we did without being detected is more than I can tell, for it was one of the worst slave towns in the country, and the law was such that no steamboat, or anything else, could take a colored person to Philadelphia without first proving his or her freedom. What makes it so astonishing to me is, that we walked aboard right in sight of everybody, and no one spoke a word to us. We went to the captain's office and bought our tickets, without a word being said to us.

At Philadelphia the three parted on the dock. Lorenzo and Zip took a ship to Europe; James walked into the city, not knowing where he was going. Coming to a shoe store, he went in and asked the white proprietor for work as a shoemaker. The man told him No, but suggested that he might find work at another shoeshop up the street, whose owner was a colored man named Simpson.

James was perhaps overcautious with Simpson, for he did not reveal his identity as a fugitive slave. Instead, he sat there talking "till most night," then asked the shoemaker for a place to sleep. That would not be convenient, said Simpson, but he had a brother who might be able to help. James, however, could not understand the address given him, and as Simpson was preparing to close his shop for the night, he felt himself as badly off as before. At this point help appeared in an unexpected way:

> My heart began to ache within me, for I was puzzled what to do; but just before he shut up, a colored minister came in; I thought perhaps I could find a friend in him, and when he was through talking with Simpson he started to go out, I followed him to the side-walk and asked him "if he would be kind enough to give me lodging that night." He told me "he could not, for he was going to church; that it would be late before the service closed, and besides it would not be convenient for him."
>
> Here the same heavy cloud closed in upon me again, for it was getting dark, and I had no where to sleep that night. Circumstances were against me; he told me "I could get a lodging place if I would go to the tavern." I made no reply to this advice, but felt somewhat sad, for my last hope had fled. He then asked me if "I was free." I told him that "I was a free man." (I did not intend to let him know that I was a fugitive.) Here I was in a great dilemma, not knowing what to do or say. He told me if "I was a fugitive I would find friends." "If any one needs a friend I do," thought I to myself, for just at this time I needed the consolation and assistance of a friend, one on whom I could rely. So thought I, "it will be best for me to make known that I am a fugitive, and not to keep it a secret any longer." I told him frankly

> that "I was from the South and that I was a runaway." He said, "you are"; I said "yes." He asked me if I "had told Simpson"; I said "no." He then called Simpson and asked him "if he knew that this to be a fact," Simpson asked me if "that was so?" I said "it was." He then told me to "come with him, that he had room enough for me." I went home with him and he introduced me to his family, and they all had a great time rejoicing over me. After giving me a good supper, they secreted me in a little room called the fugitive's room, to sleep; I soon forgot all that occurred around me. I was resting quietly in the arms of sleep, for I was very tired.

But the Underground Railroad agent into whose hands he had stumbled was not resting. He passed the word among his fellow abolitionists, and the next day, wrote James, "many of them came to see me, they talked of sending me to England; one Quaker asked me if I would like 'to see the Queen.' I told him that 'I did not care where I went so long as I was safe.' They held a meeting that day, and decided to send me to Springfield, Massachusetts; this was the fifth day after I left home. The next day, Friday morning, Simpson took me down to the steamboat and started me for New York, giving me a letter directed to David Ruggles, of New York."

In that city, with the help of a lady he encountered on the dock, James found his way to Ruggles' house, and the two "had a great time rejoicing together." He rested there through the week end, but on Monday Ruggles put him on a steamer to Hartford, with letters to a Mr. Foster in that city and a Dr. Osgood in Springfield. James was by now pretty well in the clear, although he did not think so when he went to the clerk's cabin to pay his fare:

> I asked "how much it would be?" He told me it was three dollars. I told him it was a large sum of money, more

> than I possessed. He then asked me "how much I had?" I told him "two dollars and fifty-eight cents." He told me that "that would not do, and that I must get the rest of it." I told him "that I was a stranger there, and that I knew no one." He said: "You should have asked and found out." I told him "I did, and was told that the fare would be two dollars, and that was nearly all I possessed at that time." He requested me to hand it to him, which I did, and it robbed me of every cent I had. I then took my ticket and went forward and laid down among some bales of cotton. It was very chilly and cold, and I felt very much depressed in spirits and cast down.

Penniless, hungry, and weary, the fugitive fell asleep among the cotton bales bound for Connecticut's mills. Later in the evening a waiter found him there, led him to the now deserted dining cabin, and gave him an excellent supper that "cost me nothing." A short while thereafter, he experienced a further alarm:

> Before I retired for the night, some one came through the cabin and told the way-passengers that they must come to the captain's office and leave the number of their berth before they retired for the night. I did not know what he meant by that saying; I thought it meant all the passengers to pay extra for their berths. Now, thought I, if that is the case, and I sleep in the berth all night, and in the morning have no money to pay with, I shall be in trouble sure enough. As I was very tired, I desired very much to lie down and sleep till daylight. I reached Hartford quite early the next morning, so I lay till I thought the boat was along-side the wharf; I then got up and dressed myself and looked at the number of my berth, as I was told to see what it was, so if I should meet the captain I could tell him.

As it happened, he did not see the captain anywhere. Coming on deck and wondering how he could find Mr. Foster, he began to look around:

While I was looking, I saw a colored man standing, and seemed to be looking at me; I went up to him and asked him if "he knew a man by the name of Foster?" He replied: "Yes." So he went along with me, and I found Mr. Foster's residence, by directions given; and, finding him at home, I presented the letter. After he had read it, he began to congratulate me on my escape. When he had conversed with me awhile, he went out among the friends, (Abolitionists), and informed them of my circumstances, in order to solicit aid to forward me to Springfield. Many of them came in to see me, and received me cordially; I began to realize that I had some friends. I stayed with Mr. Foster till afternoon. He raised three dollars for my benefit and gave it to me, and then took me to the steamboat and started me for Springfield. I reached there a little before night.

James now had reached the end of his appointed journey. Dr. Samuel Osgood, pastor of a Congregational church, turned out to be a genuine friend. He made James welcome in an atmosphere of Christian fellowship, found him work as a shoemaker, and saw to it that he obtained an education at a school in Wilbraham. With this training, James became an active abolitionist, making tours and giving antislavery lectures throughout southern New England. Eventually he settled in Norwich, Connecticut, as shoemaker and as pastor of a Methodist church. There he married and in due time raised a worthy family of three daughters and a son.

William Grimes, Billy Winters, and James Lindsey Smith all found a refuge in Connecticut itself, but such was not the case with the bulk of the fugitives who came into the state. For most of them, freedom lay farther north. Such a one was the young man called Charles, whose story was written down by another hand shortly after the event:[9]

About two years since, whilst on board of one of the Connecticut River Steam Boats, I observed a young well dressed colored man, whose appearance and manners particularly attracted my attention. There was something unusual in his whole bearing, and had a favorable opportunity offered, I should have made inquiries respecting him.

A few months after the above occurence, whilst attending a meeting at the office of the Connecticut Anti-Slavery Society in H——, a respectable gentleman of that city came to the door, evidently in haste and somewhat agitated, and enquired for Mr. B. After a short absence Mr. B. returned, and stated that the gentleman who had called him out, was under great anxiety on account of a young colored man who had been in his employ about three months, and who had just come to him in the deepest distress, confessing that he was a runaway slave, and stating that he had that moment seen his master and a noted slave dealer pass by, evidently in search of him and suspecting his residence. The gentleman and his family had become much interested in the young man, and were distressed at the thought of his being carried back into slavery. No time was to be lost, as Charles, (the name of the young man,) was confident he had been seen by his master. Directions were given, that he should go immediately, and as privately as possible, to a house designated in the outskirts of the city, and a gentleman present undertook to take him to F—— without delay.

I saw Charles for a few moments before he left H——, and when my eye first fell on him, I recognized the young man who had attracted my observation on board the Steam Boat. . . . Now, when I knew that he was a slave, that one, who I could not but feel was endowed by his Maker with qualities, (to say the least) equal to any that I myself possessed, that such an one should, in this land of boasted freedom, and in Connecticut too, be claimed as a slave, and be compelled to flee before his fellow man, though guilty of no crime, this greatly increased my interest, and I felt that there was a law, infinitely superior to any human laws, that called upon me to assist him in this his extremity.

The friend who had undertaken to convey him to a place of safety, was not long in keeping his appointment; and, all whose interest had been excited, breathed more easily when assured that Charles was, for a time certainly, out of danger. They were soon convinced too that promptness had probably saved him, as an officer was searching that vicinity in a few minutes after his departure.

Charles had one day's rest in F——, when Mr. B. came from H—— in great haste, and advised that he be immediately removed to some other place, as large rewards were offered for his apprehension, and search would no doubt be made here. I shall not soon forget Charles' quivering lip nor his expression of eye, when told that he could not remain here; that the pursuers were on his track. Had the baying of bloodhounds fallen upon his ear, his spirit could not have sunk more within him. This feeling, however, was but for a moment. A rigidity of muscle, and a determined expression soon followed, and no one could for an instant suppose that it was an idle threat, when he said, "I will die rather than go back to slavery."

Charles' trunk had been sent to my care, and at about ten o'clock, one of our most respectable citizens, with a worthy colored man, a resident of the town, called for the trunk with Charles. The tones of his voice, and the pressure of his hand, as I bade him "good bye," touched my heart; and it was also affecting to see the disinterested benevolence of those, who had undertaken on a night of almost pitchy darkness to guide this poor stranger to a place of safety. They found a willing friend in a secluded part of the town, who secreted him for a few days, when

> another devoted friend of the slave, rode forty miles, between nine o'clock in the evening and daylight the next morning, placing the poor fellow entirely out of danger. He remained in this last place some weeks, whilst negotiations were pending between Dr. Parish and the master; which, however, did not result successfully, and poor Charles was obliged to leave his country for Canada, where he arrived in safety. Queen Victoria has thereby gained a valuable subject, and we have lost one, besides adding to the long list of wrong and oppression, which already disgraces us in the eyes of the civilized world, and which cries to Heaven for vengeance.

As the story of Charles and those citizens of "H——" and "F——" who helped him makes clear, the Underground Railroad in Connecticut was a well-established, going concern by the late 1830's. Among its "employees" were many solid citizens; and in some places at least, they could count on the acquiescence or even the outright help of officers of the law.

Such was the case in Meriden, where two fugitives named Eldridge and Jones came in disguise as "jockeys and grooms to the two famous racing horses Phantom and Fashion." They found refuge with Homer Curtiss, a stout Underground man, who employed them in the lock shop he ran in partnership with Harlowe Isbell. The runaways had been thus engaged for some little time when word of their whereabouts seeped back to their owners in the South. The masters thereupon wrote to the sheriff in Meriden, offering him a reward if he would kidnap the pair and return them to bondage. The sheriff did nothing of the sort; instead, he relayed the message to Meriden's leading abolitionist, the Reverend George Perkins. The latter then wrote the owners to tell them that "under no circumstances would they be allowed to regain possession of the men."

The matter did not end there, however. Presently one of the owners appeared in Meriden and "demanded of Mr. Curtiss that he give up the men, blustering and threatening the intervention of the U. S. government." Curtiss, replying bluntly that he had no intention whatever of surrendering the fugitives, "ordered the man from his premises." Getting nowhere with the locksmith and receiving no cooperation from the local authorities, the slaveowner returned home, leaving Eldridge and Jones behind him.[10]

In Meriden it was a sheriff, in Plainfield it was a judge who sought to act against the slave-catcher. The case had its origin in the little village of Hampton, where in 1840 a young Negro girl arrived and found employment. Although they realized that she was probably a runaway, the townspeople accepted her readily enough. After a time, one Doit Price appeared to seize her as a fugitive slave, filing a claim in the manner prescribed by law at the Plainfield court. He alleged that the girl was the property of his mother; but he could not produce the supporting materials required by Connecticut's Personal Liberty Law. The case was continued until the next day. At the appointed hour, Price reappeared with a document—which the defense attorney, in a pre-trial conference, immediately recognized as a fake. He advised Price to forget the girl and leave town via the stage that was about to depart for Norwich; and Price, caught in a blatant forgery, did so at once. The judge, when he learned of this development, was not content to let matters rest; he directed the sheriff to apprehend Price immediately and return him to court. But the order came too late. The slave-catcher, now himself a fugitive from justice, had already made his escape. As for the girl who was the cause of the action, the community's abolitionists entrusted her to Samuel J. May in Brooklyn, who saw her safely on the road to Canada.[11]

Perhaps the most notable of the runaways who came to Connecticut was the Reverend James W. C. Pennington, pastor of a Hartford congregation and holder of a doctor's degree from the University of Heidelberg, whose story is told elsewhere in this book. The most spectacular, however, were the more than forty fugitives who arrived in New Haven in 1839, not from the American South but from a foreign country. These were the captives of the *Amistad*.

CHAPTER 4

THE CAPTIVES OF THE *AMISTAD*

THERE wasn't any doubt about Antonio, the mulatto cabin boy. He was a slave, property of the late Captain Ramón Ferrer of the schooner *Amistad*, and he was perfectly willing to return to bondage in Cuba. But what of the forty-odd Negroes, Cinque and Grabbo, Banna and Tami and the rest? Were they to be treated as runaway slaves; or as pirates and murderers; or as free men who had asserted their right to liberty by direct action? And what of the *Amistad* herself, her cargo of merchandise, and the claims to salvage brought forward by Lieutenant Gedney and others?

Such were the questions that confronted Andrew T. Judson—the man who had led the attack on Prudence Crandall's school—late in the summer of 1839. Before they were finally answered, years later, the affair of the *Amistad* had engaged the attention of three sovereign governments, a former American President, a future governor of Connecticut, several Yale professors, a seaman from Sierra Leone, many abolitionist leaders, and hundreds of ordinary citizens especially in New Haven and Farmington. It had supplied antislavery men with some of their best opportunities for propaganda, and it had established in Farmington the climate of sympathy that made that town so important a transfer point on the Underground Railroad.

The story began in the West African backlands.[1] There, in April of 1839, slave raiders seized Cinque and other members of the Mendi tribe, drove them to the coast, and chained them in the 'tween-decks of a blackbirder bound for the West Indies. For two months the captives endured the horrors of the Middle Passage; but they were a hardy group, for less than twenty of them died en route while more than fifty survived.[2] Landed at Havana in mid-June, they were promptly sold as slaves to two Cubans named Pedro Móntez and José Ruiz.

Among these victims of the slave trade was one older man, as well as three young girls and several boys, but the majority were vigorous men in their twenties. They were not a tall people—none over five feet six inches—and in color they ranged from ebony to dusky brown; one or two were "almost mulatto bright." [3] Cinque, strongly made and athletic, with a remarkable firmness of bearing and a commanding presence, was their acknowledged leader. Grabbo, second in authority, was scarcely less impressive.

The sale of these people in Cuba was completely illegal, but such happenings were common enough. Spanish law permitted the keeping of slaves in the colony but not their importation. Any slave brought from abroad was legally free the moment he set foot on shore; and a mixed British and Spanish commission, established by treaty between the two powers, sat in Havana to rule on cases involving slave ships taken at sea. In practice, however, the law was a dead letter. The mixed commission's powers covered only the high seas; what happened in territorial waters or ashore was the business of the Cuban colonial government.

Through a widespread network of graft and corruption, those who knew the ropes could receive official title to even the newest imports from Africa, and all it cost was ten dollars a head.[4] There was reason to suspect that the United States consul in Havana was involved in these practices.[5]

Móntez and Ruiz obtained the necessary papers. Then they embarked their purchases on the schooner *Amistad* (the name meant "friendship") for the coastwise run to Puerto Principe. Since the voyage was not a long one, they did not confine their bondsmen; that was a mistake. When two of the Africans went to the water cask without leave, they were whipped for it; that too was a mistake.[6]

None of the captives understood Spanish, but Banna knew a few words of English and several could speak a little Arabic. And the slave Antonio, cabin boy on the schooner, had some knowledge of the Mendi tongue. Thus the Negroes were able to ask the ship's cook where they were going. And the answer, meant but not received as a brutal joke, was understood by all: they were going to be killed and eaten.[7]

That was the fatal mistake, for it touched off an insurrection. Under the leadership of Cinque, the Africans armed themselves with long, heavy knives used for cutting sugar cane and rose in revolt on the second night of the voyage. They killed the cook; they cut down Captain Ferrer, but not before he had killed one of them and injured several others; they wounded Móntez, seized Ruiz and Antonio, and drove the rest of the crew to the boats. Now masters of the vessel, they meant to return home. Africa, they knew, lay two months distant toward the rising sun; and they forced the Spaniards to act as navigators and sail in that direction. By day, when the sun was up, Móntez and Ruiz did as they were bidden, holding the schooner on an easterly course; but by night they veered north and west, hoping to be picked up and rescued by some passing ship.[8]

For two months the *Amistad* wandered the ocean in this manner. Water and provisions ran short; ten or more of the Negroes died at sea. At length they made a landfall in the vicinty of Montauk Point, Long Island. After tacking about for two or three days, the schooner dropped anchor and Cinque went ashore with some of his followers. With Spanish money they had found on board, they bought food and water, a bottle of gin, and two dogs. They also asked if this country made slaves and if there were any Spaniards there. The answer to both questions was No; whereupon Cinque whistled and all his people jumped up and shouted in joy. They then asked one of the Long Islanders, Captain Harry Green of Sag Harbor, if he would steer them to Africa, and he let them believe he would do so the next day.[9]

Now the United States brig *Washington*, Lieutenant Thomas R. Gedney commanding, came upon the scene. Engaged in coastal survey work, Gedney had noticed the *Amistad*, and her appearance led him to believe she might be aground or in distress. He sent a party to board the schooner; and its officer, finding only Negroes armed with cane knives on deck, took control of the vessel at gun point. Móntez and Ruiz, released from below decks, immediately claimed and were accorded protection. The Negroes ashore were seized and returned to the *Amistad*. Cinque jumped into the sea and started swimming, but he was lassoed and brought back by a boat's crew. Free country or not, the Africans were captives again.[10]

Lieutenant Gedney brought his prize into the nearest port, New London, where she and the Africans were put in the custody of the United States marshal. In the United States District Court—where Andrew T. Judson was the recently appointed judge—Gedney and certain Long Islanders filed libels for salvage. Móntez and Ruiz, advised by the Spanish consul at New York, entered a claim for the return of their slaves. The Negroes, charged with piracy and murder, were housed in the New Haven jail. And the story got into the newspapers—mostly as told by the Spaniards and Antonio, for Banna's English was fragmentary.[11]

The abolitionists at once swung into action. Within three days they set up a committee consisting of the Reverend Simeon S. Jocelyn; the Reverend Joshua Leavitt, editor of *The Emancipator;* and the wealthy New York merchant Lewis Tappan. They issued a public appeal for funds; they engaged Roger S. Baldwin of New Haven as counsel for the Africans; they sought the help of John Quincy Adams, former President of the United States and now a member of Congress; [12] and they tried to find an interpreter. In this they had invaluable assistance from Professor Josiah W. Gibbs, professor of Hebrew in Yale College. He visited the Africans in jail repeatedly, and from them he learned the Mendi words for the numbers one to ten. Then he scoured the waterfronts of New Haven and New York in search of a seaman who could understand those sounds. Thus he came upon James Covey, a Mendi-speaking sailor and a former slave from Sierra Leone, whom he brought to New Haven on September 9. At last the Africans were able to tell their story in full. Gibbs also set about learning their language and was soon able to speak with them himself.[13]

By this time the Spanish minister in Washington, acting on behalf of his government, had interested himself in the affair. In a formal note on September 6 he demanded the extradition of the Negroes to stand trial in Cuba for piracy and murder. At his instance, the United States district attorney filed further claims in Spain's behalf to the schooner, the cargo, and the alleged slaves in the District Court; this action, taken in accordance with the existing commercial treaty between the two nations, superseded the individual claims. Thus the *Amistad* and her captives were quickly enmeshed in a web of legalisms.[14]

The first charge to be decided was that of piracy and murder. Committed by Judge Judson to the Circuit Court, it came before Judge Smith Thompson in the middle of September; and he made short work of it. He instructed the grand jury that, since the alleged crimes had been committed on a Spanish vessel on the high seas, no United States court had jurisdiction to deal with them. As for the Negroes, he ruled that the question of their freedom or servitude was rightly before the District Court, where it must be decided. Meanwhile, he said on September 23, the blacks must remain in custody.[15]

All the autumn, therefore, while diplomatic and legal maneuverings went on behind the scenes, Cinque and his people remained in the New Haven jail; but since Judge Thompson had ruled that they had committed no crime against American law, their treatment was hardly that of ordinary prisoners. They received a constant flow of visitors, not only their attorneys and abolitionist friends but also many who came because of mere curiosity. They had regular instruction—in Christian doctrine among other subjects—from members of the Yale faculty. Strolling on the Green on pleasant days, leaping about, turning handsprings, and performing other "wild feats of agility," they delighted the crowds of onlookers. They received gifts of American clothing, with whose unfamiliar intricacies they struggled in good humor; the girls, it was reported, thought that shawls were meant to be wound around the head, like turbans. By their cheerful good nature they won

The Reverend
Samuel J. May

The Reverend
Amos G. Beman
Beman collection

FOUR ANTISLAVERY LEADERS

Prudence Crandall

Nathaniel Jocelyn

Cinque. The portrait by Nathaniel Jocelyn.
Courtesy of the New Haven Colony Historical Society

many friends and much popular sympathy. Newspapers kept the public posted on their personal interests and habits. *The Liberator*, for example, reported this item taken from the New Haven *Register:*

> We understand that some of the abolition ladies visited the jail on Thursday morning, and went through the delightful and refreshing task of kissing several of the negroes! Whether Cinque and Graubo were honored with their favors, we know not—but the former has expressed a partiality for his "non-resistant" guests.

Pendleton the jailer was one of the first to recognize the attraction to these dark prisoners; and, in order to gain money to buy them additional comforts, he charged admission to their quarters.[16]

Among these Africans, the one who commanded the greatest attention was Cinque. His impressive physique, his noble bearing, and his unquestioned authority well merited the sobriquet by which he came to be known—"the Black Prince." Reproductions of his portrait by Nathaniel Jocelyn, abolitionist brother of the Reverend Simeon S. Jocelyn, were widely distributed in the New Haven area.[17]

Despite their growing number of well-wishers, the legal status of the Negroes remained precarious. The Spanish minister was still pressing for their extradition, and at least some members of President Van Buren's administration looked favorably on his request. But the Cabinet decided to leave the question in abeyance until the case had been decided by the District Court.[18] Judge Judson, it was felt, would make the right decision. He was known to be no friend of Negroes, and he had been appointed to his office by the current Administration, which was sympathetic to the slavocracy.[19] Presumably he would order the return of the *Amistad* captives to their claimants. In anticipation of this decision, a United States Navy vessel was sent to New Haven, to take the Negroes back to Cuba immediately Judson so ordered.[20]

Somehow the abolitionist committee learned of this development and prepared countermeasures. A group of them, of whom Nathaniel Jocelyn was one, laid plans to free the captives from jail, by force if necessary, and to spirit them out of the country on a ship of their own.[21] Meanwhile, John Quincy Adams had been at work on the case, examining the legal points and precedents involved and corresponding with the committee.[22] The British government, too, got wind of the affair and made representations to Madrid on behalf of the Negroes.[23] Much was at stake when the hearings began in the District Court in January 1840.

The inquiry lasted a week, before a crowded courtroom. So far as the salvage actions were concerned, there was little doubt as to the facts; but as to the status of the Negroes, the facts themselves were in question. Móntez and Ruiz asserted lawful ownership of these people; and their claim was backed by passports, issued in Havana on June 27 and signed by the Captain General of Cuba, in which the Africans were identified by Spanish names and were declared to be *negros ladinos* (literally, "smart blacks"—a term used to designate slaves long resident in the island) and the property of the two Spaniards. On the face of things, these papers were legal proof of ownership. But the Negroes, through their counsel, had petitioned for their release, stating that they were free-born Africans who had been unlawfully captured and sold into slavery. Moreover, there was before the Court a deposition from James Covey, describing his conversations with the *Amistad* captives and stating his belief that they told the simple truth. A further deposition, from Richard R. Madden of the mixed British-Spanish commission in Havana, perhaps carried more weight. Madden described in detail the net of chicanery by which "Bozal negroes," as newly imported slaves were called, were freely bought and sold under false papers with the connivance of the Cuban authorities. He further recounted his brief talks in Arabic with some of the *Amistad* men, and his conviction that they were indeed Bozals and hence free under Spanish law. Judson was faced on the one hand with official documents; on the other, with knowledgeable testimony indicating that the documents were fraudulent.[24]

Finally the judge handed down his rulings on January 23. Antonio, the *Amistad*, and the cargo—less salvage payments—were to be returned to their owners. The salvage claim of Lieutenant Gedney was upheld, those of the Long Island men denied. As to the Negroes, "Cinquez and Grabeau shall not sigh for Africa in vain. Bloody as may be their hands, they shall yet embrace their kindred." [25] They were in fact free men. As such, they were to be "delivered to the President of the United States by the Marshal of the District of Connecticut, to be by him transported to Africa" as provided by law in such cases.[26]

The United States attorney was not at all satisfied with this ruling. He at once moved an appeal to the Circuit Court, which in April upheld Judson's decisions. Again there was an appeal, to the Supreme Court, which would be the final authority.[27] For the Negroes, this meant more months of waiting in relatively mild detention. For their friends, it meant preparation for a further court case; and now John Quincy Adams joined Roger S. Baldwin in the thick of the fight.

The former President was well over seventy years of age but still deeply engrossed in public affairs. From the beginning he had been interested in the fate of the *Am-*

istad captives. As early as October 1, 1839, he wrote: "But that which now absorbs great part of my time and all my good feelings is the case of the fifty-three African negroes taken at sea, off Montauk Point, by Lieutenant Gedney"; and his diary for the next eighteen months is dotted with references to the affair.[28] He had studied the legal precedents, he had badgered the Administration with demands for its correspondence with the Spanish minister, he had pried deeply into the activities of the American consul at Havana, and he had given Baldwin the benefit of his advice. But he had also been carrying a full load of work as a member of the House of Representatives and chairman of several of its committees, so that he had taken no active part in the previous court hearings. Now, at the urging of Ellis Gray Loring and Lewis Tappan, he agreed to appear with Baldwin as counsel at the Supreme Court hearing, set for January 1841. He dug more deeply than ever into all aspects of the case, studied the scrapbooks of newspaper clippings that were the fruit of the abolitionists' propaganda efforts, conferred with Baldwin in person, and visited the captives in New Haven.[29] A few weeks later the boy Ka-le sent him a letter, stating in painfully learned English the case as the Africans saw it:[30]

> Dear Friend Mr. Adams:
>
> I want to write a letter to you because you love Mendi people, and you talk to the grand court. We want to tell you one thing. Jose Ruiz say we born in Havana, he tell lie. We stay in Havana 10 days and 10 nights, we stay no more. We all born in Mendi—we no understand the Spanish language. Mendi people been in America 17 moons. We talk American language little, not very good; we write every day; we write plenty letters; we read most all time; we read all Matthew, and Mark, and Luke, and John, and plenty of little books. We love books very

much. We want you you to ask the Court what we have done wrong. What for Americans keep us in prison. Some people say Mendi people crazy; Mendi people dolt, because we no talk American language. Merica people no talk Mendi language; Merica people dolt? They tell bad things about Mendi people, and we no understand. Some men say Mendi people very happy because they laugh and have plenty to eat. Mr. Pendleton come, and Mendi people all look sorry because they think about Mendi land and friends we no see now. Mr. Pendleton say Mendi people angry; white men afraid of Mendi people. The Mendi people no look sorry again—that why we laugh. But Mendi people feel sorry; O, we can't tell how sorry. Some people say, Mendi people got no souls. Why we feel bad, we got no souls? We want to be free very much.

Dear friend Mr. Adams, you have children, you have friends, you love them, you feel very sorry if Mendi people come and carry them all to Africa. We feel bad for our friends, and our friends all feel bad for us. Americans no take us in ship. We on shore and Americans tell us slave ship catch us. They say we make you free. If they make us free they tell true, if they no make us free they tell lie. If America people give us free we glad, if they no give us free we sorry—we sorry for Mendi people little, we sorry for America people great deal, because God punish liars. We want you to tell court that Mendi people no want to go back to Havana, we no want to be killed. Dear friend, we want you to know how we feel. Mendi people *think, think, think*. Nobody know what he think; teacher he know, we tell him some. Mendi people have got souls. We think we *know* God punish us if we tell lie. We never tell lie; we speak truth. What for Mendi people afraid? Because they got souls. Cook say he kill, he eat Mendi people—we afraid—we kill cook; then captain kill one man with knife, and cut Mendi people plenty. We never kill captain, he no kill us. If Court ask who brought Mendi people to America? We bring ourselves. Ceci hold the rudder. All we want is make us free.

Your friend,
Ka-le

In the middle of January Adams had a visit from Henry Stephen Fox, minister of Great Britain. He had heard, said Fox, that the Court would deliver up these unfortunate men to the Cuban claimants—a decision that would not be pleasing to Her Majesty's Government. Adams advised him to address a note to the Secretary of State, requesting the President's intervention if the case should turn out thus.[31]

The hearing before the Supreme Court was first delayed by the absence of Justice Joseph Story, then interrupted by the sudden death of Justice Philip Barbour. It began on February 20, lasting until March 2. The case for the United States—that is, for the return of the Negroes to slave status—was presented by Attorney-General Henry D. Gilpin, who based his contention on the passports issued by the Captain General of Cuba. For the captives, Baldwin spoke first. He was "sound and eloquent . . . powerful and perhaps conclusive"; but Adams was "apprehensive there are some precedents and an Executive influence operating on the Court which will turn the balance against us." [32] When his own turn came to speak, the former President built his argument about a single theme —justice—stressing his view that "an immense array of power—the Executive Administration, instigated by the Minister of a foreign nation—has been brought to bear, in this case, on the side of *injustice*." His argument, extending over two days, occupied more than eight hours; yet he was not too well pleased with his own performance.[33]

He need not have worried. The decision of the Supreme Court, handed down on March 9, was written by

Justice Story. It upheld the lower courts as to the salvage claims, the *Amistad* and her cargo, and the status of Antonio, who all this while had been detained as a possible witness. Then it spoke of the African captives. After reviewing the facts and the applicable laws and treaties, it concluded with these words: [34]

> Upon the whole, our opinion is that the decree of the Circuit Court, affirming that of the District Court, ought to be affirmed, except so far as it directs the negroes to be delivered to the President, to be transported to Africa . . . and, as to this, it ought to be reversed: and that the said negroes be declared to be free, and be dismissed from the custody of the court, and go without day.

This decision delighted the abolitionists, and the Negroes were overjoyed, kneeling in thanks to God once their initial incredulity had been dispelled. Gedney too was pleased, for he received as salvage one-third of the value of the *Amistad* and her cargo, which had long since been sold by court order. The Spanish claimants, however, continued to press for indemnities through diplomatic channels, but without success; the last of a series of measures to grant them relief died in Congress as late as 1858. As for Antonio, who had professed a willingness to return to slavery in Cuba, eighteen months in the United States had changed his mind. On the eve of his delivery to the Spanish authorities he slipped away and sought protection from Lewis Tappan, who sent him to freedom via the Underground Railroad.[35]

Now Cinque and his people were free at last; but what could they do? They had no money, no means of earning a livelihood in America. They had no way of getting back to Africa, as they wished. Adams believed that the United States government was "bound in the forum of conscience to send them home at its own charge" and probably should "indemnify them liberally for eighteen months of false imprisonment"; [36] but nothing came of this suggestion. The quondam captives remained, in fact, dependent on their abolitionist friends.

Their friends did not fail them. With renewed vigor, they set about soliciting money for the relief of the Negroes, some of whom were taken about New England by Lewis Tappan in a series of fund-raising meetings. But most were removed to a quiet Connecticut village where they could live in peace while their affairs were being arranged. That village was Farmington.[37]

Farmington was an excellent choice. It was easily reached from Hartford by road and from New Haven by canal, yet it was sufficiently out of the way to be placid and largely self-contained. Its two thousand inhabitants included only a few apologists for slavery, while among the 110 members of its two antislavery societies were many of the town's leading citizens. It was already the scene of Underground Railroad activities. To this haven the captives, now free men all, were brought in the spring of 1841.[38]

Samuel Deming and Austin F. Williams were among the local citizens who arranged for the reception and care of the so-called "Mendi Indians," but many others helped. The men were lodged in a barracks "at the rear of the old Wadsworth House . . . adjoining the cemetery," where they speedily made themselves at home; the three girls lived with local families.[39] A school was established for them in the upper floor of the Bidwell & Deming store, where Professor George E. Day of Yale continued their instruction; their progress in reading, spelling, and arithmetic, achieved under such unpropitious circumstances, made a very favorable impression. Nor was the good of their souls neglected, for they were taken to church services in a body.[40]

These visitors from a far continent added an exotic touch to the quiet life of the village. At first, stories were abroad to the effect that the Negroes were cannibals and hence dangerous, but they proved to be the most gentle of people, wandering freely about the town and making friends with everyone.[41] They soon became welcome visitors in many homes, and they were particularly popular with the children, who found delightful companions in these "big sable playmates." In later years one Farmington boy recalled "how this same Black Prince used to toss me up and seat me on his broad shoulder while he executed a barbaric dance on the lawn for my entertainment"; and again: [42]

> A broad flight of steps then led down from the southern piazza of my father's house, and I distinctly remember seeing the athletic Cinquez turn a somersault from these steps and then go on down the sloping lawn in a succession of hand springs heels over head, to the wonderment and admiration of my big brothers and myself.

The Africans also excelled as swimmers, and in warmer weather they spent many hours splashing about in the canal. There, in August, tragedy struck. Grabbo, also known as Foone, drowned while swimming in Pitkin's Basin, despite his proficiency in the water. Some believed he was seized with a cramp; some held that he made a futile attempt to extricate from the Basin the body of "young Chamberlain, who had been drowned," and that, entangling himself in the dam, he lost his life too. Still others thought it a case of suicide, brought on by despondency over his long separation from wife and family in Africa.

In any case, a monument was erected to his memory in the nearby cemetery.[43]

Not all the "Mendi Indians" took part in such athletic activities. Fourteen-year-old Tami, straight and lithe, with a soft voice and a sweet smile, loved to talk of the simple life in her home country, of the beehive straw houses and the village games she remembered so well. She took great pleasure in tending a little flower garden and was delighted when she succeeded in getting some pineapples to grow. But she too knew a dark moment: [44]

> One night after all had retired to their rooms, Tamie came to my door and when I opened it, she stood there the picture of despair; taking my hand she led me to a north window in her room where she exclaimed "I think we never see Mendi any more." The banners of an extremely brillant *Aurora Borealis* were flashing in the sky and she was sure they would be destroyed but was reassured when I told her that at certain seasons we often had those lights.

Thus the spring and the summer and the autumn passed, while the Negroes waited at Farmington and the abolitionist committee worked on the problem of getting them back home. First the committee members tried to enlist the help of the American Board of Commissioners for Foreign Missions, to whom they proposed an antislavery mission to the Mendi country, to be financed in part by the funds they had raised. When this approach proved futile, the abolitionists established their own "Mendi Mission," with the Reverend William Raymond and the Reverend James Steele in charge. After a public farewell meeting at New York's Broadway Tabernacle on November 27, 1841, the captives of the *Amistad* at last took ship for Sierra Leone and the homes from which they had been snatched nearly three years previously. The mission thus established endured for many years. Margroo or Sarah, one of the three girls, grew up to become a teacher in its school, and Cinque was its interpreter at the time of his death in 1879.[45]

Of those who had helped the captives in their dark days, John Quincy Adams continued to serve in Congress until his death in 1848, a crusty fighter for justice up to the end. Roger S. Baldwin became governor of Connecticut in 1844, advocating votes for Negroes and a law to hinder slave-catchers in the state. Four years later, as a member of the United States Senate, he voted against an appropriation to satisfy Spanish claims for indemnity in the *Amistad* case. The abolitionists used the affair as a perfect occasion to close their own ranks and to create widespread sympathy for the helpless children of Africa. And the people of Farmington, fully awake now to the evils and injustices of slavery, converted their town into the most important crossroads on Connecticut's Underground Railway.[46]

CHAPTER 5

A HOUSE DIVIDED

THE AFFAIR of the *Amistad* Negroes unquestionably stimulated Connecticut's traditional Yankee devotion to independence, and it aroused widespread sympathy for those who were held as slaves, whether in Africa or in the American South. All over the state, people who believed in freedom made their views increasingly plain, their voices increasingly heard during the next decade.

Such a one was Maria W. Chapman, whose poem "Connecticut" began with the following words: [1]

Come, toil-worn, and care-worn, and battle-worn friends!
Ye bound with the bondman, till tyranny ends!
From the glimmer of dawn on the waves of the sea,
To the shadows of sunset, wherever ye be,
Take courage and comfort! Our land of bright streams
And beautiful valleys, awakes from her dreams,
At the sound of your voices, and calls from its grave
The Spirit of Freedom, to shelter the slave.

Another outspoken opponent of slavery was the Reverend George W. Perkins of Meriden, who as a Congregational clergyman was a member of the dominant religious institution of the time. In 1845 he submitted to the General Association of Congregational Ministers of Connecticut the following resolutions: [2]

1. That no man is bound in conscience to obey the slave law.

> 2. That it may be matter of judgment and expediency what measures should be taken and what risks incurred in aiding the colored men to escape from bondage . . . the right to give such aid, we hold to be undeniable.

The Congregational body as a whole, however, was not ready to endorse such a strong statement in support of the abolitionist movement and of the Underground Railroad. The Reverend Mr. Andrews refused to vote for any resolution that described slaveholding as a sin. The Reverend E. Hall, while stating that "he abhorred slavery totally from the bottom of his heart," nevertheless opposed the Perkins resolutions as "rank Garrisonism." The New York *Observer*, commenting on the proceedings, took a similar view. "The resolutions introduced by Mr. Perkins," its editor said, "were the most ultra and untenable ever heard of in any ecclesiastical body." The Association's members were apparently of similar mind, for the resolutions were overwhelmingly defeated.[3]

Such were the feelings of Connecticut's most numerous and powerful religious group; for the Congregational Church, although it contributed abolitionist leaders, also supplied some of the most ardent defenders of slavery. Among other denominations, the Quakers, Baptists, and Methodists were the most active in the cause of abolition;[4] the Catholic Church, however—mindful of being criticized for espousing the idea of a strong central government—accepted slavery as a "matter of local concern," and therefore it "advocated state rather than federal control."[5]

At this time, too, the abolitionists—or some of them—stepped directly into the political arena. The followers of William Lloyd Garrison took no part in this action. With their leader, they thought of the Constitution of the United States as a document of slavery, hence worthy of no respect; and they felt bound in conscience to ignore it and the government established under its terms, refusing to vote in any election. But by no means did all antislavery men agree with this position. Many believed that political action within the existing framework of American government was not only proper but necessary in the abolitionist cause. Men of this view, after a series of preliminary gatherings in Ohio, Western New York, and elsewhere, met in convention at Albany in the spring of 1840. From this meeting there emerged a new political organization, the Liberty Party. Its candidate for the Presidency was James G. Birney, attorney and sometime slaveholder in Alabama, who under the influence of Theodore Weld had become first an advocate of colonization, then of total emancipation. He was now one of the most influential and respected leaders of the abolition movement. In the election of 1840, Birney polled only some 7000 of the 2,400,000 votes cast; but the Liberty Party was nonetheless the political seed which sprouted into the Republican Party and led to the overthrow of slavery two decades later.[6]

In Connecticut, the Liberty Party had scarcely more success than it did on the national scene. In the 1842 election, Francis Gillette of Bloomfield was its candidate for governor. He received but 1319 votes—a mere handful, but a significant straw in the political wind. By 1845 the Liberty Party voters had increased to more than 2000, indicative of a rising tide of antislavery feeling in the state.[7]

Perhaps as a result of that growing sentiment for freedom, the General Assembly in 1848 enacted a bill providing that "no person shall hereafter be held in slavery in this State" and that all the slaves freed by the measure—in fact, only six in number—were to be supported for life by their former owners.[8] This act of abolition created small stir; there was no official pronouncement of universal freedom, no celebrations or mass meetings either in support or in protest, for slavery had long been a dead letter in Connecticut.

Antislavery propaganda, symptomatic of the age's "restless agitation for the betterment of civilization,"[9] grew in quantity and in outspoken boldness during the 1840's. A leading voice was that of the *Charter Oak*, which had been merged with the *Christian Freeman* and which was now edited by William H. Burleigh, "self-educated genius—farmer, printer, journalist, and lawyer," who had been active in the Liberty Party in Pennsylvania. By 1847, he was boldly calling for greater activity on the Underground Railroad:[10]

> If one aids the slaves to escape he has pointed a fellow-being to his inalienable birth-right, Liberty. He has remembered those in bonds as bound with them—he has done an act which brings him nearer to the heart of God. . . . As long as men are capable of perceiving the distinction between right and wrong, so long will the uncorrupted heart and conscience side with the slave in his efforts to be free,—and the good and the brave will stand ready to aid him in his work of self-deliverance.

That such propaganda had its effects is not surprising. The number of convinced abolitionists increased; and it was said that, if the black race were petted anywhere in the world, it must have been in Connecticut, Massachusetts, and Rhode Island. In some circles—even among persons not notable for humane attitudes and behavior—it became almost the fashionable thing to show sympathy for the Negro in distress. One instance involved a Hartford man who had "superintended the sale of sixty white paupers and was some time after appealed to on behalf of a runaway slave. His 'phelinks' were so wonderfully stirred by the color of the applicant that he gave him $10, took him home, clothed and fed him, at an expense equal to what he had sold a white pauper fellow-townwoman for under the hammer. This virtue, however, proved its own reward, since the 'runaway slave' turned out to be a knavish wood-sawyer from a distant town, who was making a raise on the 'fugitive dodge.' "[11]

Nonetheless, so far as much of Connecticut was concerned, abolitionists were unpopular and free Negroes were held in contempt.[12] Under the law, they occupied a sort of second-class status. The state constitution of 1818 granted them citizenship but denied them the franchise, which was limited to free white males. It was only natural, in these circumstances, that the Southern point of view commanded widespread sympathy, especially in the business community.

Cotton was a principal reason. It provided a close commercial tie between the Southern planter, who depended on slave labor, and the New England mill owner, who depended on a crop grown by slaves. In 1818 there were 67 cotton mills in Connecticut; by 1845 the number had grown to 136, and textile production was a leading industry of the state.[13] The consumption of cotton was tremendous. It was a major item of cargo on the steamers that regularly traveled between New York and Hartford, via Long Island Sound and the Connecticut River. A single concern, the Russell Manufacturing Company of Middletown, required 3100 bales a year to feed the 15,000 spindles in its three mills. The proprietors of such establishments were naturally not inclined to hold views or to encourage activities that would interfere with the smooth flow of their commerce, particularly when the South itself constituted an important market for their goods. Hartford and Connecticut, it was said, were so closely con-

The Reverend George W. Perkins

Levi Yale

Photo courtesy the subject's granddaughter, Mrs. Laura Churchill

FOUR UNDERGROUND AGENTS

Benjamin Douglas

The Reverend Samuel W. S. Dutton

The Chaffee House, Windsor
Photo by the Author

TWO UNDERGROUND STATIONS

The Coe House, Winsted
Photo courtesy Mrs. William Barrett

nected with the cotton fields that the abolitionists there found it difficult to do their work.[14]

Yankee peddlers, too, had a part in creating sympathy for the Southern position. These men for decades past had been engaged in distributing Connecticut's small-scale products all along the eastern seaboard, from Maine to Georgia. Traveling generally by wagon, they sold their goods from door to door, not only in towns but on isolated farms and plantations as well, and they often enjoyed the overnight hospitality of those who purchased their wares. Some of these peddlers are known to have been active in the operations of the Underground Railroad, even transporting black passengers hidden beneath the goods in their red carts.[15] Others came back from their trips with an entirely different reaction: [16]

> Connecticut clock peddlers who went South . . . to vend their wares among the planters, were often so desirous of pleasing those of whom they sought patronage that they did not scan too closely the workings of the "peculiar institution." These peddlers often made a "good spec" at their business and were hospitably entertained by those who bought their time-pieces. So they came back with their original antislavery notions modified; or some of these peddlers confessed to a "change of views" on the question and of these, some were even ready to help catch the runaways.

Connecticut in the 1840's, then, was a state of divided mind, where the antislavery speaker might find hecklers as well as sympathizers among his audience in the lecture hall, while he and his property might be subject to any kind of harassment at any time. Thus, in Mystic and Naugatuck, squirt guns were used to dampen the ardor of abolitionist speakers; and Abby Kelly, who campaigned for abolition as tirelessly as for women's rights, had a hymn-book hurled at her head while waiting to speak at a church in East Bridgewater.[17]

Among the leaders of proslavery opinion were men of property, leaders in the professions and in business. Such at least was the case in Waterbury, as one antislavery spokesman reported: [18]

> I have spent most of the day in Waterbury. There is, perhaps, no place in America where manufacturing, in its every variety, is carried on as here. In wood, in iron, in brass, in wool, in every thing almost, there are mills and manufactures of incredible extent. But the conservatism of the people is beyond the power of language to express.
>
> The first person with whom I spoke (a truly civil and polite gentleman, near the depot) told me there were few except true Whigs and Democrats in town; and he added, "I don't believe there is one among them all who would not aid in the return of a fugitive."

Sometimes the opposition to antislavery speakers expressed itself in truly mean and despicable ways. An experience of the escaped slave James Lindsey Smith, on a lecturing trip with Dr. Hudson, was perhaps typical: [19]

> When we were in Saybrook there was but one Abolitionist in the place, and whose wife was sick. As we could not be accommodated at his house, we stopped at a tavern; the inmates were very bitter toward us, and more especially to the Doctor. I became much alarmed about my own situation; there was an old sea captain there that night, and while in conversation with the Doctor, had some very hard talk, which resulted in a dispute, or contest of words; I thought it would terminate in a fight. The captain asked the doctor, "what do you know about slavery? All you know about it I suppose, is what this fellow (meaning me) has told you, and if I knew who his master

was, and where he was, I would write to him to come on and take him." This frightened me very much; I whispered to the Doctor that we had better retire for the night. We went to our rooms. I feared I should be taken out of my room before morning, so I barred my door with chairs and other furniture that was in the room, before I went to bed. Notwithstanding, I did not sleep much that night. When we had arisen the next morning and dressed ourselves, we went down stairs, but did not stay to breakfast; we took our breakfast at the house of the man whose wife was sick. We gave out notice, by hand-bills, that we would lecture in the afternoon so we made preparation, and went at the time appointed. The hall was filled to its utmost capacity, but we could not do much, owing to the pressure that was so strong against us: hence we had no success in this place. We went to the tavern and stayed that night. The next morning we went about two miles from this place to the township, and stopped at the house of a friend; one of the same persuasion. He went to the school committee, and got the use of the school-house. We gave out notice that there would be an anti-slavery lecture in the school-house that night. When it was time for us, word came that we could not have the school-house for the purpose of such a lecture.

We thought that we would not be out-done by obstacles. The man at whose house we were stopping cordially told us that we might have the use of his house; so we changed the place of the lecture from the school-house to his house. The house was full; and we had, as we thought, a good meeting. At the close of the lecture the people retired for home. After awhile we retired for the evening, feeling that we had the victory. The next morning the Doctor went to the barn to feed his horse, and found that some one had entered the barn and shaved his horse's mane and tail close to the skin; and besides, had cut our buffalo robe all in pieces; besides shaving the horse, the villains had cut his ears off. It was the most distressed looking animal you ever saw, and was indeed to be pitied. The Dr. gathered up the fragments of the buffalo robe and brought them to the house; it was a sight to behold!

We intended to have left that day, but we changed our minds and stayed over another meeting. The house was crowded to excess that evening; at the close of the service the Doctor told how some one had shaved and cut his horse, and brought out the cut robe and held it up before the people, saying: "This is the way the friends of slavery have treated me. Those who have done it are known, but I shall not hurt a hair of their heads. I hope the Lord may forgive them." The people seemed to feel very badly about it.

While Smith continued to bear witness against slavery on the lecture platform, other leaders of Connecticut's Negroes were pressing their claims to full-scale citizenship. Despite the recommendation of Governor Baldwin after his election in 1844, they were still denied the right to vote; the General Assembly in 1847 defeated a measure that would have given them the franchise. Among the spokesmen for the state's colored community who particularly resented this condition of affairs was Selah Mills Africanus of Hartford. Born in New York City in 1822, he had been taught by his father to guide his life by three principles: religion, learning, and liberty. A persuasive speaker and a fervent champion of his people, he issued a stirring call to arms in a proclamation addressed to the "Colored Men of Connecticut": [20]

Brethren:—We propose to meet you in Convention, in the city of New Haven, on Wednesday, the 12th day of September, 1849, to consider our Political condition, and to devise measures for our elevation and advancement. Action on our part is imperatively necessary to secure the acknowledgement of our rights, and the enactment and administration of impartial laws affecting us, by the proper State authorities. Now as a body, we have no political existence. We are dead to citizenship, struck down by an unrighteous State Constitution, and our life spark quenched by a Cruel and unreasonable prejudice. But a voice is sounding through all lands, quickening and energizing the slumbering millions! Shall not we hear it and live also?

The shouts of hosts, battling for Freedom, are wafted to us continually over the waves. Shall we not swell the sounds? The hearts of all true lovers of Liberty and Human Progress, are beating high with hope; shall we sit alone desponding and inactive? We have reason to believe that the night is far spent, and an auspicious day is dawning upon us. Evidences of progress are numerous and increasing in our own States; shall we not prepare for the crisis?

We bid you come, then, from the four corners of the State—from the valley of the Housatonic and the Connecticut—from the borders of free Massachusetts and the western bounds of impartial Rhode Island! Let the dwellers on our southern shores, who witness daily the mighty pulsations of Old Ocean, come up as bold and irresistible, and roll on the tide wave of Liberty. Let resolute and hopeful men of every profession and occupation come. Age and Youth—the sons of ease and the sons of toil—the land holder and the landless—there's a welcome and work for all! Come in the strength and fear of God, and in the certainty of ultimate success by His blessing on our united efforts.

In accordance with this summons, the Connecticut State Convention of Colored Men assembled in New Haven on the appointed day. With Jehiel C. Beman of Middletown as president, the nearly one hundred delegates proceeded to discuss their problems and what steps might be taken. One of the subjects considered was "giving the

Bible to the Slaves," on which the fugitive Henry Bibb spoke at length. But the major topic of the assemblage was the question of Negro suffrage, which was demanded in a series of resolutions adopted by the Convention.

Despite their sincerity and the obvious justice of their case, these resolutions produced no immediate result. Even as late as 1857, the voters of Connecticut were unwilling to extend the franchise to their colored fellow citizens. In that year an amendment to the state constitution, laid before the people in referendum, was defeated by a count of 19,148 against to 5553 for—a margin of approximately three and a half to one.[21] Not until the Fifteenth Amendment to the federal Constitution came into effect in 1870 were Connecticut's Negroes at last assured the right to cast ballots.

By that time, some of Connecticut's Negroes had ceased to care. In the dangerous period that opened with the adoption of the Fugitive Slave Law of 1850, they had followed the Underground Railroad out of the country.

CHAPTER 6

"THIS PRETENDED LAW WE CANNOT OBEY"

THE SPLIT between North and South became wider and more serious as the number of runaway slaves became ever greater. It has been estimated that in the decade of the 1840's over a thousand fugitives annually escaped from what abolitionists liked to call "the land of whips and chains."[1] These runaways represented, among other things, a serious financial loss to slaveholders; a good slave in a good market might be worth $1000 or even $1500, though the average was considerably less. It was not surprising that Southern representatives in Congress constantly moved for a strengthening of the existing fugitive slave laws. A contributing factor was the decision of the Supreme Court in the case of Prigg *v.* Pennsylvania in 1842; for that ruling, while maintaining that the power to legislate on fugitives lay solely with Congress, also held that the states and their officials were not obliged to enforce the federal statutes. This decision touched off a new wave of "personal liberty laws" in Northern states, which in turn led to increased Southern pressure for a new Congressional enactment.[2]

Meanwhile, dark clouds were hovering over the Rio

Grande. American settlers in Texas, many of them slaveholders, had declared their independence of Mexico and had won it in battle in 1836. They now sought annexation by the United States, a prospect that disturbed many Northerners as much as it delighted many Southerners. Since the Missouri Compromise of 1820, the balance between slave and free states had been maintained by admitting two new states at a time, one in each category. If Texas came in by itself, the slave power would predominate; and the fact that Mexico would regard annexation as "equivalent to a declaration of war" would obligate the North to accept the resulting imbalance.[3]

The Southerners had their way. Texas was admitted to the Union in 1845, war with Mexico followed, and the United States by its victory gained vast new lands stretching all the way from the high prairies to the Pacific—New Mexico, California, and what is today Arizona.[4] Would these territories be admitted as slave states or as free ones? Controversy over this question exacerbated the growing sectional conflict and became a major national issue. At length those two masters of *quid pro quo* politics, Henry Clay of Kentucky and Daniel Webster of Massachusetts, worked out what many thought was a solution. This settlement, known as the Compromise of 1850, was adopted by Congress on September 18 of that year, despite great debate and disagreement. It embodied these chief provisions:[5]

1. The size of Texas would be somewhat reduced by allotting some of its territory to New Mexico, for which Texas was to be recompensed by the United States government;
2. California would be admitted to the Union as a free state;
3. New Mexico and Utah would be admitted, when ready,

as either slave or free, according to the determination of their settlers;

4. The slave trade would be abolished in the District of Columbia;
5. A new and strict fugitive slave law would be enacted.

The Fugitive Slave Law of 1850, adopted as a result of the compromise, was a drastic act indeed. It deprived the accused fugitive of any right to a trial by jury. Worse still, it provided that he could not even testify in his own behalf. Laying the jurisdiction of fugitive cases in the hands of federal commissioners appointed for this purpose, it directed United States marshals to apprehend alleged runaways, under pain of a fine of $1000 for failure to do so or for permitting a fugitive to escape. It permitted anyone at all to have an alleged runaway seized, without a warrant, and to bring him before a commissioner. That official had summary power to decide the case, and he was recompensed by a fee—ten dollars if the prisoner was adjudged to be an escaped slave, only five dollars if he was declared free, so that a finding of slavery was to the commissioner's advantage. On one hand the law provided no penalty for false claiming a freeman as a fugitive from slavery, and on the other, it set a fine of $1000 and a prison sentence of up to six months on anyone who sheltered an alleged runaway or who helped him escape. Further, "all good citizens" were commanded to "aid and assist in the prompt and efficient execution" of the law.[6]

This measure, in short, stacked the cards in favor of the claimant. It made every law-abiding citizen a potential slave-catcher, and it afforded not the slightest protection to the free Negro whom any slave-hunter cared to seize. It was an open invitation to kidnaping.

The South, naturally enough, endorsed the new law heartily, for it made the rendition of fugitive slaves more certain and it guaranteed the preservation of slavery as well.[7] Such a law had been sought especially by the border states—Missouri, Kentucky, Virginia, and Maryland—which adjoined the free states of Iowa, Illinois, Indiana, Ohio, and Pennsylvania, and which had consequently lost the greatest number of runaways to the Underground Railroad. But if the states of the Deep South had lost fewer bondmen, they were nonetheless in favor of the new law.[8]

In the North, too, this measure found outspoken supporters—among businessmen who had Southern connections, among persons of conservative mind, and among politicians who had strong partisan ties with their Southern counterparts. Thus it was that a well-organized union meeting was held in New Haven on October 24, 1850, to endorse the new law as a gesture of loyalty to the Constitution and to the "American System"—protection for the South's cotton and slaves, a flow of raw materials for Connecticut's mills, a counterflow of manufactured goods back to the plantation states. Addressing this meeting, the Reverend N. W. Taylor of Yale declared that it was "lawful to deliver up fugitives for the high, the great, the momentous interests of the South." Another speaker, by no means disagreeing, regretted that it might not be easy to live up to all obligations: "We have made some underground railroads—and have permitted it to be done—it is our duty to prevent their establishment. But how? That's the question. Alas, that property should take to itself wings and fly away." In the end, the meeting produced a petition stating that "any alteration of the Compromise Measures adopted at the last Session of Congress is not only inexpedient, but that it is the duty of every good citizen of this Republic to support and vindicate the same." Not less than 1746 signatures were appended to this document.[9]

Within the next few months, Connecticut's major political parties expressed more or less similar views. In November, the Whigs took the position that though the Fugitive Slave Law "was objectionable in some of its features and ought to be modified," yet "the provisions of the Constitution relative to delivering up fugitives were binding."[10] In the following February, an assembly of Democrats in Hartford stated its support of the law in unequivocally worded resolutions:[11]

> That we regard the law in relation to fugitives from service, as an act necessary to carry out the provision of the Constitution on that subject, a provision of the Constitution which is mandatory in its character, and which was adopted by the unanimous vote of the Convention which framed that instrument.
>
> That we hold in undiminished veneration the Constitution of the United States—that we will abide in good faith by all its compromises—and that we have no sympathy with those who, to evade its provisions, appeal to a "higher law" that teaches discord and disunion, and sectional hatred, and the violation of that Constitution under which this country has arrived at its present greatness and power.

Some of the state's newspapers also felt that the law must be upheld and obeyed. Thus Hartford's *Courant* stated editorially on October 19, 1850: "Let us bear in mind the language so lavishly bestowed upon the nullifiers of the South. . . . All laws passed in constitutional form must be obeyed until they are repealed. Any other course is criminal, any other doctrine leads to direct anarchy."[12] And the New Haven *Palladium*, taking a moderate position, found itself attacked by the same city's *Register* and the Hartford *Free Soil Republican*, for opposite reasons. First, the *Palladium* said on October 26:[13]

We regret to hear that a fugitive slave was arrested in Boston, yesterday. An attempt was made to take two of them, only one was captured. . . . If it appear that he is a fugitive we presume Bostonians will immediately raise the requisite funds to purchase his freedom. The Garrison men, however, it is probable will not contribute a penny because [they are] too conscientious to appropriate it for the purchase of a slave, for such an act, they say would be recognizing the legality of the slave institution. The poor slave, however, will doubtless be more thankful for the practical benevolence that frees him than for that which lives in a beautiful theory but brings forth no good fruit.

This statement brought a prompt blast from Jesse G. Baldwin, editor of the *Free Soil Republican,* who accused the *Palladium* of "passive obedience" to the Fugitive Slave Law.[14] The *Palladium* answered with an accusation of its own: [15]

The abolitionists themselves are responsible for the increased sufferings, and the present hard lot of the poor slaves. . . . The fugitive slave law, itself, is a direct consequence of the efforts of abolition kidnappers to steal away the negroes from the service of their masters —it is the abolitionist who exposed the fugitive in the free states to imminent danger of being returned to slavery.

Still trying to maintain a middle ground, the *Palladium* now turned its fire on its proslavery contemporary, the *Register:* [16]

We are surprised at the Register's course in regard to the fugitive slave law. Instead of uniting with other presses, which advocate the maintenance of order, it appears disposed to cavil even at a suggestion that the law is not the most perfect thing ever devised in human

> council. . . . One of its worst features is its retrospective or backward operation. If it had applied only to slaves escaping after the passage of the Act, it would not have been so cruel, nor have been in spirit, (we do not say it is in fact) an ex-post-facto law. . . . The fugitive slaves have, in good faith, settled and married among us, when under other circumstances, they would have settled in some other country where they would have been safe. To break up families under such circumstances is a grievous wrong.

That was too much for the *Register* to take in silence. It promptly charged that the *Palladium* had "found an ally in the New York Herald, in its deprecation of the delivering up fugitives." It then went on: [17]

> Suppose some one robs the editor of the Palladium of his printing press, and through some flaw in the indictment or the malice or prejudice of others, he is unable to recover it—and that the Legislature should so amend the law as to secure to our neighbor the certain protection of his property—and the thief should set up the cry that it was an ex-post-facto law, and that he ought to be allowed to keep what he had stolen, and only be answerable for future delinquencies? Can the editor of the Palladium say in his heart, that he would submit to such a scoundrelly plea, or admit for an instant its justice? Not he. It is no excuse to say that we at the North hate slavery; that there is a "higher law" than the Constitution; that our sympathies are with the fugitives.

The basic division in views among Connecticut's journals, reflecting those of the state's citizens, was succinctly expressed by two newspapers in Norwich. Said the *Tri-Weekly:* "Repeal, repeal, repeal! Let not the slave catchers pollute our soil!" To which the *Aurora* countered: "Who is going to deliver the slave then? The Constitution must be upheld." [18]

To many citizens, however, all this newspaper talk seemed more a battle of wits than an exchange of meaningful ideas. Holbrook Curtis, a "Conscience Whig" of Watertown, put his finger on a crucial aspect of the law and on the danger to which it might lead: "Our people at the North will not all of them readily be made Slave Catchers. I fear the folly and weakness of a few will be the means of enticing a Civil War." [19]

Selah Africanus of Hartford, speaking for Connecticut's Negro community, saw both legal and moral objections to the act, which he said "violates the spirit and letter of the Constitution, in the form and manner of seizures and arrests, in its requirements upon good citizens, in imposing excessive fines, in crushing the Habeas Corpus, and in depriving the person arrested of a trial by a jury of his peers." Furthermore, he contended, "It contravenes the Law of Nature, which is the foundation of all human laws, and which, being dictated by the Almighty himself, is of course superior in obligation to any other. Therefore, this enactment of Congress is both unjust and unreasonable, consequently becomes of no binding force, is null and void. Let it be placed among the abominations!" [20]

Connecticut's abolitionists, naturally, were not slow to express their opposition. Meeting in Hartford in early October, they filled American Hall to more than capacity. Speaking to this group, A. M. Collins expressed their position and purpose in a firm and explicit manner: [21]

> We sympathize with the fugitive from southern slavery in our own community, and with all such as in a manly and courageous spirit, are thus achieving their own freedom, that we will give them shelter, food, and clothing as deserving objects of our charity, and that we will use our utmost endeavors to secure to them the enjoyment of the scanty privileges left to them by law.

The Reverend George W. Perkins of Meriden, whose opinion of slavery had been made clear in his resolutions laid before the General Association of Congregational Ministers five years earlier, could not remain silent in the face of this new fugitive slave bill, reflecting as it did the power and determination of the slavocracy. Even before the measure became law, he had preached an almost inflammatory sermon at Guilford, under the title "Conscience and the Constitution." In this address, he set forth the view that the citizen was bound to obey two rightful authorities, the Constitution of the United States and the law of God; "but in case of conflict between the authority of the U. S. and the authority of God, obey God and disobey the United States." This, he said, was in effect the position taken by martyrs and reformers in all ages. "The early Christians were all lawbreakers—the Puritans were lawbreakers—our Pilgrim fathers were lawbreakers—our revolutionary fathers were lawbreakers." The friends of the fugitives therefore, bearing in mind the precept "Let the oppressed go free . . . betray not him that wandereth," were and must be lawbreakers too.[22] Now that the Fugitive Slave Law of 1850 was a reality, Perkins presided over a protest meeting at Middletown. Pointing out that the Bible speaks "the heartiest and most incendiary language of rebuke to the slaveholder," he drove through a resolution declaring that the law was unconstitutional, because it was contrary to the law of God and because it forbade upright citizens "to render the common offices of humanity to those who are escaping from bondage." [23]

Other churchmen than Perkins considered the new law odious. The Methodist Missionary Society, meeting in New London, condemned its "barefaced hypocrisy" in denying the fugitive the right of trial by jury while allowing "his claimant this privilege in the most unlimited manner." The meeting resolved to show resistance to tyrants and obedience to God, and to use "all lawful means for the repeal of this most atrocious and infamous law." [24]

It remained for the farmers of Middlefield, however, to state the case as the plain people saw it. Meeting under the leadership of William Lyman, they put the basic issues into the simplest terms, and they stated the only conclusion a self-respecting freeman could reach. This is the resolution they adopted: [25]

> This Fugitive Slave Law commands all good citizens to be slave-catchers: good citizens cannot be slave-catchers any more than light can be darkness. You tell us, the Union will be endangered if we oppose this law. We reply that greater things than the Union will be endangered, if we submit to it: Conscience, Humanity, Self-Respect are greater than the Union, and these must be pursued at all hazards. This pretended law commands us to withhold food and raiment and shelter from the most needy—we cannot obey.

This resolution was indicative of the rising tide of righteous indignation that swept Connecticut in the wake of the 1850 law.[26] The members of the General Assembly were not slow to hear the rumblings from the grass roots, and in a matter of months they expressed their opinion. The resolution they adopted admitted that Congress had the right to legislate concerning "delivering up of fugitives," but it maintained that Connecticut itself had the right to grant alleged runaways a fair trial by jury.[27] A few years thereafter, with Free Soil men sitting among its members, the Assembly enacted a new personal liberty law, under the title "An Act for the Defense of Liberty in this State." Adopted in 1854, the measure provided a fine of $5000 and five years' imprisonment for anyone who falsely swore that any free Negro was a fugitive slave.[28] Other acts forbade public officials to aid in the apprehension of alleged runaways; provided for jury trials; and required two witnesses to support any testimony as to services due.[29] Thus it became clear that, no matter what some segments of its press and its business population might think, official Connecticut meant both to make the work of the slave-hunter difficult and to protect the state's free Negroes.

In view of the sweeping privileges granted to slave-catchers, the colored people of the North indeed needed protection. Beginning in the autumn of 1850 a great Negro exodus, set off by the Fugitive Slave Law, saw "thousands of people of color crossing over into Canada" from all the Northern states between the Atlantic and the Missouri River, while thousands more moved from one state to another. In the next decade, the Negro population of British North America increased by 50 per cent, from "about 40,000 to nearly 60,000." [30] The flight from Connecticut had started by mid-October, when five persons left Hartford bound for Canada.[31] Even the Connecticut Colonization Society, despite its earlier proslavery leanings, played an important role at this time. Under its auspices, in 1851, the barque *Zeno* carried twenty Connecticut Negroes to Liberia—double the number that had left the state for Africa in all the years from 1820 to 1850.[32]

How many fugitive slaves were living in Connecticut at this time it is impossible to determine. Census returns for 1850 show a Negro population of 7693—some 400 fewer than a decade earlier—of whom 6244 were natives of the state.[33] But no figures are available to show how many of the remaining 1449 Negroes were freemen from other states, how many runaway slaves. A paragraph in a Middletown newspaper, however, suggests what was probably the general situation: [34]

> This law is creating great excitement in many sections of our neighborhood. The number of fugitives is many more than was suspected. Hundreds have come north, settled down and reared families. They have become respectable and useful members of the community, and have acquired a large circle of acquaintances and friends. None can see them arrested by strangers on the testimony of strangers, and carried to bondage without strongly interested feelings.

The Fugitive Slave Law touched even the small, self-sufficient village of Deep River, where William Winters had been living for two decades. Now, "because it was known that Massachusetts was more friendly to escaped slaves than Connecticut," he made his way to New Bedford. There he remained for a dozen years or more, not returning to Deep River until President Lincoln signed the Emancipation Proclamation.[35]

The effect of the new law on James Lindsey Smith was even more dramatic. For seven years he had been a resident of Norwich, earning his living as a shoemaker and giving antislavery lectures throughout southern New England. Now the fear of recapture seized him, and he was "haunted by dreams which were so vivid as to appear really true." In one of these nightmares, he dreamed that his owner had come for him and had taken him back to Virginia. His wife, when he told her the story in the morning, was even more upset than he, for she believed in dreams. Smith went to his shop that day in a thoroughly disturbed state of mind. And in mid-morning, as he glanced through a shop window at the passengers just off the Norwich-Worcester train, whom did he see—or so he thought—but the former master himself! The shoemaker was, he confessed, "pretty well frightened out of my wits. What to do I did not know. This man certainly walked like him, had whiskers like him; in fact, his whole general appearance resembled him so much that I was sure he had been put on my track. I peeped out at him as he passed my door and saw him go up the steps leading to the office of the U. S. Marshal, then I was sure he had come for me. I could do no more work that day."

All day Smith lurked in his shop, telling his fears to customers who came in. And they showed themselves to be not only customers but friends. Despite the ready services of the Underground Railroad, they advised him not to leave Norwich. One man offered him a revolver in case he needed to defend himself, for Smith was "determined never to be taken back alive." Another went to the United States marshal to ask what he would do if he were required to seize Smith as a fugitive; and the officer replied that he would resign his post rather than comply with that demand. A third customer, the town crier, checked the register of every hotel "to see if a man by the name of Lackey was registered there"; it was night before he reported that no such name could be found. Smith was safe in Norwich, but it was a long time before the effects of his horrible dream wore away.[36]

Thus the people of Norwich, by their readiness to help a threatened fugitive, showed how little regard they had for the Fugitive Slave Law, how determined they were to frustrate its operations and to assure freedom for the runaway. All over the state—all over the North—the general reaction was the same. Devout abolitionists, for many of whom their cause had the aspect of a divinely sanctioned crusade, felt the new law to be "offensive in the sight of God." Many ordinary citizens, not heretofore active in the movement, viewed it in the same light. With the fugitive's need for help now much greater than it had been, he found more and more people ready to assist him in his flight, more and more places where he could obtain rest and succor on the road to freedom. Effective as it had been, the Underground Railroad now found its traffic greatly increased, in some areas as much as tenfold.[37] This was, perhaps, the last result that the framers of the Compromise of 1850 had expected, but it was what happened—conclusive evidence, if any were needed, that the Middlefield farmers echoed a general sentiment in their ringing pronouncement: "This pretended law we cannot obey."

CHAPTER 7

NEW HAVEN, GATEWAY FROM THE SEA

The Fugitive Slave Law of 1850 gave the Underground Railroad its greatest impetus; but the lay of the land, together with the disposition of cities and villages, determined the main routes into and through Connecticut. Unlike Pennsylvania and the states along the north bank of the Ohio River, the Nutmeg State had no common border with any territory where slavery was legal. Fugitives traveling overland had to come in through either New York from the west or Rhode Island from the east; a network of routes, entering from both directions, brought the runaway into and through Connecticut on his way northward to freedom. But the coast of Long Island Sound and the central artery of the Connecticut River offered a number of entry points for those who came by water.

To any slave who could find his way to a Southern seaport, the ocean offered an opportunity for escape. As William Grimes found early in the century, many Yankee sailors and captains "forgot to be microscopic in the inspection of their craft." A runaway who could steal aboard an outbound ship and hide himself among the cotton bales might well rest undisturbed—though perhaps not unseen—for the duration of the voyage to some Northern port.

He might, like Grimes, find that a space had been left vacant for him when the cargo was stowed; that the crew supplied him with food and water; that they helped him get safely ashore when the journey's end was reached.[1]

Some of the vessels that thus transported hidden cargo were owned and sailed by Northern Negroes who had regular connections with the Underground Railroad. In other cases, it appears that the carrying of a fugitive was a matter of chance or of the inclination of an individual ship's officer or crew member. At any rate, organized or not, the number of escapes by sea was sufficient to arouse the South to preventive measures. Thus in 1854 South Carolina enacted a law to the effect that "all coloured men, free-born British subjects and others, are liable to be seized on board of vessels entering, and to be imprisoned on landing in any of the ports of this State, even though they may be driven into them by stress of weather." This measure further provided that such seamen were "liable to be sold into Slavery if they were unable to pay the jail fees." [2]

Slaves who fled from the South by sea might go on a vessel bound for Europe, but the greater number arrived at such Northern ports as Philadelphia, New York, and Boston. Connecticut's focus for this traffic was New Haven. That city housed a devoted band of abolitionists, and it became an important center of Underground Railroad activity, as both terminus and forwarding point. Inbound fugitives entered the city by sea or overland from the direction of New York. For those going farther, a principal route led eastward to Deep River; another, with alternate branches, had Farmington as its goal. But New Haven itself was journey's end for a number of fugitives, who had been coming in and settling since the days of William Grimes.

In the decades before the Civil War, the city expanded rapidly. Its population, less than 15,000 in 1840, grew to more than 20,000 by 1850 and 39,000 by 1860.[3] It had an interesting variety of racial groups. There were Scots weavers in the carpet mills, while English, French, Welsh, and German immigrant laborers flocked to the carriage factories. The Irish, "with bellicose energy," built the four railroads that entered New Haven, and there were German Jews who, with thrift and ambition, prospered in merchandising establishments.[4]

For the city's Negroes, for the most part just emerging from slavery either in the South or in Connecticut itself, job opportunities were not numerous. Many worked as manual laborers, many more as domestic servants. A small but notable group made their mark as barbers. Few Germans were trained in this profession, and no one would "let a wild Irishman approach his face with a razor in his hand." William Grimes had followed this trade, and his friend "Barber" Thompson, also a fugitive slave, was known as "the greatest barber in America." Following the tradition set by them, Negroes constituted all the barbers there were in New Haven in 1840 and "two thirds of the whole dozen barbers" in 1850.[5]

Despite the comparative prosperity of the barbers, a proportion of the city's Negro inhabitants were beset by the evils of poverty—poor and ill-lighted housing, too often in cellars; overcrowding; and as a result, moral laxity. Missionary societies worked hard to better the lot of these unfortunates. Hannah Gray, a Negro mission worker, was especially diligent in collecting money for the underprivileged slum-dwellers and for the support of fugitives who had gone on to Canada. Funds for this purpose were promptly sent to the Canadian Missionary Society, as were other gifts—for example, a barrel of Bibles and household goods from the New Haven Juvenile Society in 1852.[6]

Another zealous friend was the Reverend Simeon S. Jocelyn, founder (in 1828) and first pastor of the city's original house of worship for colored people, the Temple Street Church. Unfortunately, his plan for a "Collegiate school on the manual labor system" for Negroes was wrecked on the rocks of public opposition in 1831. He was one of the founders of the New Haven Anti-Slavery Society, which by 1837 had fifty members with Mrs. Leicester Sawyer as secretary. Runaway slaves could always look for spiritual and material help from this group; for Jocelyn, in addition to his other activities, was a devoted Underground manager.[7]

His brother Nathaniel Jocelyn, the artist who painted Cinque's portrait and stood ready to release the *Amistad* captives from jail by force, was also an active agent of the Underground Railroad. His commodious house sheltered many a fleeing bondsman, although only his intimates knew of it. In fact, he and Mrs. Jocelyn, as host and hostess, served and protected Underground travelers throughout the day "without telling the children who their guests might be." [8]

Another faithful Undergrounder was the Reverend Samuel W. S. Dutton, pastor of New Haven's North Church. His home at 113 College Street was an established station. Fugitives who went to him were directed to rap in a peculiar, gentle way on his kitchen door; whereupon those Negroes already in the house were expected to admit the newcomers, "usually two but sometimes one." These runaway guests were provided with a place to wash and a good meal. They were then taken to the attic, "where they slept all day on beds provided for them." At night, after another meal, they were concealed under the load in a hay wagon and sent on their way.[9]

Other known agents were Amos Townsend, cashier of the New Haven Bank, and the Reverend Henry Ludlow. In this city, too, Roger S. Baldwin first demonstrated his sympathy with the runaway slave. One of his earliest cases, just after he had begun the practice of law, involved a matter of this kind. An alleged fugitive in New Haven had been seized, bound, and hauled aboard a vessel "to be taken to New York and Kentucky." One of the man's friends went to Baldwin in great anxiety and asked him to handle the case. The young lawyer, despite pressures against him, at once obtained a writ of habeas corpus and brought the accused before a judge of the Superior Court for a hearing. Since Baldwin was able to establish conclusively that "there was no legal evidence that the man was a fugitive slave," he won his case and the prisoner was released.[10] From this start, Baldwin went on to represent the *Amistad* captives before the United States District and Supreme Courts; to serve as governor of Connecticut; and to sit for his state in the United States Senate.

Among these Underground leaders of New Haven, not least was the Reverend Amos G. Beman, first Negro minister of the Temple Street Church. Arriving in 1838 from Hartford, where he had been a teacher in a school for colored children, he noted in his diary: "This day I landed in this city from Hartford—how long I shall stay, I know not. Resolved that I will, while in this city, endeavor to glorify God—and seek the good of immortal soul." He soon became a zealous manager of the New Haven Vigilance Committee and an agent of the Underground Railroad. The full range of his activities in the latter capacity is not a matter of record, but he described one instance as follows: [11]

> On the sixth instant [January 1851], we had the pleasure of receiving and sending on her way an interesting pas-

> senger from the land of chains and whips by the underground railroad—notwithstanding it was said by one of the orators in the Union Meeting that "we have made some underground railroads—and permitted it to be done—it is our duty to prevent their establishment." But who will blot out the North Star?

Beginning in that same year, Beman submitted many reports on activities in New Haven to *The Voice of the Fugitive*, an antislavery newspaper published in Detroit. In these writings, he frequently made use of cryptic phrases —"concert of the enslaved" for the Underground Railroad, "our friends" for fugitive slaves. He discussed at length the Colonization Society of Connecticut, maintaining that it was haunted by the "increase of the colored population to the white" but adding that, as a result of the recent territorial acquisitions from Mexico and of the vastly increased flow of immigrants from Ireland and Germany, "the growth of the colored population could not keep apace to the whites." He saw New Haven's newly arrived Negroes beginning to put down permanent roots: [12]

> Within a few months several of our friends have purchased real estate and paid for it. Several who have never taken any interest in this matter have shown praiseworthy zeal to secure for themselves a Home. Many "Elevation Meetings" are held in order that they may voluntarily testify to trials and tribulations of their bondage.

He saw, too, that despite all obstacles, the cause of abolition was making headway among New Haven's citizens as the full implications of the Fugitive Slave Law of 1850 sank deeper into public consciousness: [13]

> The free soil vote has increased considerable in this city —and the monthly "concert of the enslaved" and the nominally free, the flying fugitive, and for the happiness

> and prosperity of those, who have found a home in Canada—every month, it increases in interest and promises to continue so for some time.

Beman was a true prophet. The "free soil vote" grew throughout the state to the point that, in 1856, Connecticut's six electoral votes went to the newly formed, anti-slavery Republican Party. Nonetheless, there were many who looked on abolitionists and Undergrounders as "an inflammatory group stirring up trouble and perhaps endangering the Union." Some of the citizens had profitable business connections with Southern planters, who were good customers for the locally made wagons and carriages. Some had pleasant social relations with Southern boys at Yale, with their sisters in New Haven schools, and with their families who came North to spend the summer on the shores of Long Island Sound.[14] A larger number, perhaps, opposed anything that smacked of abolition for more deep-seated and more sinister reasons, of which New Haven was said to afford a classic example:[15]

> They disliked or pretended to dislike slavery; but they thought that, "seeing there was a law" against helping fugitive slaves on their way, the law should be obeyed. But the opposition in that state to the business of the Underground road sprang also from the imbred hatred of many people of the state for the negro. This hatred had come down from former generations. It had been carefully kept through all the stages of its transmission; it had been fostered with the fondness given a favorite child; it had been guarded as a precious treasure; it had been prized as a sacred jewel.

George Beckwith, teacher and member of the Baptist Church, encountered a direct example of such prejudice. A colored lady of New Haven approached him and asked if he would teach her sons, to which he readily agreed. As soon as his decision became known, he was met everywhere with sidelong glances and "significant frowns," but his purpose remained unaltered. Then, within forty-eight hours after he had admitted the Negro boys to his school, he was visited by a group of parents—including some of his fellow parishioners—who demanded an explanation. Beckwith would not admit that any explanation was needed, and this refusal led to a threat. If he did not dismiss the colored boys, these parents would withdraw their own sons. Undaunted, the teacher suggested that that would be the best alternative.[16]

Against such a background, the Underground Railroad operators went on with their work, receiving their "friends" and passing them along to agents in nearby communities. Outbound routes from New Haven radiated north, northeast, and east; stationmasters used alternate lines as circumstances at the given moment indicated was best. Conveyances were not always available for the passengers, and as a result—whenever it was deemed wise—some of them walked the distance to the next station.

The route eastward from New Haven followed the Old Stage Road and led to Deep River or Chester, where the fugitive might find refuge with Deacon George Read or with Judge Ely Warner and his son Jonathan. Along the way he might find help in Guilford; its antislavery society had 123 members, and the pastor of its Congregational church, the Reverend Mr. Dutton, was an outspoken abolitionist. Too outspoken, in fact, to be continuously useful to the cause; since he insisted on employing his church building for antislavery meetings, the trustees dismissed him from his pastorate.[17]

The main Underground line from New Haven ran northward to Farmington by either of two alternate routes.

Fugitives who traveled on foot occasionally lost their way, wandering off in the direction of Plymouth. Those who had better directions or who journeyed under the care of a conductor might follow the main line through Meriden or the side road by way of Southington.[18]

On the Southington branch, Carlos Curtiss was a most active worker. Bearded, energetic, and persistent, he looked what he was—a farmer and a rugged individualist. Many a day he drove his full hay wagon over the dirt road to New Haven; many a night he made the return journey with dark passengers concealed beneath the load. Back at his farm on the South End Road, the fugitives were fed a good meal by Mrs. Curtiss. They then went to the barn, where a trap door in the floor opened into a cellar six feet deep and ten feet square. Once his guests were ensconced in this hideout, Curtiss rolled his wagon over the trap door to hide it from curious neighbors. With straw for their beds, the runaways remained in the little cellar until evening returned. Then they were ready for another ride. Again they concealed themselves under the wagonload of hay; again Curtiss hitched up a team and drove through the darkness; and on this second leg of the trip, he took his charges all the way to Farmington. Thus it was that, night after night, this determined Connecticut farmer went about "the work his conscience told him was right." [19]

On this westernmost route from New Haven, there were other Southington citizens who kept the traffic moving. In after years, Martin Frisbie recalled "a colored farer toward freedom who was lodged and fed in a house by his older brother and their mother" under rather risky circumstances. Nearby lived an uncle "who kind though he was to his deceased brother's widow and sons, would have informed officers of the law against them had he suspected them of harboring a fugitive negro." Knowing this man's attitude, and remembering the fine of $1000 to which they would be liable for helping a runaway, the Frisbies were somewhat hesitant when a weary fugitive came to their house and appealed for help. Mother and older son conferred, and their "humane feelings conquered their fears." They decided to take the risk and shelter the man; and they warned Martin not to say anything about it to the uncle. Thus harbored and fed for several days, the runaway was sent on his way to Farmington.[20]

Despite the activity of Carlos Curtiss on the Southington line, most of the fugitives who left New Haven were taken or sent on the branch that ran through Meriden. Their first way station was North Guilford, where the Reverend Zolva Whitmore, the Congregational minister, directed the Underground work of the Bartletts and others of his parishioners. An incident of his activity was told years after the event:

> Those still living remember that one Sunday evening he helped a darkey on his way to the next station, carrying him concealed in a load of hay on a farm wagon. The Whitmores and their antislavery friends were strict observers of the Sabbath. But they doubtless thought that aiding a fugitive slave on his way toward freedom was one of the "acts of necessity and mercy" that were allowed even by the most Puritanical of Sabbatarians. One of the minister's daughters asked her mother: "What is papa going off with that load of hay Sunday night for?" And the answer was: "Daughter, please don't ask any questions." The girl when grown was informed of the meaning of this Sunday evening hay carting.

By no means all of Whitmore's flock approved of his Underground labors. Finally, after twenty-five years of service, he was compelled to resign his pastorate. He then removed to Massachusetts, where he labored "a score of years, dying at a good old age, esteemed by all who knew him and respected there and by his antislavery friends in Connecticut for what he did for the oppressed."[21]

The path of the runaway led northwest from North Guilford to Meriden, where there were at least three stations. One of these was the home of Levi Yale, "a man of very pronounced views against slavery, and one who had the courage of his convictions." The oldest of a number of children whose father died early, he was running his mother's farm before he was thirteen; from the age of sixteen he supported the family by teaching in winter and farming in summer. In time, he served his town and state as first selectman and as a member of the General Assembly. Many runaways, it was said, found "food and harbor" at his farmhouse. In the center of town, Homer Curtiss and Harlowe Isbell conducted an Underground station in their lock shop, where they sheltered the fugitives Eldridge and Jones among others. But perhaps the most effective agent in Meriden was that fiery advocate of immediate emancipation, the Reverend George W. Perkins.[22]

Through the decade 1844–1854, this dedicated minister of the Congregational Church often secreted fugitives in the attic of his house or in his barn. According to the later recollections of his daughter Frances, most of these were men or boys, but some were women. She remembered other details too:[23]

> My aunt, Miss Frances Perkins (1839–1918) used to tell me that as a child she remembered "a black face peering in the window" and then disappearing. She also told of hearing how her father harnessed his horse himself in the night and drove away, returning some time next day. I have no idea where the next station was located, but it would seem very likely to be in the neighborhood of Hartford—a three hour drive from Meriden with a good horse. I understand that escaped slaves were generally made

comfortable in some out-house or stable in order to make escape more possible in case of search.

The stop to which Perkins took his passengers probably was the way station operated by Milo Hotchkiss in Kensington. A few miles beyond it the "Stanley Quarters," in the northern part of New Britain, formed a more important center. Here many active Undergrounders were ready to succor the fleeing fugitive—DeWitt C. Pond, Alfred Andrews, David Whittlesey, the Henry Norths, the Stanleys, the Harts, and the Horace Booths.[24] New Britain, in fact, was a long-time center of antislavery activity. Mrs. Minerva Lee Hart was "an abolitionist before there was an antislavery society"; and when her husband and others were mobbed for their opinions, she saw the event as a proof that "God was bringing one of His mighty human problems to solution." [25] Many other citizens of the town "joined the movement headed by William Lloyd Garrison, in violent opposition to the principles of slavery, no matter what the difficulties of settling the question." [26]

Some of these devoted Undergrounders suffered for their convictions and actions. On a night in October 1857, Mrs. Henry North's barn was set on fire by incendiaries; the flames consumed the building with twenty tons of hay and several sleighs and wagons, and George Hart, who was inside at the time, had to run for his life. At the same time the barn of Horace Booth, with forty to fifty tons of hay, was destroyed by an arsonist fire. Rewards were offered for the apprehension of the perpetrators, but it is not on record that they were ever caught.[27]

But no threats, no violence, deterred the workers for human freedom. As long as there was need of their services, they continued to receive passengers from down the line and to forward them to the center of Connecticut's Underground network. That center was Farmington.

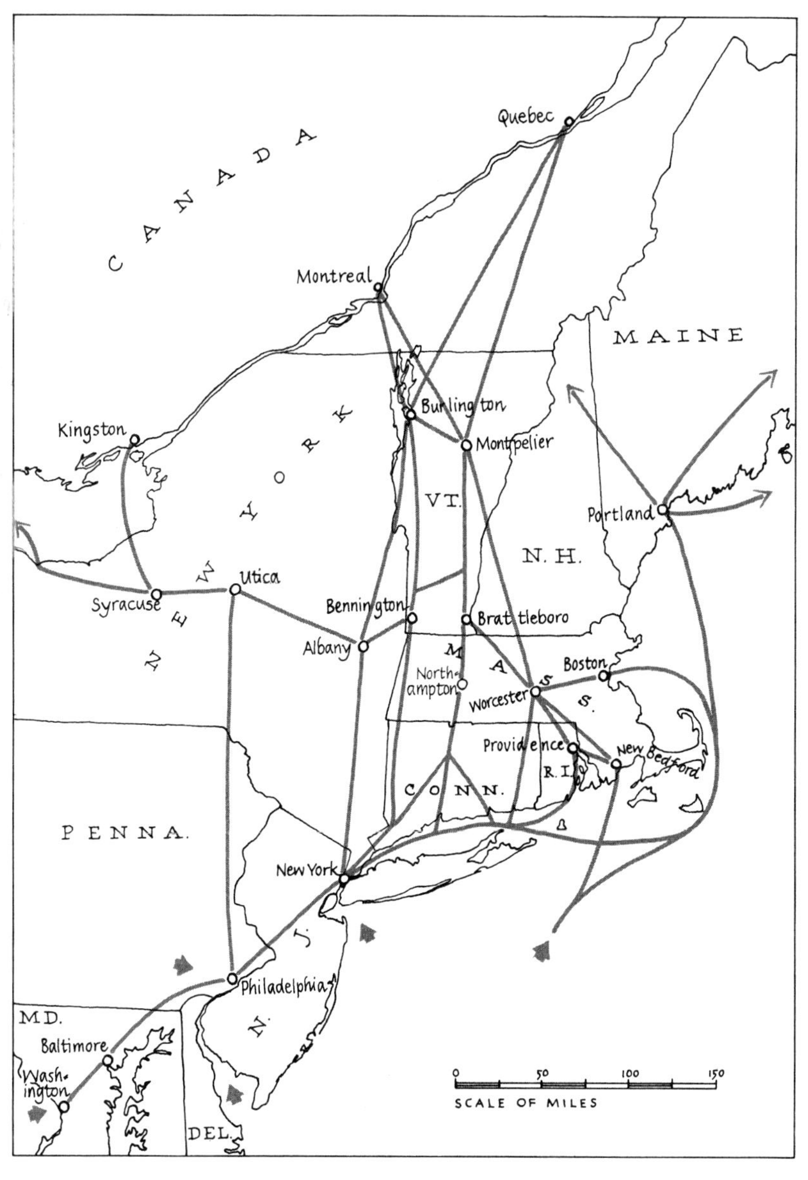

Principal Underground Routes in the Northeast

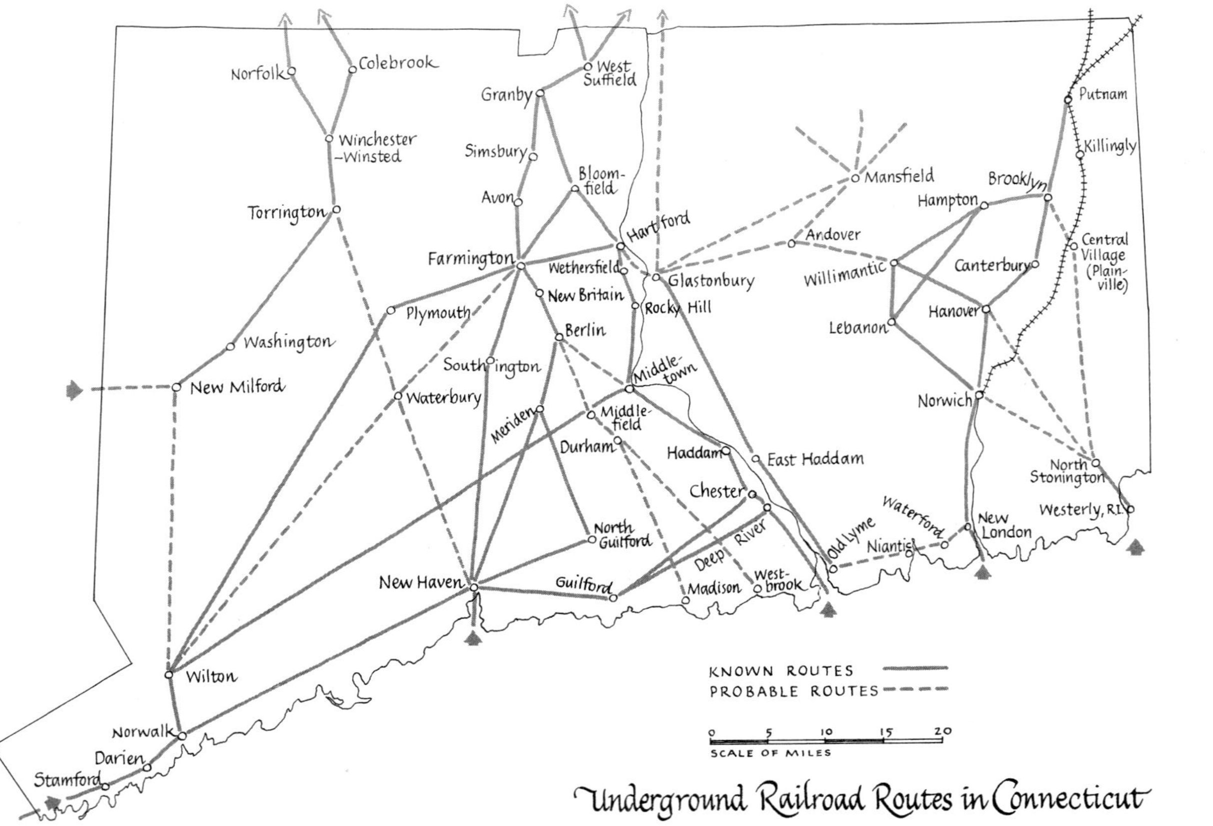

Underground Railroad Routes in Connecticut

CHAPTER 8

WEST CONNECTICUT TRUNK LINES

WHILE some fugitives entered Connecticut from the sea, at New Haven or another port, the majority came by overland routes. Pennsylvania, whose southern border was the Mason-Dixon line, received thousands of runaways from the contiguous states of Virginia, Maryland, and Delaware; and Philadelphia, with its large Quaker population and its long-established Underground apparatus, became a most important haven and forwarding station for refugees from slavery. Between 1830 and 1860, more than 9000 slaves are said to have been helped on their way to freedom in that city.[1] A great proportion of these were sent on, by rail or steamer or road, to New York City, where the Vigilance Committee, in existence by 1835 and operated mainly by Negroes, gave them protection and help. The Reverend Amos Beman, who addressed this group at one of its anniversary meetings, summarized its role in the work of the Underground Railroad:[2]

> Those who come with fear and trembling and apply for aid, are flying from the cruel prison house—the dark land of their unpaid toil—the ground stained with their blood and wet with their bitter tears—they have journeyed with scant food, guided by the pale light of the

> North Star—the sombre night has been their day—the cold damp earth their cheerless bed—the dreary day has been full of danger and alarm—every stirring leaf spoke to them of the slavehunter—every sound told them of the bloodhound. . . . At this point, this Committee find them tormented by overwhelming anxiety. . . . To stay here would be to be in a state of continual jeopardy—for this is the slavecatcher's hunting ground; and it is for such persons, thus situated, that this committee asks your efficient aid in shielding the flying slave.

The flow of fugitives through New York was constant, and constantly increasing. The Reverend Charles B. Ray, one of the Vigilance Committee's outstanding Negro workers, reported that "more than four hundred persons, escaped from slavery" came into the city during the year 1849; and after the passage of the Fugitive Slave Law of 1850, the place "became more active than ever in receiving and forwarding" the runaways.[3]

From Manhattan, fugitives journeyed farther by any one of several means, going in any one of several directions. Some voyaged by boat to New England ports—New Haven, Hartford, and others. Some went across the East River to Long Island, where there were points of refuge. Many followed the Hudson River northward, by a route whose branches might take them straight to Montreal, or westward through Central New York and across Lake Ontario to the region of Kingston, or eastward via a number of laterals into Connecticut, Massachusetts, or Vermont. Still others traveled the path of William Grimes, northeast along the Sound shore and so across the state line at Greenwich.[4]

Those who came by this route found protection at the Underground station operated by Benjamin Daskam in Stamford. He had several different hiding places at his disposal, to be used as discretion indicated; he once concealed a runaway in a neighbor's barn, while another was secreted in the belfry of the Presbyterian church. He acted as a conductor also, taking his charges in a hay wagon to a man named Weed in Darien.[5]

East of Darien, there was a station in Norwalk, but who operated it remains unknown. It may have been the house of David Lambert, which had a secret stairway from beneath the gambrel roof to a dark cellar, from which in turn a tunnel—literally underground—led to a nearby salt-box house. This building is believed to have been used as a hideaway for freedom-bound fugitives.[6] It is logical to suppose that, from this point, some runaways followed the Sound to New Haven, but the locations of stations along this route, and the names of their proprietors, have not come to light.

A known route took the refugee north from Norwalk to Wilton, where William Wakeman was an earnest abolitionist and active Undergrounder for many years. In the late 1830's he invited the Reverend Nathaniel Colver, the touring antislavery lecturer, to speak at his house before "immense crowds." He was still at his work for the enslaved, with redoubled effort, after the Fugitive Slave Law of 1850 was adopted.

Wakeman was both station-keeper and conductor. He was in touch by mail with other Underground operators, who sent him coded letters announcing the arrival of passengers—sometimes as many as five or six in a single party. He gave them lodging and food; when the neighbors saw him "carrying wood to the guest chamber and Mrs. Wakeman carrying trays of her best food, they knew that during the dark hours of the preceding night one or more dusky guest had arrived." As a conductor, Wakeman was bold and tireless, taking his "packages of hardware and dry goods" to places as distant as Plymouth and Middletown—trips of forty and fifty miles as the crow flies, farther than that by road. For this purpose, he sometimes used a hay wagon and traveled by night; at other times he openly worked on the dangerous day shift. One local historian reported on his activities in the following rough notes:

> Anti-slavery underground railroad. There is no stowaway in cellar. Wm. Wakeman helped the fugitives openly. One man he afterwards heard of arrived in Canada and doing well. He drove away one man and 2 women in broad daylight, black as they could be—to another station in Plymouth . . . was merely threatened for his duty but never molested.[7]

It is possible, though it is not verified, that some of Wakeman's trips went no farther than Waterbury, where Deacon Timothy Porter and J. M. Stocking both maintained Underground stations. The Plymouth operators, to whom Wakeman presumably made his deliveries, included Joel Blakeslee, Ferrand Dunbar, and William Bull. They not only handled passengers from Wilton; they also had to keep watch for unaccompanied fugitives on foot who had lost their way on the western line between New Haven and Farmington. The Plymouth "minute men" had to set these wanderers on the right track, which took them a dozen miles eastward to Farmington.[8]

In addition to the lines out of Wilton, western Connecticut had other Underground Railroad tracks which it is not possible to trace in their entirety. The locations of stations and the names of their keepers spring easily to view; not so the names of the conductors or the routes that were followed. Indeed the routes themselves, in this area as throughout the North, were constantly changing; new branches were opened and old ones closed, tracks shifted and stations relocated, as convenience and safety might dictate.

Thus it is known that New Milford was a center of Underground work; but whether fugitives came to this town by traveling northward from the vicinity of Wilton, or eastward via a lateral from the Hudson River line in New York, or both, remains unclear.[9] In any case, the sins of colonial slavery in the area "were somewhat atoned for in after years by the zeal of Abolitionists in aiding runaways to reach Canada and freedom." There were several stations here, one of which was the house of Charles Sabin. Another was the home of Augustine Thayer. He and "his good wife devoted their lives to the Abolition cause. They helped many poor slaves on their way, rising from their beds in the night to feed and minister to them and secreting them till they could be taken under cover of darkness to Deacon Gerardus Roberts' house on Second Hill and from there to Mr. Daniel Platt's in Washington."[10]

Among the first real abolitionists of Washington was Frederick W. Gunn, who in 1837 opened a private school in the village. The project was not successful. Many citizens felt that he would infect his scholars with his well-known antislavery views, for which he was the target of much criticism. The local minister "thundered against him from the pulpit, excommunicated him." In the face of this opposition, Gunn left the town and accepted a teaching post in Pennsylvania. In the same year, Abby Kelly, a noted abolitionist speaker of the Quaker faith, visited Washington. While sojourning there and delivering antislavery lectures, she met the sort of heckling that greeted most women who spoke in the abolitionist cause. The same local minister hurled invectives at her in his Sunday sermons; he described her as a second Jezebel, who "calleth herself a prophetess, to teach, and to seduce my servants to commit fornication." Coming to the point, he concluded, "Let your women keep silence in the churches, for it is not permitted unto them to speak." Miss Kelly, "fair, comely, and of the noblest character," left Washington for good. But several years later, when the local climate of opinion was more favorable to abolitionists, Gunn returned to his native village and founded The Gunnery—a school, he said, to make men of boys, where the most important subject was "self-direction and self-government." The direction of runaways on the road to freedom, however, remained Gunn's private affair.[11]

Despite this educator's good work, that of Daniel Platt and his wife was more important. They, with a few others who were concerned over the slavery issue, "were the centre of a storm of persecution by which less heroic souls would have been overwhelmed." Nonetheless they persevered, accommodating "many a trembling black refugee" on their farm. Their son Orville—who lived to serve twenty-six years in the United States Senate—later recalled that "the slaves stayed, as a rule, but a short time, though some remained several weeks until it was learned through the channels of communication among Abolitionists that their whereabouts was suspected." They were then forwarded to either of two destinations—to Dr. Vaill on the Wolcottville Road or to Uriel Tuttle in Torrington.[12]

The latter town was something of a center of antislavery sentiment. It was the birthplace of the abolitionist firebrand and martyr, John Brown. Its antislavery society had forty members as early as 1837; and it was said that, when this body held its initial meeting in a barn, it "was not the first time that strangers found shelter there because there was no room in the inn." Yet, curiously, Uriel Tuttle was the only Underground stationmaster here of whom a record survives.[13]

At Winchester, a few miles north of Torrington and close to Winsted, there was a small but active antislavery society. Noble J. Everett was its secretary; Jonathan Coe, a member who lived in nearby Winsted, managed a well-patronized Underground station at his house.[14] Another station may have been the home of Silas H. McAlpine, poet, philanthropist, and abolitionist of Winchester; in the foundation wall of his house was a hidden crypt that was possibly a hiding place for fugitives, but there is no positive evidence that it was so used.[15] Notwithstanding these few records, there is reason to believe that the two towns formed a busy jumping off point for the fugitive. A local historian who had lived in the era of Underground activity later wrote that "antislavery sentiment had become more pervasive and incisive in our town than in any other in Western Connecticut before the outbreak of the rebellion." [16] Parker Pillsbury, visiting the area in the early 1850's, felt the pulsation of that sentiment: [17]

> After two weeks of wandering over a desert of pro-slavery indifference and hostility, a spot such as Winsted is a real oasis, a "Delectable Mountains" resting place to an anti-slavery agent. Almost every where, there will be one family to give me a good and welcome home; but beyond that, in Connecticut, we need not look for sympathy and support, except in very few and rare instances.
>
> In Winsted, there is a little band of chosen spirits. Their love to God is manifested not by reverencing holy days, holy houses, or holy ministers, but by acts of benevolence and humanity to his suffering children. They are mostly hard laboring mechanics, eating none but the bread of patient industry; and they are a noble example of what working men and women can and ought to be.

> . . . In short, they constitute one of the most gallant and valuable auxilliaries in our warfare to be found any where in New England.

Beyond this point, there were stations to the north in Colebrook and to the northwest in Norfolk. Who were the Underground agents in Colebrook remains unknown, but there were certainly several of them. One may have been J. H. Rodgers, secretary of the ninety-member antislavery society in 1836. But if the names of the agents have been forgotten, word-of-mouth tradition has preserved the location of several of the stations they used. It is also reported that there was a network of Underground byways in this vicinity and that residents of Norfolk were responsible for paving many of them.[18]

Norfolk had been hospitable to runaway slaves as far back as the 1790's, when more than a dozen different citizens had cooperated in sheltering young James Mars and his family. Even in the 1850's there were old-timers in the village who remembered how James and his brother had been spirited from house to house until a settlement could be reached with their owner, Parson Thompson. One of those who knew the Mars story was Deacon Amos Pettibone, whose forebears had owned the tavern in which the Mars family found their first refuge. The Deacon actively carried on the family tradition, and quite openly too. It was later recalled that, on one occasion, he brought "a young runaway slave whom he had kept overnight" to a neighbor's home, so that the children could see "the scars on the runaway's ankles, where he had worn irons"—a vivid though wordless lesson in the cruelties that flourished under the system of Southern slavery.[19]

For the fugitive traveling through northwestern Connecticut, Norfolk was the last stop in the state. From here, he was sent across the Massachusetts border to New Marlboro, thence over to the Housatonic River line through Stockbridge and Pittsfield to Bennington, Vermont. At that junction point a well-traveled route came in from Troy, New York; and from it, the road ran north through Rutland and Burlington to freedom beyond the Canadian border.[20]

CHAPTER 9

EAST CONNECTICUT LOCALS

To a significant extent, the Underground Railroad lines of East Connecticut received their passengers from neighboring Rhode Island. The people of that small state had had their own experiences with slavery, by which some of them had prospered. Merchants of Newport had figured prominently in the international slave trade before its abolishment in 1810, buying Africans from slave raiders in their native land and transporting them to the auction blocks of North America; the foundations of the city's fashionable society rested on fortunes made in this commerce in human flesh. Many businessmen of Providence also had proslavery views. Yet in the religiously tolerant atmosphere of Roger Williams' sometime colony, anti-slavery Quakers and Baptists had achieved a powerful voice. Due largely to their influence, the state's legislature in 1784 enacted that all children born into slavery from that time onward should be free; and thereafter, the slaves became fewer and fewer while the "free people of color" increased rapidly in numbers. By 1840 there was a steady stream of runaways passing through Rhode Island. Both Quakers and Baptists worked diligently in their behalf—and quite openly too. For instance, in 1849 the Baptists of the Pond Street Church, Providence, used the pages of the local *Gazette* to solicit donations of money for the work of the Underground Railroad.[1]

Fugitives who came into Rhode Island almost without exception made the first stage of their voyage by water. Stowing away among the cotton bales bound for Northern mills, or invited on board ship by Underground agents among the crewmen, they fled by sea from Southern ports to landing places in Rhode Island itself or in neighboring Massachusetts. Their fate when they came ashore, said a conscientious Quaker lady who was party to such events, "depended on the circumstances into which they happened to fall." If some were caught, it appears that many more achieved their longed-for freedom:[2]

> A few, landing at some towns on Cape Cod, would reach New Bedford, and thence be sent by an abolitionist there to Fall River, to be sheltered by Nathaniel B. Borden and his wife, who was my sister Sarah, and sent by them to my home at Valley Falls, in the darkness of night, and in a closed carriage, with Robert Adams, a most faithful Friend, as their conductor. Here, we received them, and, after preparing them for the journey, my husband would accompany them a short distance on the Providence and Worcester railroad, acquaint the conductor with the facts, enlist his interest in their behalf, and then leave them in his care. They were then transferred at Worcester to the Vermont road, from which, by a previous general arrangement, they were received by a Unitarian clergyman named Young, and sent by him to Canada, where they uniformly arrived safely.

Another Quaker station in Rhode Island was the house of Charles Perry, in Westerly. When nightfall came, fugitives who took shelter with him were spirited over the state line to the home of his brother Harvey in North Stonington. Harvey Perry was prepared for mishaps as well as normal Underground Railroad business; in his cellar was "a well-concealed black hole," to be used as an emergency hideout when an alarm was sounded. Another station-keeper in this town, whose name has not been recorded, "so ingeniously arranged his woodpile that it served as a safe retreat for fugitives when danger threatened." [3]

Leaving either of these two places of safety, the runaway found himself conducted or sent through a network of hideaways spreading among the isolated and scattered villages of eastern Connecticut. To this maze of lines and stations there were other possible entry points too. One of these, of minor significance to the East Connecticut pattern, was Old Lyme, at the mouth of the Connecticut River. Some of its traffic in runaways flowed up the river valley toward Hartford. But there was also an eastbound line along the Sound toward New London and Norwich.[4] Fugitives on this route might find shelter at a house in Niantic. This station's operator remains unknown, but the building still stands. According to local tradition, slaves who arrived here made their presence known by tapping on the windows; coming inside, they were hidden from view in the base of a huge chimney.[5]

It is probable that another station was maintained just east of Niantic in Waterford, and that its manager was Nehemiah Caulkins, carpenter, hater of slavery, and fiery advocate of abolition. When he attacked the South's "peculiar institution," Caulkins had reason to know what he was talking about. For eleven years, from 1824 to 1835, he spent the winters working at his trade on plantations in North Carolina, among slaves and their masters. Thereafter, revolted by the cruelty and exploitation he had seen and feeling impelled to awaken the conscience of the North "in behalf of human freedom," he set down a factual—and coldly horrifying—account of his observations. This was published as a contribution to Theodore Weld's great abolitionist anthology of 1839, *American Slavery As It Is*—a book that, distributed by the tens of thousands, was a powerful means of bringing converts to the antislavery cause.[6]

From the home town of this influential spokesman for freedom, the fugitive might find his way a few miles eastward to New London, or somewhat farther northward to Norwich. The former, then prospering as a whaling port second only to New Bedford, was the center of an active abolition movement. Here was published a periodical whose name declared its orientation—*The Slave's Cry*. Here, in 1844, was held a meeting "to hear the experience of the fugitive—John—who is just from the land of whips and chains—J. Turner, likewise a fugitive, was speaking when we arrived." [7] It is not recorded how John and J. Turner reached the city—possibly by ship, for New London's ocean trade was extensive. Strangely, the identities of the Underground operators remain unknown, although the Hempstead house, oldest in the city, is said to have been a station.[8]

The runaway heading inland from New London would logically make for Norwich, a dozen miles away; it could be reached either by boat up the Thames River or by following the northbound road. Norwich was also a short distance from North Stonington, and it is probable that some of Harvey Perry's erstwhile guests made it their next stop. The town, lying where the Shetucket and Yantic rivers joined to form the drowned estuary called the Thames, was something of a seaport in its own right. Its two antislavery societies, for men and for women, had Alpheus Kingsley and Miss F. M. Caulkins as their respective secretaries. It was the home of James Lindsey Smith, escaped slave, shoemaker, and abolitionist lecturer, who was so highly regarded that the United States marshal offered to resign his position rather than turn Smith over to slave-catchers. Yet so discreetly did its Underground Railroad agents do their work that their identities remain undiscovered.

Norwich was something else, too. It was the terminus of the Norwich and Worcester railroad line, in whose cars the Undergrounders of New London County frequently forwarded their riders to operatives in Massachusetts. With his passage money supplied him and with the help of the railroad conductor enlisted in his behalf, the fugitive rode the rails in broad daylight, for the one daily northbound train left the terminal at 7:30 A.M.[9]

For those who did not travel by train, a patchwork of Underground stations lay in an arc northwest, north, and northeast of Norwich. The precise routes connecting them are not fully known; presumably the fugitives traveled now one road, now another, as safety or convenience indicated. There was a station, of unknown management, at Lebanon; it sent passengers northeast to Hampton, and probably also to Willimantic, due north and much nearer at hand. There were known agents in the village of Hanover, in what was then Lisbon township. There were others at Canterbury and at Plainfield.

At Central Village in the latter township lived Wesley Cady, station-keeper and conductor. Using an old covered wagon, he drove southward in the evening, ostensibly on his way to market but actually headed for an Underground depot down the line—whether North Stonington, Norwich, or some unremembered place nearer at hand is unknown. In the morning he returned home with a cargo of dark passengers hidden beneath the wagon cover; and if the neighbors knew of this traffic, it was not by Cady's wish. Some years later, his son W. W. Cady stated that "the children were never allowed to know anything about it for fear they might tell and a person's life and property was not safe if it was known that he harbored a slave." [10]

Plainfield was a gateway to Windham County, where abolitionist sentiment was more widespread and more strongly held than in any other part of Connecticut.[11] It was the home of two antislavery societies, the one for men having ninety-four members and that for women numbering forty-three in 1837. In both of these bodies "three or four towns were represented, among them the far famed town of Canterbury." This was the village, only four miles from Plainfield, in which Prudence Crandall had undergone her martyrdom; and the hue and cry raised against her made slavery a topic of controversy in every hamlet in that part of the state. The people of Windham County, it was reported, "read with candor" about the persecution of Miss Crandall and her supporters; "others even who began to read with prejudice against them, the publishers of fanatics, found their prejudice wearing away; and several who were at first strongly opposed to Miss Crandall's scheme" became "most zealous and active Abolitionists." [12] It is known that members of the Crandall family were Underground agents in Canterbury. It is known also that some fugitives reached this town from other points than Plainfield—specifically, from Hanover.

In that country village, runaways were taken in charge by Levi P. Roland and William Lee, who was a deacon of the church and secretary of the antislavery society. These men, presumably farmers, forwarded their guests either northwest to Willimantic or northeast to Canterbury. William Lee's son Samuel later stated that these routes were active from 1840 onward, and that "I occasionally piloted a colored man from my father's to my brother's two and a half miles distant." One fugitive settled in Hanover and lived there for many years; but when a villager told him he was being sought by slave-hunters, he pressed onward to Canada.[13]

For runaways traveling north in eastern Connecticut, the main line ran through Brooklyn, Killingly, and Pomfret to Uxbridge or Worcester, Massachusetts. Yet those journeying through Hanover generally reached Brooklyn via a roundabout route through Willimantic and Hampton, rather than by the more direct way through Canterbury. The reasons for this apparent detour are unclear, but the fact is well established. At Willimantic, John Brown, J. A. Conant, and J. A. Lewis were active stationkeepers, receiving fugitives both by wagon and on foot—possibly including some from Lebanon as well as those from Hanover. They directed their visitors to Hampton, where three more agents awaited them—Ebenezer Griffin and Phillips Pearl, farmers, and Joel Fox, mason. All of these were conductors as well as stationmasters, and Brooklyn was the destination to which they took their passengers under wagonloads of hay. One runaway transported by Fox is known to have been carried from Brooklyn to Danielson, where he was put aboard the Worcester train.[14]

The Brooklyn agents who raised the funds for this refugee included George Benson, a man named Whitcomb, and others. They were working in the tradition established by the Reverend Samuel J. May, who as early as 1834 was receiving fugitives at this town and sending them across the state line to Uxbridge or Worcester.[15] The local antislavery societies numbered fifty-three men and twenty-two women respectively. Brooklyn was a busy station, for most of the East Connecticut lines converged here, probably including a direct track from Wesley Cady's station in Central Village. The operators here, if they could not make

The Reverend
James W. C. Pennington

The home of Francis Gillette in Bloomfield, used as an Underground Station.

Photo by the Author

use of the railroad line from Danielson, might forward their charges to either Prosper Alexander in Killingly or to agents in Putnam.[16] In the latter town, there was a secret cell in a building later occupied by the Masonic Club: this was well patronized by northbound fugitives.[17]

In this quarter of the state, Underground managers obviously maintained a very close bond with the station-masters in Uxbridge, Worcester, and Boston. Interesting was an account that a member of West Killingly's anti-slavery society forwarded to the *Liberator:*

> A female, representing herself to be a slave, escaping from Maryland, giving her name Ellen, and aged 19 years, stayed at my house last Friday night, and took the 8 o'clock morning train, Saturday, for Boston. The friends of the slave in this village [Danielsonville] raised money sufficient to carry her to Boston, and some more I advised her to leave the cars at Brighton and walk into Boston, and to the Anti-Slavery Office, 21 Cornhill. She designed calling on you. We have been sorry since she left that we did not invite her to remain with us, as we feel that no slave could be taken here, and rather wanted the issue tested. She was a fine looking and intelligent girl, neat and agreeable. Feeling very anxious for her safe passage through this 'piratical Egypt,' I take the liberty of writing to request you to communicate to me information of her arrival in Boston, if such is the fact.

It was later learned, to the chagrin of abolitionists, that this female fugitive was an impostor, who assumed the names of Helen in Ohio, Orlena in Detroit, Ellen in Connecticut, and Mary in Worcester.[18]

Beyond Killingly and Putnam, the obvious track of the fugitive led into Massachusetts, very likely to Uxbridge. It was a gathering point for runaways, as the South Carolina abolitionist lecturer Angelina Grimke noted in a letter to Theodore Weld early in 1838: "We met two very interesting ones in Uxbridge—a mother pining after her son in bondage, a son upon whom she had seen 500 lashes inflicted, after which he was given to her to rub with a solution of salt and pepper. And a young man, whose heart yearned over his sister in slavery."[19] From this community, fugitives went on to Worcester or Boston, thence by the established route through Vermont to Canada.

From the foregoing details, it becomes apparent that the East Connecticut locals, with all their detours and intertwinings, in a general way followed or paralleled the valley of the Thames and Quinebaug rivers from the Sound northward into Massachusetts. Yet there were two points of abolitionist activity in the area whose places in the pattern remain unclear. One was Mansfield, north of Willimantic, which could boast the largest antislavery society in the state—in 1837, 300 members, headed by Dr. H. Skinner, out of a total population of approximately 2400 men, women, and children.[20] The other was Andover, some ten miles west of Willimantic in the direction of Hartford. On a side road near this village, the Hendee house had "mysterious secret closets and a tunnel from the cellar to a thicket, one hundred feet from the house . . . a relic of the 'Underground Railroad' days."[21] Who managed this station, if indeed it was one, is unknown; and whether its dark lodgers moved eastward to Willimantic, or northward through Mansfield, or westward through Hartford to the grand junction at Farmington, can only remain a subject of speculation.

CHAPTER 10

VALLEY LINE TO HARTFORD

BESIDES the vessels that brought fleeing slaves to landings at New Haven, New London, and other salt-water ports, not a few river steamers, transporting with their cargo those same stowaways, sailed up the Connecticut River. In its great river, flowing 400 twisting miles from its source in New Hampshire to the Sound at Old Saybrook, the state possessed a central waterway which from earliest times had been a major artery of traffic. Almost every town along the Connecticut, from its mouth to the head of navigation, was a center of boat-building and a port for fishermen, river boats, or even ocean-going vessels. Old Saybrook, Middletown, and Hartford were important centers of overseas shipping. Old Lyme, it is said, "once knew a time when every dwelling housed a captain's family." [1]

Many times the boats that sailed these inland waters carried more than merely legal cargo and freeborn passengers. Abolitionist shipowners like Jesse G. Baldwin of Middletown found room on their craft for any fugitive that needed it.[2] The steamers that after 1824 regularly plied the route from New York to Hartford, carrying Southern cotton to Connecticut's mills, also brought

Southern runaways to Connecticut's freer air. James Lindsey Smith and the fugitive Charles were only two of those who made part of their journey to freedom in this way. When the river steamers were first used to transport refugees, and whether the plan was instigated by Hartford's Underground workers or by those in New York, remain uncertain; but as Smith's narrative shows, the runaway was directed to the river steamer and had his fare paid by agents in Manhattan.

Despite the importance of water-borne traffic, it is probable that most fugitives who followed the valley line did so by going along the river's banks. Old Lyme, on the eastern side near the stream's mouth, was an Underground Railroad center of "great activity." [3] How many of its handsome old houses, many of them dating from the eighteenth century and occupied by the families of seafaring men, were actual stations is undetermined. The Moses Noyes house, on the west side of Lyme Street, was one of them; [4] it is logical to suppose that there were others. The agents in this locality sent some of their guests eastward in the direction of New London, but others went upstream along the Connecticut River, at this point flowing from northwest to southeast.

The precise route of those riverside travelers who followed the east bank remains a matter of conjecture. Certain homes in East Haddam apparently afforded them protection and rest; details are lacking, but there is sufficient reason to believe that the descendants of Captain James Green, who owned the Blacksmith Arms at East Haddam Landing, furnished one of these havens.[5]

The foremost shipbuilders in Middlesex County were to be found in East Haddam; Gideon Higgins and George E. and William H. Goodspeed were most prominent among them. Higgins, it is said, was not only a master designer of ships but also a devout abolitionist, "a radical," and "uncompromising in his convictions." Making his home at Chapman's Landing, where the Goodspeed Opera House now stands, he no doubt performed many acts of charity for the nearly famished stowaways who stepped into his parlor from the gangway.[6] Though the Goodspeeds were not described as having Higgins' proclivities, yet from one of the vessels they constructed, the *Hero*, a fugitive slave made a hairbreadth escape from his owner:[7]

> Among the colored men employed upon the *Hero*, was a fugitive slave. His 'master,' wishing to use the new law to arrest him, took passage in the *Hero*, thinking to catch the man upon reaching Hartford. But at East Haddam, the hunted man felt moved in spirit to go ashore and examine the country. When the boat reached Hartford, the hunters could not find him. They sought diligently, but in vain.

Whether this slave, having baffled his pursuers, received the humane assistance of Gideon Higgins, or through his own courage and ingenuity fell into the company of friends at the Blacksmith Arms on Main Street, is not a matter of record.

Nor is there any clue as to what accommodations existed for him in the long reach from that point to Glastonbury. The latter town was the home of Mrs. Hannah Smith, a staunch abolitionist, who with her daughters conducted antislavery rallies in her dooryard on pleasant evenings. She was sensitive to the needs of Connecticut's free Negroes, for she noted that on November 12, 1849, "Mr. Beman, a colored man, called to bring a pamphlet about their Convention."[8] That Mrs. Smith also entertained fugitives in flight is more than probable. A person of her strong abolitionist views could hardly have failed to do so at need, but no discreet Underground agent would enter such facts in her diary. Where the trail led beyond Glastonbury can only be guessed—possibly eastward to Andover, possibly straight north or across the river to Hartford, some five or six miles away. In any event, traffic on the Connecticut's eastern bank was light compared to that which followed the western side.[9]

That shore could be reached by the fugitive at a number of points—across the river's mouth from Old Lyme; direct from the sea at Old Saybrook or ports farther up the river; and overland by the established Underground line from New Haven to Deep River or by dimly traceable laterals that ran inland from Madison and Westbrook toward Middletown. Saybrook, as James Lindsey Smith had found, was none too hospitable to abolitionists and their "friends"; but the case was otherwise in Deep River, where Deacon George Read was ever ready to help the runaway who, like Uncle Billy Winters, stood in need of his assistance. Equally committed to the succor of the fugitive were the Warners, father and son, in nearby Chester. Underground agents of undetermined identity were active in Haddam, a few miles upriver, and in Durham, some little distance west of that point. All of these lines—the river road and the laterals west of it—converged in the area of Middletown.[10]

Within that city itself, abolitionist and Underground activity was considerable, with Jesse G. Baldwin, the Reverend Jehiel C. Beman, and Benjamin Douglas among the leaders.[11] Middlefield, at the time an outlying area of the township of Middletown rather than a legal entity, was a notable center of antislavery feeling. This was the community whose citizens, under the leadership of William Lyman, so ringingly stated their defiance of the Fugitive Slave Law of 1850. Among those who rallied about him were David Lyman, Alfred and Russell Bailey, James T.

Dickinson, Marvin Thomas, and Phineas M. Augur—all of them dirt farmers except perhaps Augur, who was a town official and a land surveyor. The farm of William Lyman constituted the chief Underground station in the district if not the only one; it was well established and well patronized.[12] Augur, who designed the first accurate map of Middlefield, was an active conductor; and on various occasions, over the roads he knew so well, he escorted fugitives to other stations on their route to freedom.[13] He could take his imports west to Meriden, northwest to Kensington or New Britain, east to Middletown, or north in the direct line to Hartford. In any case, the ultimate destination was likely to be Farmington.

For those who went straight north from the Middletown-Middlefield area, way stations existed at Rocky Hill and at Wethersfield. Jesse G. Baldwin of Middletown, in his occasional role as a conductor, is known to have taken passengers in their direction; [14] but who maintained them, and precisely how they fitted into the intricate network that was the Underground Railroad, are matters as yet undiscovered.

Contiguous to Wethersfield was the important city of Hartford, metropolis of central Connecticut and, with New Haven, co-capital of the state. Abolitionist views were not universal among its citizens. Its Whig and Democratic politicians tended to soft-pedal the slavery issue for fear of offending Southern members of their parties, and its manufacturers had strong business reasons for not wishing to disturb their Southern customers. The city was the site of the annual meetings of the Connecticut Colonization Society. It had been the scene of a race riot in 1835, when home-going Negroes were attacked by white roughs as they left church. Nonetheless it was the center of much effective antislavery work, in which it was closely linked to neighboring Bloomfield and, especially, Farmington.

Some of that work took the form of the publication of abolitionist periodicals. At one time or another, Hartford was the headquarters of three of these—the *Free Soil Republican*, the *Christian Freeman*, and the *Charter Oak*, the two latter being merged in the mid-1840's under the editorship of William H. Burleigh. The city was also the location of annual meetings of the Connecticut Anti-Slavery Society and of such special gatherings as that called to protest the Fugitive Slave Law of 1850. In fact, its reputation as an antislavery center was well established by 1839. In that year, when the Circuit Court was considering the case of the *Amistad* captives, District Attorney Holabird wrote to the State Department: "I should regret extremely that the rascally blacks should fall into the hands of the abolitionists, with whom Hartford is filled." [15]

Most prominent among the antislavery men in the area was unquestionably Francis Gillette, who lived for some years in Bloomfield and later in Hartford. Although trained in the law, he never practiced it, instead spending his efforts on his ancestral farm and in working for social causes—temperance and educational reform as well as the abolition of slavery. His wife was a sister of John Hooker, a lawyer and leading antislavery man of Farmington; hence he was connected by marriage with Mrs. Hooker's brother and sister, Henry Ward Beecher and Harriet Beecher Stowe.[16] Gillette was among the incorporators of an insurance firm known as the American Temperance Life Insurance Company, which later became the Phoenix Mutual. He was also chairman of the board of trustees of the Connecticut state normal school at its foundation in 1849 and for many years thereafter. For causes like these, both in private life and in the political arena, he was a ceaseless campaigner. Twice he was elected to the General Assembly, in 1832 and in 1838, when he supported the bill that would have given Negroes the right to vote. He ran for governor on the Liberty Party ticket in 1842 and several times thereafter. In 1854 a coalition of Free Soilers, Whigs, and temperance voters sent him to the United States Senate to fill out the unexpired term of Senator Truman Smith. In his year there, he was able to vote against the Kansas-Nebraska Act and to make his voice heard as a ringing spokesman against slavery.[17]

Gillette's home in Bloomfield was a commodious house built by himself "of unhewn stone brought from the nearby mountain-side." More than once, it is reported, he here "welcomed and gave shelter for a night to the flying slave, whose stories and songs, as he warmed and cheered himself by the fire, made a lifelong impression upon his young listeners."[18]

In 1853, Gillette and his brother-in-law Hooker jointly purchased a hundred-acre property, known as Nook Farm, on the Farmington road—then just outside Hartford, afterward well within the city limits. Here, in houses built on streets newly opened, sprang up the homes of a distinguished group of cultural and civic leaders—among them Joseph R. Hawley, a lawyer who became a Union general and a United States Senator; Charles Dudley Warner, essayist and long-time editor of the Hartford *Courant;* in due time Harriet Beecher Stowe herself; and, later, a rough-hewn writing man from the West named Samuel L. Clemens. Recalling this community in after years, Hooker felt that he "ought not to omit William Gillette, then a boy growing up among us, the son of my sister, who has since become distinguished as an actor and playwright."[19]

In his new surroundings, Gillette first occupied the original farmhouse for several years, then built himself "a large and very pleasant house on the same street." The entire community became a center of Hartford's intellectual and social life, where visitors outstanding in public affairs and in literary and philanthropic activities were frequent.[20] Perhaps not so frequent—and certainly less conspicuous—were the dark travelers who came in secrecy, found shelter and food in Gillette's barn, and went on their way never knowing that they had enjoyed the hospitality of a United States Senator.[21]

Hartford's Underground operatives other than Gillette were men less in the public eye; and so far as the record is concerned, largely anonymous. They included the "Mr. Foster" and "friends"—many in number but not otherwise identified—who helped James Lindsey Smith get through to Springfield. There were also the "Mr. B." and the several unnamed gentlemen of "H——" who spirited Charles to "F——" and thence to safety. In their own day, when their activities for the runaway were illegal, it would not have been prudent to give their names; but they did not hesitate to rejoice publicly when "four fresh fugitives reached Hartford" in October 1850 and were dispatched safely to Canada.[22]

Among the fugitives who came to Hartford, an undetermined number sought to make the city their permanent home, and there were many residents prepared to help them find a place in the community. Charles, during his three months of comparative safety in Connecticut, had been employed by a "respectable gentleman" who became much interested in him and put him on the Underground Railroad when that step became necessary. At about the same time, a fugitive girl whose name is not recorded found an even better friend in her employer, Elisha Colt. Walking in the street one day, this woman met her former owner's nephew; but instead of threatening her, he greeted her in a friendly manner. His family, he said, had forgiven her for running away, and to prove it, he had a gift of clothes for her in his room; would she come with him to get them? So smoothly did he speak that she went along as asked. But, once in the room, the young man locked the door and let the girl know that he meant to arrest her as a fugitive slave. She managed to break away, however, by leaping desperately through a window. By good fortune, she fell onto an awning below rather than onto the street, escaping without serious injury. When Colt learned of this, he went to work at once in her behalf, holding her in safety until he could make a financial arrangement with her claimant and purchase her freedom.[23]

Hartford was also home to one of the most distinguished of all fugitives from bondage, the Reverend James W. C. Pennington, D.D. Born a slave in Maryland in 1809, he escaped at the age of twenty and made his way to Philadelphia. There an elderly woman directed him to a Quaker, identified only by the initials W. W., who greeted the runaway with the words: "Well, come in and take thy breakfast, and get warm, and we will talk about it; thee must be cold without any coat, come in and take thy breakfast and get warm." These words from a stranger, spoken with "an air of simple sincerity and fatherly kindness," as Pennington later recorded, made "an overwhelming impression" on his mind. He remained with this man for some time; and here he took the first steps in the direction he was to follow so successfully. "It was while living with this Friend, and by his kind attention in teaching me, that I acquired my first knowledge of writing, arithmetic, and geography." After six months of this training, Pennington went to Long Island, where he taught two years in a Negro school. Then, having a thirst for further education, he removed to New Haven, where he hoped to study theology at Yale. For reasons not clear —possibly because he lacked the necessary prerequisites in formal training—he was not admitted to the theological school. Nevertheless he was permitted to pursue his studies "by sitting with the classes though not participating." In this way he managed to study history, astronomy, algebra, philosophy, logic, rhetoric, and systematic theology.[24]

Pennington received a license to preach in 1838 and began a long career as pastor of the Talcott Street Congregational Church, Hartford. He became an outstanding minister, "widely known and very much respected by the clergy of the city, as well as by the people generally." Twice he was elected president of the Hartford Central Association of Congregational Ministers, a group comprising some twenty of the leading clergymen of that domination. He went as a delegate to the General Convention for the Improvement of the Free Coloured People, the World's Antislavery Convention, and the World Peace Convention. The latter two met simultaneously, in London, in 1843. Thus Pennington made his first visit to England, where he preached as visiting minister in many Dissenting churches. He exchanged pulpits with fellow ministers in Connecticut also—among others, with Dr. Noah Porter of Farmington, whose parishioners were "astonished, some of them shocked, by seeing one of the blackest of men in their pulpit."[25]

All this while, Pennington's status as a runaway slave was known only to the Philadelphia Quakers who had first befriended him. Not even his wife was told the truth, lest she be troubled about his safety. Pennington himself, however, was "burdened with harrassing apprehensions of being seized and carried back to slavery"—the more so as the troubled 1840's increasingly foreshadowed a coming crisis. At length he could stand the strain no longer. He went to John Hooker, who was still living in Farmington, and told him the facts: that his original name was Jim Pembroke; that he had run away from his owner, Frisbie Tilghman of Hagerstown, Maryland; and that he wanted to purchase his freedom.[26]

Hooker was glad to handle the case. First he sent Pennington to Canada for safety's sake. Then he wrote Tilghman a letter asking what price he would accept for the slave's freedom. Tilghman replied that although "Jim Pembroke" was "a first-rate blacksmith, and well worth $1,000," he would take half that amount to settle the matter. He also implied that he had some knowledge of his erstwhile bondsman's new name and occupation. The asking price was considerably higher than the sum available to meet it, and Tilghman's implication was a sign of possible danger. On Hooker's advice, Pennington went from Canada to the British Isles.

In all, he was abroad about two years; the Fugitive Slave Law, passed soon after his departure, made it impossible for him to return safely until Tilghman's claim was satisfied. Pennington's name was already familiar to British abolitionists, and his autobiography had been published in London. His character and intellectual accomplishments won him warm friends wherever he went. His greatest honor came in Germany, where, on a visit to the University of Heidelberg, he was awarded the degree of doctor of divinity, in a ceremony that included the following words:

> You are the first African who has received this dignity from a European University, and it is the University of Heidelberg that thus pronounces the universal brotherhood of humanity![27]

Pennington replied in a graceful speech, in which he declared his personal unworthiness of the honor but accepted it as a representative of his race.

While England entertained this Negro minister and Germany honored him, Scotland provided him with the most practical help. A group of abolitionists there made it their business to obtain his legal freedom. Forming themselves into a committee for the purpose, they set about raising the necessary funds. Then they instructed Hooker to resume negotiations with Tilghman and to carry them through, whatever the cost might be.

The lawyer's next letter to the Maryland man, however, brought an answer from a stranger. Tilghman, it said, had died; the writer was the administrator of his estate; and to settle the affair promptly, he would accept $150. He added that, under the law, he had no power to manumit; he could only sell the slave, and who would the purchaser be? With his reply, Hooker sent both the money and a bill of sale to himself; and when it came back from Maryland, duly receipted, ownership had been lawfully transferred to this Yankee abolitionist who was a descendant of the Reverend Thomas Hooker and a brother-in-law of the author of *Uncle Tom's Cabin.* Hooker kept the document for a day "to see what the sensation would be." Then he executed and had entered in the Farmington town records a deed of manumission, whereby he set free "my slave, Jim Pembroke, otherwise known as the Rev. James W. C. Pennington, D.D."

Thus Pennington became legally a free man, able to return home and to resume the pastorate in which he so long served his flock and shed luster on his adopted city. By his own efforts he had fled to freedom, achieved a high place in the world, gained international honors, and finally cleared his position in the eyes of an unjust law. It was perhaps only fitting that, when he needed an agent to negotiate for him, he found that agent not in Hartford but in Farmington, where so much of Connecticut's Underground Railroad activity was centered.

CHAPTER 11

MIDDLETOWN, A WAY STATION

In the decade before the Civil War, Middletown presented a peaceful scene of horse-drawn vehicles rolling along the tree-lined streets. It was not unusual to see a Negro hackman quietly speaking to his team as they climbed the slope toward Wesleyan University's brownstone buildings, or a Negro laborer working with pick and shovel on the right of way of the New York and Boston Rail Road, then under construction. Generally, however, a decent living did not come easily to these people just emerging from slavery, among whom were not a few fugitives from Southern bondage. In 1850, most of the 149 Negroes in the city were seamen, laborers, or—unfortunately—paupers, though one had an estate valued at $2000.[1]

There had been something of a Negro population in Middletown since 1661, a decade or so after the first settlement, when sea captains brought a few African slaves from Barbados and sold them at auction. The slave trade never became as important here as it was in New London, Boston, and some other ports; but it is recorded that John Bannister, Newport merchant, was pleased in 1752 to find Middletown purchasers for "the finest cargo of Negro men, women, and boys ever imported into New England." [2] The number of slaves had risen by 1756 from its original handful to 218 in a total population of 5664. Middletown then ranked third among Connecticut towns in Negro inhabitants, but hardly anyone at that time "held more than two slaves." [3]

If one of these bondsmen was sold, the purchaser was likely to be someone in a nearby town or in Middletown itself. In 1777 Joseph Stocking signed a document that transferred ownership of one Silvia to George Wyllys: [4]

> Know all men by these presents that I Joseph Stocking of Middletown in the County of Hartford and State of Connecticut for the Consideration of Thirty Pounds lawful Money received to my full satisfaction of George Wyllys Esquire of Hartford in the County aforesaid do give grant Bargain and sell & convey and deliver to the said George Wyllys Esqr his Heirs and Assigns a certain Negro woman slave name Silvia of the Age of twenty three years.

At about the same time a colored woman named Pegg was sold by Theophilus Woodbridge of Middletown to Benjamin Arnold of the same place. Arnold later brought suit against Woodbridge, claiming that the seller had represented the slave as enjoying the best of health, although he knew she suffered from epileptic fits. Arnold won the case in court, and an award of damages was upheld on appeal.[5]

Just as those who bought slaves were sometimes dissatisfied with their purchases, so the slaves were sometimes unhappy with their owners. One in Middletown went so far as to emasculate his master's son. This presented a legalistic puzzle for the Superior Court at Hartford, where the offender was brought to trial, "for there existed no law covering such a crime." Finally the Court invoked the Mosaic injunction of "an eye for an eye and a tooth for a tooth." The slave was punished accordingly.[6]

Connecticut's laws for the gradual emancipation of slaves had taken full effect in Middletown by 1830. But many Negroes, although they had achieved freedom in a legal sense, were the victims of discrimination, living in a sort of half-caste status in the least desirable parts of the town. A Wesleyan University man, identified only by the initial "K," reported on this situation in 1840:[7]

> One cold, bleak, November evening, I knocked at the door of a miserable block, in one of the darkest lanes in town, and enquiring for the person of whom I was in pursuit was directed up stairs, till reaching the attic, an emaciated colored female answered my summons, and welcomed, with the most grateful acknowledgements, my visit to her desolate home. There were a few expiring embers upon the hearth, over which two small children sat shivering. The furniture of the room consisted of a broken chair, an old chest, a straw pallet in one corner, and a much used family Bible. . . . I saw that I had interrupted her evening meal, and requested her to proceed without noticing me. She gathered her little ones around the old chest, and brought a plate, containing a few crusts of bread, as their intended repast.
>
> As she sat down, awhile, she remained lost in thought, now and then a tear dropping down upon her cheek; then raising her eyes to heaven and clasping her hands . . . she burst forth, "All these blessings, Lord, and Christ too?" As I left that humble paradise, I thought I had discovered the essence of that command, "Whether ye eat, or drink, or whatsoever ye do, do all to the glory of God."

Like that poor woman, Middletown's Negroes found comparatively few of the citizens who cared in the least about their welfare. In fact, the temper of the city was predominantly sympathetic to slavery and opposed to abolition or anything that smacked of it. Although slavery was a blightful condition, declared a Middletown editor, it was impracticable to give the slaves their freedom. "They know not the value of liberty . . . and any external interference, while it has no influence in meliorating their condition, exasperates their masters, and weakens our bond of Union." [8] The colonization movement was strong, and Willbur Fisk, first president of Wesleyan University, was one of its leaders; in his opinion, the proper place for people of color was Africa, where they could unfold in their natural habitat. Middletown, he boasted, was the seat of "the earliest Colonization Society in Connecticut . . . for the ladies of the city, to their honor be it spoken, have long had a society in successful operation, the earliest in Connecticut, if not in New England." [9] To people like these, the presence in their midst of Negroes—in 1830, 209 altogether, as against 6683 whites—threatened the amalgamation of the races.[10]

The Negroes, almost to a man, wanted no part of the colonization scheme. Instead, they looked to the antislavery movement for help in their quest for full American citizenship.[11] In Middletown, the first antislavery organization was a direct outgrowth of their own work. In 1828 a group of colored people gathered at the home of George W. Jeffrey, a laborer, where they organized the African Methodist Episcopal Zion Church. Its building was erected on Cross Street near Mount Vernon Street, close to the Wesleyan campus; and when the Reverend Jehiel C. Beman became its pastor in 1831, it found its guiding spirit. Beman came from Colchester and was proud of the origin of his name. His father, once a slave, had chosen it on obtaining his freedom; for, as he said, he had always detested slavery and wanted to *be* a *man*, so now he would adopt a name that declared his newly won condition.[12]

The minister's home was near the church on Cross Street, where he lived with his wife Clarissa and their family. Mrs. Beman was among those who, on April 2, 1834, organized the Colored Female Anti-Slavery Society of Middletown—the second women's abolition society in the United States. This forward-looking group not only sought the end of slavery but also worked for "mutual improvement and increased intellectual and moral happiness" among free Negroes.[13] William Lloyd Garrison, visiting the Bemans on a tour through Connecticut in the early 1830's, was greatly impressed with their faith and their work in freedom's cause. "It was with as much difficulty as reluctance," he said, "I tore myself from their company." [14]

A son of this dedicated couple was Amos G. Beman, then a young man about twenty years of age. He had received some primary schooling from Miss Huldah Morgan, a colored schoolmistress, and through his own efforts he had acquired further learning. Now, with the newly opened Wesleyan University almost in his dooryard, he wished to complete his formal education. Wesleyan provided teachers for the Zion Church's Sunday school, but its Joint Board had ruled that "none but male white persons shall be admitted as students of this institution." [15] Charles B. Ray, who later became an efficient Underground operator in New York, was unable to obtain any instruction there. Amos Beman, more fortunate, found among the students a friend who "was aroused to assist the persecuted." This was Samuel P. Dole.

Dole, who had reported on Ray's difficulties to Garrison's *Liberator*, offered to teach Amos three times a week. For six months Amos followed the course of instruction laid out by Dole. Though he was a constant victim of "horseplay and name-calling" from many of the students, yet he kept on with his work. Then, one day, he received a letter:

> Middletown, October 5th, 1833
>
> To Beman, Junior:
>
> Young Beman:—A number of the students of this University deeming it derogatory to themselves, as well as to the University, to have you and other colored students recite here, do hereby warn you to desist from such a course; and if you fail to comply with this peaceable request, we swear, by the Eternal God, that we will resort to forcible means to put a stop to it.
>
> Twelve of Us

Apprehensive, Amos immediately relayed this letter to his tutor Dole, who later wrote down his actions and his findings:

> The letter was given to our teacher; the President being absent, it was also shown to two of the Professors. One of them, with a significant toss of the head, passed by on the other side; the other stated that bating the profanity, it expressed the sense of a by-law enacted by the Board of Trustees at their last meeting—by subsequent inquiry, we have found it even so. The resolution was moved and supported by ardent Colonizationists.[16]

This was clearly the handwriting on the wall. Amos Beman dropped his studies in Middletown and went to Hartford, where he taught a primary school for colored children for the next four years; thereafter he moved to New Haven and the ministry where he did such important work for the antislavery cause. A year after he had gone, Wesleyan's Joint Board countermanded its ruling against Negroes and opened the doors of the college to male students without regard to race.[17]

Meanwhile, abolitionist sentiment was beginning to stir among the citizens of Middletown, and for this Jesse G. Baldwin was largely responsible. He was a native of Meriden, born on a farm there in 1804, and in his late teens he became an itinerant peddler of silver and plated ware. In this vocation he traveled extensively, especially in the South, where he saw the horrors of the auction block. With his mind firmly set against the evils of slavery, he came to Middletown in 1833, where he opened a store dealing in "Yankee notions" and also began the manufacture of cotton webbing on a small scale. In later life he branched out into other lines—banking, insurance, and shipping. He was a man who kept his own counsel; it was said of him that he "did not let his left hand know what his right hand doeth." [18]

Deep-seated was Baldwin's hatred of slavery, and it became a guiding principle in both his business and his personal life. The cotton he used was not purchased in the American South, but from a Quaker settlement in the West Indies where all the laborers were free. The sugar served in his household came from "distant lands where there were no slaves." When he traveled, he "carried loaf sugar with him, which was made by free men, and, when taking meals at hotels, he would sweeten his tea with the sugar he carried, taking a lump or two from his vest pocket and dropping it into his tea." [19]

Soon after his arrival in the city, Baldwin was instrumental in organizing the Middletown Anti-Slavery Society. The initial meeting took place in 1834, in the Guild & Douglas shop at William and Broad streets. Here friends of the slave gathered to hear fiery abolition speeches and to formulate a set of by-laws that squared solidly with rank Garrisonism. Meanwhile an angry mob of pro-slavery sympathizers gathered outside. From jeers and catcalls they passed to physical violence, hurling stones and eggs through the windows at the men gathered within. Then someone shouted: "Water would do no harm to a dirty abolitionist!" No sooner said than done; the mob obtained buckets and began dousing the members with water. Mayor Elijah Hubbard was summoned to the scene, but his reading of the Riot Act could not abate the uproar. When the abolitionists tried to get away, they were seized and roughly handled: "Edwin Hunt was tumbled up Main Street to the Mansion House, where he was later rescued. Father Bunnell was kicked over the park, and Deacon Lewis was chased across a lot. . . . The Reverend Mr. D. Dennison and Mr. Dole were kicked and hounded through William Street to Main." [20]

In spite of this violent treatment, the Middletown antislavery men reassembled at a later date to carry on their business. At a meeting on October 22, 1837, held at the First Methodist Episcopal Church, they adopted these resolutions:

1. That the principles and practices of slavery are diametrically opposed to the principles and practices taught in the Bible.
2. That John Wesley and the founders of the M. E. Church were Abolitionists and intended that the Church should be an Abolition as well as a temperance Church.
3. That the great and rapidly increasing number of slave holders in the M. E. Church is cause of grief and alarm and calls upon every friend of the purity and prosperity of the Church to raise their united voices in remonstrance against it and their persevering efforts for its overthrow.

At the meeting's end, the members sang, to the tune of "Auld Lang Syne," an anthem beginning as follows:

I am an abolitionist!
I glory in the name;
Though now by slavery's minions hissed,
And covered o'er with shame:—
It is a spell of light and power—
The watchword of the free—
Who spurns it in this trial hour,
A craven soul is he.[21]

Despite its enthusiastic beginning, the antislavery movement in Middletown made little headway. In August of 1838, President Willbur Fisk of Wesleyan was writing to a correspondent in Covington, Georgia: "Abolitionism in Middletown is on the wane. It has in a great measure consumed its energies by the intensity of its own fires. Unless they can get some new martyrs or some *Go*, they will have to stop operations for want of materials." [22] Nine months later, as revealed in the minutes of the Anti-Slavery Society for May 1, 1839, the organization could count on the financial support of only eleven members: [23]

> We the undersigned agree to pay monthly, to the Treasurer of the Middletown Anti-Slavery Society, or his order, the sum affixed to each of our respective names during the year commencing May 1, 1839:

Jesse G. Baldwin	$52.00
Ira Gardiner	3.00
Chauncey Wetmore	12.00
A friend	5.00
I. W. M. Ree	12.00
Chas. B. Clark	2.00
Dea. Woodward	1.00
Richard Warner	5.00
Richard S. Rust	3.00
Benjamin Douglas	3.00
William Mitchell	5.00

This list reveals, not surprisingly, that Jesse G. Baldwin was not only the driving force of the abolition movement in Middletown but its chief monetary backer as well. He was more than that; he was also a station-keeper and conductor on the Underground Railroad. His two schooners, built in 1848, the *W. B. Douglas* and the *Jesse G. Baldwin*, are believed to have carried runaway slaves as well as their ordinary cargoes.[24] In his home at 15 Broad Street, Middletown, one of the rooms was used as a hiding place for fugitives; this chamber was occupied in after years by his grandson Henry Sill Baldwin, to whom the old abolitionist frequently told stories of the operations of the secret road to freedom. Some of these concerned the elder Baldwin's work as a conductor, when he would "hitch up his horses" and drive the refugees to a further station on the route through Rocky Hill and Wethersfield to Hartford and Farmington.[25]

There is no record that Alanson Work carried on Underground activities in Middletown, but he was surely an unflinching witness for the abolitionist faith. A native of Woodstock, Connecticut, he lived in Middletown from the early 1820's to about 1840; here he was married in 1825 to Miss Amelia A. Forbes, and here in 1832 was born their son Henry Clay Work, who became famous as the composer of "Marching Through Georgia" and such temperance ballads as "Father, Dear Father, Come Home With Me Now." [26] Several years later, Work took his wife and four children to Quincy, Illinois, where by 1841 he had become involved in the antislavery activities that centered about the Mission Institute there. Across the Mississippi River lay Missouri, a slaveholding land; the young men who were "pursuing a course of training for the Christian ministry" at the Institute could hear, from the other side of the stream, "the crack of the Overseer's whip" and the cries of the beaten slaves. Alanson Work, together with his student friends James E. Burr and George Thompson, resolved to free at least some of these poor sufferers from their misery. They devised a plan to cross into Missouri, abduct two slaves with whom they had been in touch, and send them northward by the Underground Railroad line out of Quincy. But once they reached the west bank of the river, they were seized by a group of angry Missourians, who marched them off to prison. Swiftly they were brought to trial on three counts: stealing slaves, attempting to steal slaves, and intending to make the attempt. The verdict was guilty; the sentence, twelve years in the penitentiary.[27]

Abolitionists of the more zealous sort often thought of themselves as sharing in spirit the fetters of the slave; Alanson Work now wore fetters in hard reality. Chained in his prison cell, he wrote in his journal:[28]

> The Lord hears prayers; blessed be his name. My chain feels light this morning. Oh! let me not trust in man. Last evening being monthly concert for the oppressed, we "remembered those in bonds, as bound with them." After lying down to rest, and while thinking of those bound in more galling chains than ours, we overheard a conversation, by which we learned that six slaves had crossed the Mississippi, the night before, and that some persons were preparing to go to the river to intercept other fugitives. Gladly will I wear this chain till it galls my ankle to the bone, if thereby the slave may go free.

Work continued to make friends among his fellow prisoners, even some who were incensed against his abolitionist principles; meanwhile he suffered his harsh imprisonment with Christian resignation. Finally, on the basis of his exemplary behavior, he was released after three years, six months, and seven days, on condition that he return to

Connecticut. Burr remained in jail a year longer, while Thompson served five years of his twelve-year sentence.[29]

Safely back in his native state, Work did not forget the bondsmen for whom he had suffered, and he was disgusted with the apathy toward the slavery issue that he saw around him. In 1846 he expressed his views in a letter to the *Charter Oak:* [30]

> We are here in Middletown, and although much farther from the poor slave than we were a few months ago, still we do not intend to forget him. Having tasted a little of the bitter cup which he has to drink, we hope to remember him as bound with him. I do not see or hear of much doing in this place for the slave. I hear of no Liberty meetings—no concerts—no prayer meetings, or prayers for the slave, and if there is any sympathy for him, (with a few exceptions) it appears to be locked up in the breast that contains it. I have thought, should the slaveholders come here into Connecticut, and take one out of every family (the father, perhaps) and take him off to the South and shut him up in their Penitentiaries, O Sir, we should have Liberty men here then, and women and children, too. There would be praying then, and tears and sighs. And I think it would not end there, but there would be some doing too.

In spite of Work's gloomy estimate of the situation, there was "some doing" in Middletown, and the pump shop of William and Benjamin Douglas was the center of much of it. These two had come to the city from Northford in 1832, when William was twenty years of age and his brother only sixteen. William became a partner in the firm of Guild & Douglas; the firm's name was changed when Benjamin joined it in 1839 after an apprenticeship elsewhere. Together, the brothers became highly successful in the manufacture of pumps invented and patented by themselves; they maintained two plants, the former Guild & Douglas works and a pump shop nearby on William Street. After the passage of the 1850 Fugitive Slave Law, their establishment became known as the "Cradle of Liberty" because of the abolitionist work that had long centered there. Benjamin Douglas, in particular, was a leading citizen, mayor of the city from 1850 to 1856 and lieutenant governor of the state in 1861–1862.[31] But even his public standing did not entirely save him from the attacks that abolitionists had to expect. At several meetings that he attended, "stones were hurled through the windows by those who held opposite views." During the Draft Riots in New York City in 1863 he faced a greater danger, when he rescued an escaped slave named Ephraim Dixon from a mob "that would not have hesitated to take his life." After hiding Dixon for a time, Douglas "smuggled him out of the city on a ferry boat and brought him to Middletown." There he continued to befriend the man, setting him up in a barber shop of his own.[32]

The runaways who reached these Middletown abolitionists generally did so, as has been stated, by the Connecticut River line or one of its laterals; but the Underground Railroad provided a highly adaptable system. On one occasion William Wakeman brought a band of refugees—a man, his wife, and three children—all the way from Wilton to the hands of the Baldwin circle.[33] What circumstances made necessary so long a cross-country journey can only be guessed, nor is it known what happened to this particular group. In all probability, like the bulk of the fugitives for whom Middletown was a way station, they were sent by one of the several available routes to Farmington.

CHAPTER 12

FARMINGTON, THE GRAND CENTRAL STATION

FARMINGTON, in the year 1696, was a self-contained farming village whose citizens produced virtually all the things they consumed, minded their own business, and elected their own leaders. One whom they honored with public office was Frank Freeman, a Negro and a man of property. His life's partner in an interracial marriage was Maudlin, widow of Samuel Street of Wallingford; but his marital happiness was short-lived, for he died a few months after the ceremony. His estate included books appraised at over six shillings—a fair-sized library by the standards of the place and time, when one considers that that of Luke Hayes, schoolmaster and Freeman's successor as husband of the often married Maudlin, was valued at only eighteen pence.[1]

Like other Connecticut villages, Farmington had its bondsmen during the colonial period. In 1790 the township's approximately 2700 residents owned just nine slaves; and these, it appears, were treated more as domestic servants and members of the household than as chattels.[2] Ten years later there were left only two, one owned by Thomas Lewis and the other by Elizabeth Wadsworth. In 1820, after the state's gradual emancipation laws had had time to take effect, there were none.[3]

In the early years of the century, the area around the town was what it had been since the earliest settlement—a farming region. The village proper stood adjacent to the comparatively low-lying and fertile meadows along the Farmington River, which came in from the northwest and turned sharply to the north. It was linked with Hartford and New Haven by a system of turnpikes, over which stagecoaches plied between the state's two capitals. The roads were "sandy in summer, buried out of sight by snow drifts in winter, and, when these began to melt in the spring, of unknown depth." It was only natural that, when the Erie Canal opened in 1820 to become an assured success, promoters and plain citizens saw in it a model worth emulating. One result was the Farmington Canal, chartered in 1822 and opened for service in 1828, eventually linking the Sound at New Haven with the Connecticut near Northampton; a planned extension to the St. Lawrence River was never completed.[4]

This waterway, with its promise of easy communications, brought a change to Farmington's business life. Small plants sprang up for the manufacture of paper, hardware, knit goods, and carriages.[5] These last-named products were in demand in the South; but there is nothing to indicate that any local citizens developed strong ties with Southern planters, as did manufacturers in other Connecticut cities.[6] Nonetheless there were some pro-slavery residents, and almost everyone regarded the Negro as belonging to a naturally inferior order of beings. John Hooker, who was a boy in the 1820's, later wrote of "the universal disregard of the rights of colored people" in those days:[7]

> Negro was always spelled then with two "G's." The black man seemed to have no rights as a man. He was often kindly regarded by humane people, but such a thing as

> his having the rights of a man was hardly thought of. In church he sat in the negroes' pew, a pew close by the door in the lower part of the house or in the gallery. . . . When the anti-slavery movement came along it met not only with ridicule, but with persecution. Its opponents did not entertain a doubt of its ultimate failure. As the New York *Nation* says of the time, it was a few fanatics on one side and all society on the other.

Even then, however, there were those in Farmington who took to heart the words of the Declaration of Independence: "We hold these truths to be self-evident, that all men are created equal." Such a one, perhaps, was the proprietor of Phelps' Hotel, where the stage from Hartford made its regular stop. On one occasion it had among its passengers a "decently-clad black man, on his way to New Haven." Captain Goodrich, "one of New Haven's aristocracy," was waiting to board the coach; when he saw the dark passenger inside, he ordered him "with an oath" to get out, and the stage driver seconded the command. Together they forced the Negro from the place to which he had every right, whereupon the coach drove off and left him standing. But Phelps, possibly from fear that he would be blamed for the incident or possibly from a simple sense of justice, "got up a wagon and drove the man to New Haven." [8]

By 1836, when Garrison's *Liberator* had been publishing its message of freedom for half a decade, the climate of opinion was showing a change. Early in that year Farmington's antislavery society was organized, with Thomas Cowles as its secretary and with seventy men as members. There was also a women's abolition organization of forty members. Between them, they included "some of the best of the Farmington people." They held meetings, propagandized for their cause, and listened to traveling antislavery orators—among them the magnetic Quaker Miss Abby Kelly, one of the most eloquent and impassioned of speakers, and the Reverend Amos Phelps, one of the gentlest and most moderate yet most impressive.[9]

Their work was not without opposition. While the town was generally "quiet and orderly," it did contain some who upheld the institution of slavery and others who could not accept the Negro as a man and a brother. On one occasion when the Reverend Mr. Phelps was speaking at the Congregational church, "a stone was thrown with great violence through the window back of the desk at which he was speaking, which passed close by his head, and went across the hall to the wall on the other side. . . . It might have killed one whom it chanced to hit." Even as late as 1840, when Hooker invited a "respectable-looking and decently-clad" Negro to share his pew at church, "the moral shock was very great. One of the church members said that I had done more to break up the church than any thing that had happened in its whole history." Early in the following year, when Hooker opened his law office for the first time, he "encountered much unfriendliness from those who were bitter against the anti-slavery movement"; and a worldly-wise relative who lived in another town advised him that his identification with abolition would "very seriously injure my chances of getting into business." [10]

In that same spring Cinque, Tami, and the other Negroes from the *Amistad* came to Farmington to enjoy the hospitality of local abolitionists and to win supporters all over town by their constant good cheer. Their simple friendliness and almost childlike delight in the new sights about them did much to break down local prejudice against people of color. The walls crumbled further when, a few years later, Farmington's beloved and respected minister Dr. Noah Porter exchanged pulpits with the Reverend

Mr. (not as yet Dr.) Pennington, and his congregation thus learned that a man of almost ebony hue could also be an outstanding preacher.[11] These events, particularly the presence of the *Amistad* captives, created a sympathy that was "concretely expressed by some of Farmington's well-known citizens in making their homes stations of the Underground Railroad." [12]

The clandestine work, however, had been going on for some little time before this. The incident involving Charles was the first of which there is a reliably dated record; it took place in 1838. At least five Farmington residents, one of them a Negro, had parts in this affair as conductors or otherwise, and two different houses sheltered the fugitive during the several days he was secreted in the town.[13] One of these men was John T. Norton, who took care of Charles' trunk and later set down the story of the escape. He was also a good friend of the *Amistad* people, who were frequent visitors at his house, and he was the man to whom they turned for help when Grabbo was tragically drowned.[14]

Of the other Underground operatives in Farmington, then and later, not all can be identified, but they included some of the most substantial citizens: Austin F. Williams, Horace Cowles, William McKee, Levi Dunning, Samuel Deming, Lyman and George Hurlburt, and Elijah Lewis. Cowles, George Hurlburt, and McKee are known to have been keepers of stations; a colored man of unrecorded name who made his home with Hurlburt was an active messenger and conductor.[15] If John Hooker was personally involved in Underground operations, he did not admit it, but he was certainly one of the leaders of the abolitionist group.

Through the hands of these men, during the next decades, passed a constant stream of fugitives on their way from Wilton or New Haven or Hartford to stations beyond the Massachusetts line. The town was indeed the junction of Connecticut's escape routes, the Grand Central Station of its Underground Railroad lines. Most of the runaways went on after a few hours or a few days of rest, but some remained to work for the farmers, relying on them for protection and help if an attempt should be made to recapture them.[16]

From those who stayed, for a time or permanently, the villagers heard many stories of slavery and escape, saw much evidence of the brutalities of the "peculiar institution." One of the runaways, who worked for a local farmer, exhibited on his back the marks of a fearful scourging with a raw lash.[17] Another, in town for a short stop only, had a story that illustrated only too well the slaveholder's complete indifference to the human rights and feelings of his bondsmen: [18]

> He was born and raised in Virginia, and married a slave girl there who belonged to his master, and had three or four small children. At this time slaves were raised in Virginia to be sold for the cotton fields of the South, a large business of that sort being carried on. This negro was working in a field, when a slave trader came along and bought him and several other negroes from his master. They were attached to a coffle of slaves that the trader was taking along, being handcuffed and fastened together. He was not allowed to go home to see his family or to get anything to take with him, but as the coffle passed his cabin, quite a distance away, his wife saw him and ran out screaming towards him. The trader upon this drew out his pistol, and, pointing it towards her, threatened to shoot her if she came another step. She stopped and the coffle passed by, too far off for him to call to his wife, and he never saw her or his children again.

All of the fugitives were, in one way or another, victims of cruelty and injustice; some of them were heroes too. Such a one was Henry, fine-looking, manly, and energetic, who lived and worked with Arthur Williams and was greatly liked by everyone who knew him. After he had been in town for some months, he encountered a fugitive from his former home in South Carolina, who had bad news. The owner had accused Henry's old mother of aiding her son's escape and had given her a terrible flogging on the naked body as punishment. Knowing full well what he would face if recaptured, Henry nevertheless decided to go back and settle accounts. He would see and comfort his mother, and he would get revenge by helping other slaves to escape. And that was exactly what he did. Somehow he managed to follow the Underground routes in the reverse direction; he reassured his mother; and he got up a company of eight others who were ready to follow him north. Among them was a young woman, the wife of one of the party, who was soon to have a child. At first she walked through the night with the others; then, as she grew more exhausted, her husband and Henry carried her on their backs, turn and turn about. After several nights of this hard going, she was utterly worn out; they all stopped to watch her die, then buried her in the darkness and pushed on. They had many perils and escapes on the way, but they all reached Canada in safety. Henry, born a slave, had certainly proved himself a bold and resourceful leader of men.[19]

Another leader, though in a different way, was George Hurlburt's Negro friend, whose name unfortunately has been lost. By channels not now traceable, he received news of incoming fugitives. On such occasions he went at night to the home of Elijah Lewis and gave a prearranged signal; then the two would go away together to pick up and guide their passengers. Sometimes these arrangements were varied. On one occasion, it is reported, Lewis met this same man with a fugitive "about nine o'clock . . . where the wolf-pit road comes out of the Hartford Turnpike"; then the three of them proceeded along the road to the Deer Cliff Farm and from there to Simsbury. Apparently this particular runaway had been picked up in or near Hartford.[20]

This same Elijah Lewis was perfectly willing to accept former slaves as permanent settlers in the area. He once sold some land to Jane and Maria Thompson, who were buying it for the fugitive George Anderson. Soon afterward, however, Anderson saw in the Farmington streets a planter from the South whom he knew to be a neighbor of his former owner. Certain that he would be recognized and seized, he changed his plans immediately and vanished from the town.[21]

That particular planter may not have been searching for runaway slaves, but there were those who did, and Farmington's Undergrounders did their work with appropriate precautions. The daughter of one of them later recalled how her father had gone into Hartford to a house where a fugitive was concealed in a wardrobe. "It was winter and sleighing. The man was put in the bottom of the sleigh and covered in such a way as to resemble a load of feed. He was brought to our barn and there passed on to another place of safety and reached Canada in due time." Another Farmington child, in later life Mrs. Hardy, was once told by her father not to answer any questions from anyone while he was away. All the long summer day she sat on the doorstep, and in common with the rest of the village she saw a horse covered with lather driven frantically through the street by a stranger. Only later did she learn that the driver was a slaveholder seeking his vanished property—and that the slave had been hidden all day in the southwest bedroom of her own house.[22]

That slave was only one of many who got safely away from Farmington to some more distant point. The canal was one possible route of escape but probably not the best one—no traffic in winter, locks where a boat might be inspected, no navigation at night. Besides, it was never extended beyond Northampton, and it ceased operations altogether in 1848. For travelers by land, Francis Gillette's house in Bloomfield was a possible way station so long as he lived there. The Chaffee house in Windsor, to the northeast, was also a station. Phineas Gabriel in Avon was an agent, escorting or directing fugitives north along the Farmington River, perhaps as far as Granby or West Suffield.[23] Someone of unknown identity operated around Simsbury, receiving passengers from Elijah Lewis and probably others.

This was the main highway into Massachusetts, and over the state line the chief receiving station was Hiram Hull's farm in Westfield. It was a busy station indeed, where the younger Hiram and his brother Liverus had the duty of feeding the fugitives morning and night—sometimes as many as twenty all at once, lodged together in the barn. Hiram Junior was responsible for the nighttime safety of the runaways as well. Locking them in the barn so that they would not be disturbed, he went to his own room for a little sleep; but near him he kept a "billet of wood about twice the size, as he remembered it, of a policeman's club," which he considered enough to deal with any trouble that might arise; he never had a pistol. In the dark hours he occasionally strolled to the barn to see that all was well. In the morning, after breakfast, the refugees went on by daylight if the coast seemed clear; otherwise they remained until evening, then proceeded to Northampton.[24]

That place, like Farmington, was something of an Underground junction, for it received not only the passengers of the Westfield line but those who came by the riverside route through Springfield. The latter city, the metropolis of western Massachusetts, had received James Lindsey Smith by boat from Hartford, and he was by no means the only one to reach it, either by water or by land. It was in fact an important center. During the 1830's the Reverend Samuel Osgood harbored many runaways, helping them to find both schooling and jobs. In this he was assisted by Joseph C. Bull, John Howland, a Mr. Church, and others.

As the flow of fugitives increased, parties were unloaded by night in the Worthington grove and taken to various houses in the city; but this practice came to be considered a dangerous one. Finally, the custom was to receive runaways in the woods of the North End. Osgood's circle secured a house in the woods for their shelter; but the Negroes never knew the names of the men under whose roof they slept.[25]

John Brown, the grim and terrible man who wrote his name in blood in Kansas and in fanatical heroism at Harper's Ferry, also had his moment of activity in Springfield. Coming here in 1851 on a tour of Massachusetts, he enlisted the help of the fugitive Thomas Thomas and organized the first Vigilance Committee in the Connecticut Valley. Its members were some forty-four Negroes; its purpose, to resist the enforcement of the Fugitive Slave Law systematically, by disciplined violence. Brown's "Agreement and Rules" gave quite specific directions for paramilitary actions, the disruption of court proceedings, and the rescue of prisoners—"and be hanged, if you must, but tell no tales out of school." What part this organization played in the Underground is unclear, but the route's activity increased after the troop was formed.[26]

Of all the agents in the Connecticut River Valley, one of the busiest was J. P. Williston of Northampton. Many of the fugitives from both Springfield and Westfield came to shelter in his barn and to eat at his table. Moreover, he gave them money for their journey—something that few other agents are known to have done. He was a temperance man as well as an abolitionist, and he suffered for his convictions; the "rum element," together with pro-slavery people, joined hands and burned his barn. To show his sentiments, he took a Negro boy into his house as a member of the family and trained him in the printer's trade. Furthermore, since the lad had musical gifts, he sang in the choir of Northampton's Old Church, of which Williston was a leading member.[27]

Another station-keeper in this area was Arthur G. Hill, who described an incident of his work as follows: [28]

> William Wilson was landed here, remained a few months, worked and earned some money, returned south secretly, was gone quite a while but finally reached here again with a grown-up son, that he had been able to guide from slavery to freedom. The two men hired a small tenement, were industrious and worked for an object. After they had saved money enough they went south to rescue their daughter and sister. After a long absence the younger man returned, the older one having been captured and returned to slavery. The younger was confident that his father would again escape and decided to wait for him here. Sure enough, in a little while the old gentleman and daughter came and after a short stay to rest and get a little money the whole party moved north to the Queen's Dominion.

The natural route for these fugitives to follow ran directly up the river valley and over the Vermont border to Brattleboro, which also received passengers from Fitchburg, Worcester, and beyond. Thus the river line at last connected with that from the Thames and Quinebaug valleys; and the passenger who had first seen Connecticut's soil at Greenwich or New Haven might make his way through Montpelier to Canada side by side with one who had entered the Nutmeg State from Westerly in Rhode Island.[29]

CHAPTER 13

THE ROAD IN FULL SWING

THE Compromise of 1850 had been intended to allay the sectional conflict over the extension of slavery to the territories; and for a time, despite Northern opposition to the Fugitive Slave Law that was one of its provisions, it seemed to succeed in its purpose. The Missouri Compromise of 1820 remained in force; no territory north of latitude 36 degrees 30 minutes would come into the Union as a slave state, and by custom new states would be admitted in pairs, one slave and one free. North and South, at least in public, maintained an uneasy truce.[1]

It did not last long. Clay and Webster, architects of the 1850 settlement, both passed from the scene in 1852, and younger men came to the fore. One of them was Stephen A. Douglas, the five-foot-tall "Little Giant" who was a Democratic Senator from Illinois. He showed scant interest in the slavery question as such, but he was an ardent expansionist who envisioned America spreading inexorably across the continent. He was also devoted to the interests of his home state and its people, and he was eager that the transcontinental railroad, already being discussed, should spring from the Middle West rather than from New Orleans, thus crossing the still-unorganized upper Louisiana Territory rather than the state of Texas. As a step toward this end, Douglas in early 1854 introduced a measure to establish territorial government in the region. In its final form, the bill provided for two territories, Kansas and Nebraska, the one contiguous to slave-holding Missouri, the other to free Iowa. It also explicitly repealed the Missouri Compromise and provided that, in line with Douglas' favorite principle of "popular sovereignty," these territories should "be received into the Union with or without slavery, as their constitution may prescribe at the time of their admission." It was expected, though not stated, that Nebraska would eventually come in as a free state, while Kansas would enter as a slave state, and almost at once. In spite of desperate Free Soil opposition, the measure went through Congress by a sectional vote, and when President Pierce readily signed it on May 30, the Kansas-Nebraska Act was the law. It was, said Senator Charles Sumner of Massachusetts, at once the worst and the best bill on which Congress had ever acted: the worst, because it was a triumph for slavery; the best, because "it annuls all past compromises with slavery, and makes all future compromises impossible. Thus it puts freedom and slavery face to face, and bids them grapple. Who can doubt the result?" [2]

One result was that, in Kansas, the fight between slavery and abolition began at once, in earnest, with deadly weapons. Missourian "border ruffians" flocked into the territory to stake out claims, while Free Soil "jayhawkers" with Sharps rifles rushed in from Northern states—among them that fierce old Ironside from Torrington, John Brown. While the battle lines formed in the West, opposition to the bill and support for the Free Soil settlers showed themselves all over the East.

In Connecticut, less than two months after the act

became law, Eli Thayer and his supporters applied to the General Assembly for a charter for the Connecticut Emigrant Aid Company, whose stated purpose was to enable emigrants from that state and the rest of New England to settle in Kansas and Nebraska. The charter never materialized, but Thayer's group was more successful in Massachusetts, where they secured passage of a measure creating the Massachusetts Emigrant Aid Society, forerunner of the New England Emigrant Aid Company. Within a year, according to the so-called "Ministers' Memorials" that it circulated in July 1855 to nearly all New England clergymen, the Company had sent out "two or three thousand settlers" who had established six towns in Kansas. When Thayer visited Hartford on November 14 of the same year, he raised $5000 to support the work; the following day, addressing a large group of citizens in New Haven, he obtained $1600 more.[3]

By that time Free Soil sentiment was running high in the latter city. Under the leadership of Charles Lines, a Kansas Company of sixty members was organized to emigrate to the territory, and many meetings were held to raise money for them and to bid them farewell. Among the speakers at the final meeting in the North Church was Henry Ward Beecher, pastor of the Plymouth Church of the Pilgrims in Brooklyn and brother-in-law to John Hooker. Despite the fact that an admission fee was charged, the church was packed. Speakers let it be known that the colonists needed rifles for protection against "bears, wolves, panthers, robbers, and murderers." Professor Benjamin Silliman of Yale pledged one Sharps rifle; the Reverend Samuel W. S. Dutton, minister of the church, pledged another, for one of his deacons who had joined the band. Beecher pledged twenty-five from his church if the number were matched at the meeting. Amid great enthusiasm, enough were promised to arm the entire company, while all present sang the "Emigrant Song" to the air of "Auld Lang Syne." Women gave boxes of clothing; men donated money for provisions. The company thereafter was known as the "Rifle Christians," and the Sharps rifle was sometimes referred to as "Beecher's Bible." [4]

These dramatic events were only symptoms of a ground swell of antislavery feeling that swept the entire state. More and more people were coming to believe that, in the words of the Reverend Leonard Bacon, a mild abolitionist of New Haven, "slavery was wrong, and that any man who hoped to extend it was doing what he knew was wrong." Officially, Connecticut declared its position by adopting a new and stronger personal liberty law in 1854—one whose true purpose was to prevent the execution of the Fugitive Slave Law of 1850. The state's Whigs were solidly opposed to the Kansas-Nebraska Act and what it stood for, and they were equally opposed to the incumbent Democratic Administration. Soon enough, the bulk of them found a more comfortable political home in the new Republican Party, which openly avowed antislavery principles. It carried the state for Frémont in 1856, but the country elected the Democratic candidate.[5]

Two days after the inauguration of President James Buchanan, Frémont's opponent, the Supreme Court handed down its far-reaching decision in the case of Dred Scott *v.* Sanford. Scott, a Negro owned by an army surgeon, had been taken from Missouri to Illinois and later to the territory of Minnesota. After his return to Missouri, he had brought suit for his freedom, on the ground of his residence in two places where slavery was illegal—Illinois, free under the Northwest Ordinance of 1787, and Minnesota, free under the terms of the Missouri Compromise.

The case, financed by abolitionists, had reached the highest tribunal on appeal.

With Chief Justice Roger B. Taney as its spokesman, a majority of the Court found against Scott, on three grounds. First, as a Negro, he was not a United States citizen but only a chattel or thing, and hence had no right to bring suit in a federal court. Second, the laws of Illinois had no bearing on his case because he was a resident of another state. Third, his stay in Minnesota was irrelevant because Congress had no power to prohibit slavery in the territories. It therefore followed that the Missouri Compromise was not only void and inoperative under the Kansas-Nebraska Act, but unconstitutional as well. Hence, slavery was national in scope, while freedom was sectional, and any part of the country might become slaveholding if slaveholders should settle therein.[6]

Whatever the elation of the South at this ruling, the reaction in Connecticut was one of shock. The Nutmeg State had had a similar case of its own—in which the ex-slave James Mars was involved in a minor role—some twenty years previously, and its court's decision had gone quite the other way. In that case, Nancy Jackson, a Georgia slave who had been brought by her owner to Hartford for a two-year stay, claimed freedom under the law of 1774 that prohibited the importation of any slave "to be disposed of, left or sold within this state"; and the Supreme Court of Errors had found in her favor. The decision in the Dred Scott case went in exactly the opposite direction, which neither the people of Connecticut nor its legislature could follow.[7]

At its session in the spring of 1857, the General Assembly made its position plain. It adopted a series of resolutions covering a number of points. As to the Dred Scott decision itself, "Nothing was decided authoritatively except that Dred Scott could not sue in a Federal Court," and "all beyond this was extra judicial and of no binding force" because "extra judicial opinions of the United States Supreme Court are not law." Supreme Court justices who volunteered opinions not necessary to the decisions before them were deserving of censure. It was a right and a duty to resist the extension of slavery into the territories. In addition to adopting these resolutions, the Assembly expressed its sympathy with "the Free State settlers in Kansas." It then enacted the last law on slavery in the state's history, one of the many in which it expressed its opinion to the federal government: [8]

> Any person having been held to service as a slave in any other state or country, not having escaped from any other state of the United States in which he was held to service or labor under the laws thereof, coming into this state or now being therein, shall forthwith be and become free.

In this legislative act and its resolutions, the General Assembly gave official expression to the views already stated by newspapers of the state, in editorials of which the following are examples:

> Never in the history of the American Government has there been so unrighteous a decision by the Supreme Court of the United States, as the one given in the Dred Scott case. It not only opens the Territory of Slavery, but allows it to exist in those States which have been called Free, as the master, by this decision, can take his property [slaves] into any State of the Union for a temporary sojourn, and then carry them back to the State from whence they came, without let or hindrance.[9]

> There is at least one point in this decision which the people in some of the States will find it difficult to com-

> prehend. It is that which declares the negro is not a citizen. In some States the negro is not a citizen. In some States the negro is a citizen, and entitled to all the priviliges of citizenship. . . . The State in which they live makes them citizens, and if they are citizens there, according to the plain Anglo-Saxon of the Constitution of the United States, they are citizens of the United States.[10]

While the General Assembly and the press gave utterance to statements like these, Connecticut's Underground Railroad found plenty of passengers. Old centers were more active than ever—in Farmington, any runaway who arrived was sure of food, lodging, and a lift [11]—and new agents joined the ranks. In New Haven, a prosperous merchant named Thomas R. Trowbridge furnished a room in his house for the use of north-bound fugitives after 1857. The Honorable Joseph Sheldon of the same city also established a station around 1860, working with the Reverend Samuel W. S. Dutton as a "most efficient coadjutor." [12] In June 1855, when a slave-hunter cornered and seized a runaway at Dayville in Windham County, "the citizens there interfered and the fugitive escaped." [13] A new station also came into being just over the state line, near Westerly, but for rather different reasons. A group of free Rhode Island Negroes, terrified by the implications of the Dred Scott decision, literally took to the woods. In a heavily overgrown, out-of-the-way spot near the Connecticut border, they set up a sort of fugitive camp of stone huts topped with roofs of saplings and sod. Here they lived and did their simple cooking in the open, with little chance of being discovered by any traveling slave-hunter; and here they began to receive newly arrived fugitives whom they sent on by established Underground lines.[14]

New stations like these, set up and managed with less

secrecy than had formerly been necessary, were evidence of Connecticut's increased tolerance toward the antislavery movement. Threatened by no tar and feathers, marched out of town by no drum and fife, abolitionist ministers now preached openly and defiantly against the encroachments of the slave power. A few weeks after the signing of the Kansas-Nebraska Act, the Reverend Charles P. Bush of Norwich began his Sunday sermon with the words: "Thou shall not deliver unto his master the servant which is escaped from his master unto thee"; and he went on to denounce the Fugitive Slave Law as "a gigantic national sin, for which every reflecting Christian must feel that we have reason to fear Divine judgments." [15] Three years later, the Dred Scott decision led the Reverend Leverett Griggs of Bristol to preach on the topic "Fugitives from Slavery." In his opinion, it was a simple Christian duty to help the runaway to freedom: [16]

> Fugitives from American Slavery should receive the sympathy and aid of all lovers of freedom. If they come to our door, we should be ready to feed, and clothe, and give them shelter, and help them on their way. If we make the Bible our rule of life,—if we are willing to do to others as we would they should do to us, we can have no difficulty on this subject.

Similarly, in a sermon titled "Slavery Viewed in the Light of the Golden Rule," the Reverend R. P. Stanton of Norwich in 1860 exhorted his congregation, in the familiar abolitionist phrase, to "remember those in bonds as bound with them"; and he described the Fugitive Slave Law as "an accursed enactment, which, it would seem, no beings but demons could enact, and no beings but demons could obey." [17]

In fact, the law was being more and more widely defied

—sometimes even by persons in official positions of law enforcement. In September of 1859, a runaway who came by sea benefited from this state of affairs. Stowing away in the cargo of a vessel at Wilmington, North Carolina, with "two pounds of crackers and a piece of cheese," he subsisted on this monotonous fare for twelve days as the ship worked north along the coast. At the mouth of the Mystic River he came out on deck, where the captain immediately apprehended him and summoned his crew. The Negro, however, managed to leap over the bow and swim ashore, where he set off for New London. The captain, convinced that he was a fugitive, followed in pursuit. In New London he succeeded in finding the man, seized him, and "brought him at once before a United States Commissioner at the Custom House." Word of this happening spread quickly through town, and Judge Brandegee of the New London Police Court hurried to the scene "with a large number of prominent citizens." He spoke directly to the runaway: "Do you wish to stay here or go free?" To go free, the man replied promptly. "Go then!" said the Judge; and despite the efforts of the officials to prevent him, "he went." [18]

Such was Connecticut on the eve of the Civil War—a state where legislature, pulpit, press, and people were firm in their opposition to slavery and where the fugitive might find help in many places, from a United States Senator or a local police magistrate, a city merchant or a village pastor, numerous farmers or any free Negro at all. Yet it was also a state where the free Negro, although recognized as a citizen, was far from enjoying the opportunities open to others. His economic state was, in general, precarious; the schooling available to him was likely to end all too soon; in the community at large he was accepted as something less than an equal. He did not even have the right to vote, and this as a matter of the popular will. In 1857 a referendum was held on the subject of extending the franchise to colored people; the result throughout the state was 5553 votes favorable, 19,148 opposed—roughly 22 per cent for, 78 per cent against. It is not surprising that Windham County, where abolition sentiment was more widespread than anywhere else in the state, cast the highest proportion of "aye" votes, but even there it was only 36 per cent. Hartford County came next, with 34 per cent for, 66 per cent against; New Haven and Fairfield counties were lowest on the list, showing only 11 and 10 per cent favorable votes respectively. The *Middlesex Republican* found this outcome deplorable:[19]

> Massachusetts, and we believe all the rest of the New England States but our own, can come, if need be, to the door of the Supreme Court of the United States and claim equal rights for the colored population. Even New York can do the same without a blush, provided they have freehold estates to a certain amount. Not so, however, with Connecticut. It makes our own cheek tingle, when we reflect, that after she permitted them to help fight the battles of our Revolution, and to man our ships of war in the last conflict with England, after also, she had allowed them the full rights of citizenship; she then, on amending or rather adopting her present Constitution excluded them wholly from the elective franchise.

Nonetheless it was evident that, although Connecticut's Yankees were generally opposed to slavery, prejudice against colored people was still widespread and powerful.

Even after the Civil War began, the Negro was for a time not allowed to play the fighting man's part. He was, according to one Connecticut view, too "frivolous, lazy, sensual, and lying to come to the aid of our government."[20]

Joseph Sheldon of New Haven, who as an Underground operator had been in position to judge the character and capacities of colored men, did not agree. Believing that the time would come when Negro soldiers would be employed, he quietly assembled a company of thirty or forty, who met at night for military drill in the basement of Music Hall. These recruits were pledged to keep their training secret, but their time came soon. In November 1863 the General Assembly authorized the organization of Negro units in Connecticut, and almost every man in Sheldon's troop became a noncommissioned officer in either the Twenty-ninth or the Thirtieth Regiment. They proved their fitness and their manhood under fire on the field of battle.[21]

By that time, of course, the Underground Railroad had ceased to exist. Its tracks were abandoned because there was no more traffic; its stations closed for want of passengers; its operators went on with their lives in whatever direction their destinies might take them. In place of the dedicated few who had escorted the lone fugitive through the night or hidden him in closet or barn, there were now thousands of young men in blue uniforms who, all unintentionally, were carrying on the work in the South itself. Everywhere that Union lines were established, there was a haven where any slave could find an end to his bondage—not because Union generals and soldiers were abolitionists but because the slave, so long as his labor remained available to the Southern master, was a valuable asset to the war effort of the Confederacy.[22] General Benjamin Butler set the pattern when in May 1861, with the war hardly begun, he refused to surrender fugitives because they were contraband. Two months later he made his position clear in a letter to the Secretary of War:[23]

> In a loyal State I would put down a servile insurrection. In a state of rebellion I would confiscate that which was used to oppose my arms, and take all that property, which constituted the wealth of that State, and furnished the means by which war is prosecuted, besides being the cause of the war; and if, in so doing, it should be objected that human beings were brought to the free enjoyment of life, liberty, and the pursuit of happiness, such objection might not require much consideration.

At the same time General John C. Frémont, in Missouri, proclaimed martial law and freed all slaves belonging to persons in rebellion. Hardly a week thereafter, on August 6, 1861, Congress passed a Confiscation Act, which made all property used to aid the rebellion subject to seizure. These actions, by generals and lawmakers, anticipated the Emancipation Proclamation, and they also made it inevitable. The Proclamation, when it came, turned what was already a practical program into an official policy. But it did more than that; it transformed the war from one whose purpose was merely the preservation of the Union to one that had the nature of a moral conflict—a war not only for territorial integrity but for the larger cause of human freedom.[24]

Not everyone in Connecticut was pleased by this development. The President, said the Hartford *Courant*, had laid the axe to the root of the tree: "The Proclamation meets our views both in what it does and in what it omits to do. Its limitations show that President Lincoln means to preserve good faith toward the loyal border slave states, so long as they are loyal, their slaves are safe." [25] The Waterbury *American* hoped that the Proclamation, "like bread cast upon the waters, will we trust, bring forth good fruits after many days." [26] But the Middletown *Sentinel and Witness* feared that "the immediate emancipation of the slaves would not aid the Negro, either morally, physically, or politically, but it would by flooding the North with Africans to compete in every department of labor with the white mechanics, and artisans, impoverish and degrade the latter." [27] The Norwich *Aurora* thought that "this Act of Lincoln's is the culmination of his stupidity." [28] The New Haven *Columbian Weekly Register*, a Democratic organ, was merely vituperative: [29]

> "God bless Abraham Lincoln" will be repeated by all the tribe of Negro worshipping fanatics, fools and fiends in human shape. History does not furnish a more palpable instance of folly than the usurpation by which the administration has undertaken the championship of the abolition fanaticism.

But to James Lindsey Smith, who knew much better than any Connecticut editor the truth about slavery, the Proclamation came as the fulfillment of a cherished dream: "Glory to God, peace on earth, and good will to men—the year of jubilee has come!" [30]

The war at last was fought to its end, and it was followed in short order by the Thirteenth, Fourteenth, and Fifteenth Amendments. Slavery was gone from the country forever; full citizenship and the franchise were guaranteed to all Americans, regardless of color, as matters of constitutional right. It is not the purpose of this book to review the sad history of subterfuge, evasion, discrimination, and segregation that has unfolded since then. But one may hope that the zealous men, black and white, who manned the Underground Railroad lines of the past have found their twentieth-century counterparts in the sit-in demonstrators and the freedom riders of today.

APPENDICES

APPENDIX 1

NARRATIVE OF MR. NEHEMIAH CAULKINS OF WATERFORD, CONNECTICUT

I SPENT eleven winters, between the years 1824 and 1835, in the state of North Carolina, mostly in the vicinity of Wilmington; and four out of the eleven on the estate of Mr. John Swan, five or six miles from that place. There were on his plantation about seventy slaves, male and female: some were married, and others lived together as man and wife, without even a mock ceremony. With their owners generally, it is a matter of indifference; the marriage of slaves not being recognized by the slave code. The slaves, however, think much of being married by a clergyman.

The cabins or huts of the slaves were small, and were built principally by the slaves themselves, as they could find time on Sundays and moonlight nights; they went into the swamps, cut the logs, backed or *hauled* them to the quarters, and put up their cabins.

When I first knew Mr. Swan's plantation, his overseer was a man who had been a Methodist minister. He treated the slaves with great cruelty. His reason for leaving the

Reprinted from *American Slavery As It Is,* compiled by Theodore Weld (New York, 1839).

ministry and becoming an overseer, I was informed, was this: his wife died, at which providence he was so enraged, that he swore he would not preach for the Lord another day. This man continued on the plantation about three years; at the close of which, on settlement of accounts, Mr. Swan owed him about $400, for which he turned out to him a negro woman, and about twenty acres of land. He built a log hut, and took the woman to live with him; since which, I have been at his hut, and seen four or five mulatto children. . . .

It is customary in that part of the country, to let the hogs run in the woods. On one occasion a slave caught a pig about two months old, which he carried to his quarters. The overseer, getting information of the fact, went to the field where he was at work, and ordered him to come to him. The slave at once suspected it was something about the pig, and fearing punishment, dropped his hoe and ran for the woods. He had got but a few rods, when the overseer raised his gun, loaded with duck shot, and brought him down. It is a common practice for overseers to go into the field armed with a gun or pistols, and sometimes both. He was taken up by the slaves and carried to the plantation hospital, and the physician sent for. A physician was employed by the year to take care of the sick or wounded slaves. In about six weeks this slave got better, and was able to come out of the hospital. He came to the mill where I was at work, and asked me to examine his body, which I did, and counted twenty-six duck shot still remaining in his flesh, though the doctor had removed a number while he was laid up.

There was a slave on Mr. Swan's plantation, by the name of Harry, who, during the absence of his master, ran away and secreted himself in the woods. This the slaves sometimes do, when the master is absent for several weeks, to escape the cruel treatment of the overseer. It is common for them to make preparations, by secreting a mortar, a hatchet, some cooking utensils, and whatever things they can get that will enable them to live while they are in the woods or swamps. Harry staid about three months, and lived by robbing the rice grounds, and by such other means as came in his way. The slaves generally know where the runaway is secreted, and visit him at night and on Sundays. On the return of his master, some of the slaves were sent for Harry. When he came home he was seized and confined in the stocks. The stocks were built in the barn, and consisted of two heavy pieces of timber, ten or more feet in length, and about seven inches wide; the lower one, on the floor, has a number of holes or places cut in it, for the ankles; the upper piece, being of the same dimensions, is fastened at one end by a hinge, and is brought down after the ankles are placed in the holes, and secured by a clasp and padlock at the other end. In this manner the person is left to sit on the floor. Harry was kept in the stocks day and night for a week, and flogged every morning. After this, he was taken out one morning, a log chain fastened around his neck, the two ends dragging on the ground, and he was sent to the field, to do his task with the other slaves. At night he was again put in the stocks, in the morning he was sent to the field in the same manner, and thus dragged out another week.

The overseer was a very miserly fellow, and restricted his wife in what are considered the comforts of life—such as tea, sugar, &c. To make up for this, she set her wits to work, and, by the help of a slave, named Joe, used to take from the plantation whatever she could conveniently, and watch her opportunity during her husband's absence, and send Joe to sell them and buy for her such things as she directed. Once when her husband was away, she told Joe to kill and dress one of the pigs, sell it, and get her some tea, sugar, &c. Joe did as he was bid, and she gave him the offal for his services. When Galloway returned, not suspecting his wife, he asked her if she knew what had become of his pig. She told him she suspected one of the slaves, naming him, had stolen it, for she had heard a pig squeal the evening before. The overseer called the slave up, and charged him with the theft. He denied it, and said he knew nothing about it. The overseer still charged him with it, and told him he would give him one week to think of it, and if he did not confess the theft, or find out who did steal the pig, he would flog every negro on the plantation; before the week was up it was ascertained that Joe had killed the pig. He was called up and questioned, and admitted that he had done so, and told the overseer that he did it by the order of Mrs. Galloway, and that she directed him to buy some sugar, &c. with the money. Mrs. Galloway gave Joe the lie; and he was terribly flogged. Joe told me he had been several times to the smoke-house with Mrs. G, and taken hams and sold them, which her husband told me he supposed were stolen by the negroes on a neighboring plantation. Mr. Swan, hearing of the circumstance, told me he believed Joe's story, but that his statement would not be taken as proof; and if every slave on the plantation told the same story it could not be received as evidence against a white person.

To show the manner in which old and wornout slaves are sometimes treated, I will state a fact. Galloway owned a man about seventy years of age. The old man was sick and went to his hut; laid himself down on some straw with his feet to the fire, covered by a piece of an old blanket, and there lay four or five days, groaning in great distress, without any attention being paid him by his master, until death ended his miseries; he was then taken out and buried with as little ceremony and respect as would be paid to a brute.

There is a practice prevalent among the planters, of letting a negro off from severe and long-continued punishment on account of the intercession of some white person, who pleads in his behalf, that he believes the negro will behave better; that he promises well, and he believes he will keep his promise, &c. The planters sometimes get tired of punishing a negro, and, wanting his services in the field, they get some white person to come, and, in the presence of the slave, intercede for him. At one time a negro, named Charles, was confined in the stocks in the building where I was at work, and had been severely whipped several times. He begged me to intercede for him and try to get him released. I told him I would; and when his master came in to whip him again, I went up to him and told him I had been talking with Charles, and he had promised to behave better, &c., and requested him not to punish him any more, but to let him go. He then said to Charles, "As Mr. Caulkins has been pleading for you, I will let you go on his account;" and accordingly released him.

Women are generally shown some little indulgence for three or four weeks previous to childbirth; they are at such times not often punished if they do not finish the task assigned them; it is, in some cases, passed over with a severe reprimand, and sometimes without any notice being taken of it. They are generally allowed four weeks after the birth of a child, before they are compelled to go into the field, they then take the child with them, attended sometimes by a little girl or boy, from the age of four to six, to take care of it while the mother, after nursing, lays it under a tree, or by the side of a fence, and goes to her task, returning at stated intervals to nurse it. While I was on this plantation, a little negro girl, six years of age, destroyed the life of a child about two months old, which was left in her care. It seems this little nurse, so called, got tired of her charge and the labor of carrying it to the quarters at night, the mother being obliged to work as long as she could see. One evening she nursed the infant at sunset as usual, and sent it to the quarters at night. The little girl, on her way home, had to cross a run, or brook, which led down into the swamp; when she came to the brook she followed it into the swamp, then took the infant and plunged it head foremost into the water and mud, where it stuck fast; she there left it and went to the negro quarters. When the mother came in from the field, she asked the girl where the child was; she told her she had brought it home, but did not know where it was; the overseer was immediately informed, search was made, and it was found as above stated, and dead. The little girl was shut up in the barn, and confined there two or three weeks, when a speculator came along and bought her for two hundred dollars.

The slaves are obliged to work from daylight till dark, as long as they can see. When they have tasks assigned, which is often the case, a few of the strongest and most expert, sometimes finish them before sunset; others will be obliged to work till eight or nine o'clock in the evening. All must finish their tasks or take a flogging. The whip and gun, or pistol, are companions of the overseer; the former he uses very frequently upon the negroes, during their hours of labor, without regard to age or sex. Scarcely a day passed while I was on the plantation, in which some of the slaves were not whipped; I do not mean that they were *struck a few blows* merely, but had a *set flogging.* The same labor is commonly assigned to men and women, —such as digging ditches in the rice marshes, clearing up land, chopping cord-wood, threshing, &c. I have known the women go into the barn as soon as they could see in the morning, and work as late as they could see at night, threshing rice with the flail, (they now have a threshing machine,) and when they could see to thresh no longer, they had to gather up the rice, carry it up stairs, and deposit it in the granary.

The allowance of clothing on this plantation to each slave, was given out at Christmas for the year, and consisted of one pair of coarse shoes, and enough coarse cloth to make a jacket and trowsers. If the man has a wife she makes it up; if not, it is made up in the house. The slaves on this plantation, being near Wilmington, procured themselves extra clothing by working Sundays and moonlight nights, cutting cord-wood in the swamps, which they had to back about a quarter of a mile to the river; they would then get a permit from their master, and taking the wood in their canoes, carry it to Wilmington, and sell it to the vessels, or dispose of it as they best could, and with the money buy an old jacket of the sailors, some coarse cloth for a shirt, &c. They sometimes gather the moss from the trees, which they cleanse and take to market. The women receive their allowance of the same kind of cloth which the men have. This they make into a frock; if they have any under garments they must procure them for themselves. When the slaves get a permit to leave the plantation, they sometimes make all ring again by singing the following significant ditty, which shows that after all there is a flow of spirits in the human breast which for a while, at least, enables them to forget their wretchedness.

Hurra, for good ole Massa,
He giv me de pass to go to de city
Hurra, for good ole Missis,
She bile de pot, and giv me de licker.
Hurra, I'm goin to de city

Every Saturday night the slaves receive their allowance of provisions, which must last them till the next Saturday night. "Potatoe time," as it is called, begins about the middle of July. The slave may measure for himself, the overseer being present, half a bushel of sweet potatoes, and heap the measure as long as they will lie on; I have, however, seen the overseer, if he think the negro is getting too many, kick the measure; and if any fall off, tell him he has got his measure. No salt is furnished them to eat with their potatoes. When rice or corn is given, they give them a little salt; sometimes half a pint of molasses is given, but not often. The quantity of rice, which is of the small, broken, unsaleable kind, is one peck. When corn is given them, their allowance is the same, and if they get it ground, (Mr. Swan had a mill on his plantation,) they must give one quart for grinding, thus reducing their weekly allowance to seven quarts. When fish (mullet) were plenty, they were allowed, in addition, one fish. As to meat, they seldom had any. I do not think they had an allowance of meat oftener than once in two or three months, and then the quantity was very small. When they went into the field to work, they took some of the meal or rice and a pot with them; the pots were given to an old woman, who placed two poles parallel, set the pots on them, and kindled a fire underneath for cooking; she took salt with her and seasoned the messes as she thought proper. When their breakfast was ready, which was generally about ten or eleven o'clock, they were called from labor, ate, and returned to work; in the afternoon, dinner was prepared in the same way. They had but two meals a day while in the field; if they wanted more, they cooked for themselves after they returned to their quarters at night. At the time of killing hogs on the plantation, the pluck, entrails, and blood were given to the slaves.

When I first went upon Mr. Swan's plantation, I saw a slave in shackles or fetters, which were fastened around each ankle and firmly riveted, connected together by a chain. To the middle of this chain he had fastened a string, so as in a manner to suspend them and keep them from galling his ankles. This slave, whose name was Frank, was an intelligent, good looking man, and a very good mechanic. There was nothing vicious in his character, but he was one of those high-spirited and daring men, that whips, chains, fetters, and all the means of cruelty in the power of slavery, could not subdue. Mr. S. had employed a Mr. Beckwith to repair a boat, and told him Frank was a good mechanic, and he might have his services. Frank was sent for, his shackles still on. Mr. Beckwith set him to work making trunnels, &c. I was employed in putting up a building, and after Mr. Beckwith had done with Frank, he was sent for to assist me. Mr. Swan sent him to a blacksmith's shop and had his shackles cut off with a cold chisel. Frank was afterwards sold to a cotton planter.

I will relate one circumstance, which shows the little regard that is paid to the feelings of the slave. During the time that Mr. Isaiah Rogers was superintending the building of a rice machine, one of the slaves complained of a severe toothache. Swan asked Mr. Rogers to take his hammer and knock out the tooth.

There was a slave on the plantation named Ben, a waiting man. I occupied a room in the same hut, and had frequent conversations with him. Ben was a kind-hearted man, and, I believe, a Christian; he would always ask a blessing before he sat down to eat, and was in the constant practice of praying morning and night.—One day when I was at the hut, Ben was sent for to go to the house. Ben sighed deeply and went. He soon returned with a girl about seventeen years of age, whom one of Mr. Swan's daughters had ordered him to flog. He brought her into the room where I was, and told her to stand there while he went into the next room: I heard him groan again as he went. While there I heard his voice, and he was engaged in prayer. After a few minutes he returned with a large cow-hide, and stood before the girl, without saying a word. I concluded he wished me to leave the hut, which I did; and immediately after I heard the girl scream. At every blow she would shriek, "Do, Ben! oh do, Ben!" This is a common expression of the slaves to the person whipping them: "Do, Massa!" or, "Do, Missus!"

After she had gone, I asked Ben what she was whipped for: he told me she had done something to displease her young missus; and in boxing her ears, and otherwise beating her, she had scratched her finger by a pin in the girl's dress, for which she sent her to be flogged. I asked him if he stripped her before flogging; he said, yes; he did not like to do this, but was obliged to: he said he was once ordered to whip a woman, which he did without stripping her: on her return to the house, her mistress examined her back; and not seeing any marks, he was sent for, and asked him if he had made her pull her clothes off; he said, No. She then told him, that when he whipped any more of the women, he must make them strip off their clothes, as well as the men, and flog them on their bare backs, or he should be flogged himself.

Ben often appeared very gloomy and sad: I have frequently heard him, when in his room, mourning over his condition, and exclaim, "Poor African slave! Poor African slave!" Whipping was so common an occurrence on this plantation, that it would be too great a repetition to state the many and severe floggings I have seen inflicted on the slaves. They were flogged for not performing their tasks, for being careless, slow, or not in time, for going to the fire to warm, &c. &c.; and it often seemed as if occasions were sought as an excuse for punishing them.

On one occasion, I heard the overseer charge the hands to be at a certain place the next morning at sun-rise. I was present in the morning, in company with my brother, when the hands arrived. Joe, the slave already spoken of, came running, all out of breath, about five minutes behind the time, when, without asking any questions, the overseer told him to take off his jacket. Joe took off his jacket. He had on a piece of a shirt; he told him to take it off: Joe took it off: he then whipped him with a heavy cow-hide full six feet long. At every stroke Joe would spring from the ground, and scream, "O my God! Do, Massa Galloway!" My brother was so exasperated, that he turned to me and said, "If I were Joe, I would kill the overseer if I knew I should be shot the next minute."

In the winter the horn blew at about four in the morning, and all the threshers were required to be at the threshing floor in fifteen minutes after. They had to go about a quarter of a mile from their quarters. Galloway would stand near the entrance, and all who did not come in time would get a blow over the back or head as heavy as he could strike. I have seen him, at such times, follow after them, striking furiously a number of blows, and every one followed by their screams. I have seen the women go to their work after such a flogging, crying and taking on most piteously.

It is almost impossible to believe that human nature can endure such hardships and sufferings as the slaves have to go through; I have seen them driven into a ditch in a rice swamp to bail out the water, in order to put down a flood-gate, when they had to break the ice, and there stand in the water among the ice until it was bailed out. I have often known the hands to be taken from the field, sent down the river in flats or boats to Wilmington, absent from twenty-four to thirty hours, without any thing to eat, no provision being made for these occasions.

Galloway kept medicine on hand, that in case any of the slaves were sick, he could give it to them without sending for the physician; but he always kept a good look out that they did not sham sickness. When any of them excited his suspicions, he would make them take the medicine in his presence, and would give them a rap on the top of the head, to make them swallow it. A man once came to him, of whom he said he was suspicious: he gave him two potions of salts, and fastened him in the stocks for the night. His medicine soon began to operate; and there he lay in all his filth till he was taken out the next day.

One day, Mr. Swan beat a slave severely, for alleged carelessness in letting a boat get adrift. The slave was told to secure the boat: whether he took sufficient means for this purpose I do not know; he was not allowed to make any defence. Mr. Swan called him up, and asked why he did not secure the boat: he pulled off his hat and began to tell his story. Swan told him he was a damned liar, and commenced beating him over the head with a hickory cane, and the slave retreated backwards; Swan followed him about two rods, threshing him over the head with the hickory as he went.

As I was one day standing near some slaves who were threshing, the driver, thinking one of the women did not use her flail quick enough, struck her over the head; the end of the whip hit her in the eye. I thought at the time he had put it out; but, after poulticing and doctoring for some days, she recovered. Speaking to him about it, he said that he once struck a slave so as to put one of her eyes entirely out.

A patrol is kept upon each estate, and every slave

found off the plantation without a pass is whipped on the spot. I knew a slave who started without a pass, one night, for a neighboring plantation, to see his wife: he was caught, tied to a tree, and flogged. He stated his business to the patrol, who was well acquainted with him, but all to no purpose. I spoke to the patrol about it afterwards: he said he knew the negro, that he was a very clever fellow, but he had to whip him; for, if he let him pass, he must another, &c. He stated that he had sometimes caught and flogged four in a night.

In conversation with Mr. Swan about runaway slaves, he stated to me the following fact:—A slave, by the name of Luke, was owned in Wilmington; he was sold to a speculator and carried to Georgia. After an absence of about two months the slave returned; he watched an opportunity to enter his old master's house when the family were absent, no one being at home but a young waiting man. Luke went to the room where his master kept his arms; took his gun, with some ammunition, and went into the woods. On the return of his master, the waiting man told him what had been done: this threw him into a violent passion; he swore he would kill Luke, or lose his own life. He loaded another gun, took two men, and made search, but could not find him: he then advertised him, offering a large reward if delivered to him or lodged in jail. His neighbors, however, advised him to offer a reward of two hundred dollars for him dead or alive, which he did. Nothing however was heard of him for some months. Mr. Swan said, one of his slaves ran away, and was gone eight or ten weeks; on his return he said he had found Luke, and that he had a rifle, two pistols, and a sword.

I left the plantation in the spring, and returned to the north; when I went out again, the next fall, I asked Mr. Swan if any thing had been heard of Luke; he said he was shot, and related to me the manner of his death, as follows: —Luke went to one of the plantations, and entered a hut for something to eat. Being fatigued, he sat down and fell asleep. There was only a woman in the hut at the time: as soon as she saw he was asleep, she ran and told her master, who took his rifle, and called two white men on another plantation: the three, with their rifles, then went to the hut, and posted themselves in different positions, so that they could watch the door. When Luke waked up he went to the door to look out, and saw them with their rifles, he stepped back and raised his gun to his face. They called to him to surrender; and stated that they had him in their power, and said he had better give up. He said he would not; and if they tried to take him, he would kill one of them; for, if he gave up, he knew they would kill him, and he was determined to sell his life as dear as he could. They told him, if he should shoot one of them, the other two would certainly kill him: he replied, he was determined not to give up, and kept his gun moving from one to the other; and while his rifle was turned toward one, another, standing in a different direction, shot him through the head, and he fell lifeless to the ground.

There was another slave shot while I was there; this man had run away, and had been living in the woods a long time, and it was not known where he was, till one day he was discovered by two men, who went on the large island near Belvidere to hunt turkeys; they shot him and carried his head home.

It is common to keep dogs on the plantations, to pursue and catch runaway slaves. I was once bitten by one of them. I went to the overseer's house, the dog lay in the piazza, as soon as I put my foot upon the floor, he sprang and bit me just above the knee, but not severely; he tore my pantaloons badly. The overseer apologized for his dog, saying he never knew him to bite a white man before. He said he once had a dog, when he lived on another plantation, that was very useful to him in hunting runaway negroes. He said that a slave on the plantation once ran away; as soon as he found the course he took, he put the dog on the track, and he soon came so close upon him that the man had to climb a tree, he followed with his gun, and brought the slave home.

The slaves have a great dread of being sold and carried south. It is generally said, and I have no doubt of its truth, that they are much worse treated farther south.

The following are a few among the many facts related to me while I lived among the slaveholders. The names of the planters and plantations I shall not give, as they did not come under my own observation. I however place the fullest confidence in their truth.

A planter not far from Mr. Swan's employed an overseer to whom he paid $400 a year; he became dissatisfied with him, because he did not drive the slaves hard enough, and get more work out of them. He therefore sent to South Carolina, or Georgia, and got a man to whom he paid I believe $800 a year. He proved to be a cruel fellow, and drove the slaves almost to death. There was a slave on this plantation, who had repeatedly run away, and had been severely flogged every time. The last time he was caught, a hole was dug in the ground, and he buried up to the chin, his arms being secured down by his sides. He was kept in this situation four or five days.

The following was told me by an intimate friend; it took place on a plantation containing about one hundred slaves. One day the owner ordered the women into the barn, he then went in among them, whip in hand, and told them he meant to flog them all to death; they began immediately to cry out "What have I done Massa? What have I done

Massa?" He replied; "D——n you, I will let you know what you have done, you don't breed, I haven't had a young one from one of you for several months." They told him they could not breed while they had to work in the rice ditches. (The rice grounds are low and marshy, and have to be drained, and while digging or clearing the ditches, the women had to work in mud and water from one to two feet in depth; they were obliged to draw up and secure their frocks about their waist, to keep them out of the water, in this manner they frequently had to work from daylight in the morning till it was so dark they could see no longer.) After swearing and threatening for some time, he told them to tell the overseer's wife, when they got in that way, and he would put them upon the land to work.

This same planter had a female slave who was a member of the Methodist Church; for a slave she was intelligent and conscientious. He proposed a criminal intercourse with her. She would not comply. He left her and sent for the overseer, and told him to have her flogged. It was done. Not long after, he renewed his proposal. She again refused. She was again whipped. He then told her why she had been twice flogged, and told her he intended to whip her till she should yield. The girl, seeing that her case was hopeless, her back smarting with the scourging she had received, and dreading a repetition, gave herself up to be the victim of his brutal lusts.

One of the slaves on another plantation, gave birth to a child which lived but two or three weeks. After its death the planter called the woman to him, and asked her how she came to let the child die; said it was all owing to her carelessness, and that he meant to flog her for it. She told him with all the feeling of a mother, the circumstances of its death. But her story availed her nothing against the savage brutality of her master. She was severely whipped.

A healthy child four months old was then considered worth $100 in North Carolina.

The foregoing facts were related to me by white persons of character and respectability. The following fact was related to me on a plantation where I have spent considerable time and where the punishment was inflicted. I have no doubt of its truth. A slave ran away from his master, and got as far as Newbern. He took provisions that lasted him a week; but having eaten all, he went to a house to get something to satisfy his hunger. A white man suspecting him to be a runaway, demanded his pass: as he had none he was seized and put in Newbern jail. He was there advertised, his description given, &c. His master saw the advertisement and sent for him; when he was brought back, his wrists were tied together and drawn over his knees. A stick was then passed over his arms and under his knees, and he secured in this manner, his trowsers were then stripped down, and he turned over on his side, and severely beaten with the paddle, then turned over and severely beaten on the other side, and then turned back again, and tortured by another bruising and beating. He was afterwards kept in the stocks a week, and whipped every morning.

To show the disgusting pollutions of slavery, and how it covers with moral filth every thing it touches, I will state two or three facts, which I have on such evidence I cannot doubt their truth. A planter offered a white man of my acquaintance twenty dollars for every one of his female slaves, whom he would get in the family way. This offer was no doubt made for the purpose of improving the stock, on the same principle that farmers endeavour to improve their cattle by crossing the breed.

Slaves belonging to merchants and others in the city, often hire their own time, for which they pay various prices per week or month, according to the capacity of the slave. The females who thus hire their time, pursue various modes of procuring the money; their master making no inquiry how they get it, provided the money comes. If it is not regularly paid they are flogged. Some take in washing, some cook on board vessels, pick oakum, sell peanuts, &c, while others, younger and more comely, often resort to the vilest pursuits. I knew a man from the north who, though married to a respectable southern woman, kept two of these mulatto girls in an upper room at his store; his wife told some of her friends that he had not lodged at home for two weeks together, I have seen these two *kept misses*, as they are there called, at his store; he was afterwards stabbed in an attempt to arrest a runaway slave, and died in about ten days.

The clergy at the south cringe beneath the corrupting influence of slavery, and their moral courage is borne down by it. Not the hypocritical and unprincipled alone, but even such as can hardly be supposed to be destitute of sincerity.

Going one morning to the Baptist Sunday school, in Wilmington, in which I was engaged, I fell in with the Rev. Thomas P. Hunt, who was going to the Presbyterian school. I asked him how he could bear to see the little negro children beating their hoops, hallooing, and running about the streets, as we then saw them, their moral condition entirely neglected, while the whites were so carefully gathered into the schools. His reply was substantially this: "I can't bear it, Mr. Caulkins. I feel as deeply as any one can on this subject, but what can I do? My HANDS ARE TIED." . . .

Emancipation would be safe. I have had eleven winters to learn the disposition of the slaves, and am satisfied that they would peaceably and cheerfully work for pay. Give them education, equal and just laws, and they will become a most interesting people. Oh, let a cry be raised which shall awaken the conscience of the guilty nation, to demand for the slaves immediate and unconditional emancipation.

APPENDIX 2

UNDERGROUND RAILROAD AGENTS IN CONNECTICUT

*(Probable agents are indicated by *)*

FAIRFIELD COUNTY

Daskam, Benjamin–Stamford
Roberts, Geradus–New Milford
Sabin, Charles–New Milford
Thayer, Augustine–New Milford
Wakeman, William–Wilton
Weed,——–Darien

HARTFORD COUNTY

Africanus, Selah*–Hartford
Andrews, Alfred–New Britain
Booth, Horace–New Britain
Clark, Dan–New Britain
Cowles, Horace–Farmington
Dunning, Levi–Farmington
Foster,——–Hartford
Gabriel, Phineas–Avon
Gillette, Francis–Bloomfield and Hartford
Hart, Norman–New Britain
Hurlburt, George–Farmington
Hurlburt, Lyman–Farmington
Lewis, Elijah–Farmington
McKee, William–Farmington
North, Henry–New Britain
Norton, J. T.–Farmington
Pond, DeWitt C.–New Britain
Smith, Hannah*–Glastonbury
Stanley, Amon–New Britain
Stanley, Noah–New Britain
Whittlesey, David–New Britain
Williams, Austin–Farmington

LITCHFIELD COUNTY

Blakeslee, Joel–Plymouth
Bull, William–Plymouth
Coe, Jonathan–Winsted
Dunbar, Daniel–Plymouth
McAlpine, Silas H.*–Winchester
Pettibone, Amos–Norfolk
Tuttle, Uriel–Torrington

MIDDLESEX COUNTY

Augur, Phineas M.–Middlefield
Bailey, Alfred*–Middlefield
Bailey, Russell*–Middlefield
Baldwin, Jesse G.–Middletown
Beman, Jehiel*–Middletown

Dickinson, James T.*–Middlefield
Douglas, Benjamin–Middletown
Lyman, David*–Middlefield
Lyman, William–Middlefield
Read, George–Deep River
Thomas, Marvin*–Middlefield
Warner, Judge Ely–Chester
Warner, Jonathan–Chester
Work, Alanson*–Middletown

NEW HAVEN COUNTY

Bartlett, A. E.–North Guilford
Beman, Amos–New Haven
Curtiss, Carlos–Southington
Curtiss, Homer–Meriden
Dutton, Samuel W. C.–New Haven
Frisbie,—— –Southington
Hotchkiss, Milo–Berlin
Isbell, Harlowe–Meriden
Jocelyn, Nathaniel–New Haven
Jocelyn, Simeon S.–New Haven
Ludlow, Henry–New Haven
Perkins, George W.–Meriden
Porter, Timothy–Waterbury
Sheldon, Joseph–New Haven
Stocking, J. M.–Waterbury
Townsend, Amos–New Haven
Trowbridge, Thomas–New Haven
Yale, Levi–Meriden
Whitmore, Zolva–North Guilford

NEW LONDON COUNTY

Caulkins, Nehemiah*–Waterford
Lee, William–Lisbon
Perry, Harvey–North Stonington
Roland, Levi P.–Lisbon

TOLLAND COUNTY

Hendee,—— –Andover

WINDHAM COUNTY

Alexander, Prosper–Killingly
Benson, George–Brooklyn
Brown, John–Willimantic
Burleigh, Charles*–Plainfield
Cady, W. W.–Plainfield
Conant, J. A.–Willimantic
Crandall,—— –Canterbury
Fox, Joel–Hampton
Griffin, Ebenezer–Hampton
Lewis, J. A.–Willimantic
May, Samuel J.–Brooklyn
Pearl, Phillips–Hampton
Whitcomb,—— –Brooklyn

The eighty-six underground agents listed are documented within this text.

APPENDIX 3

SLAVES AND FREE NEGROES IN CONNECTICUT, 1639-1860

Year	*Slaves*	*Free Negroes*
1639	1	—
1680	30	—
1730	700	?
1755	4000	?
1774	6562	?
1790	2759	2801
1800	951	5330
1810	310	6453
1820	97	7844
1830	23	8047
1840	17	8105
1850	—	7693
1860	—	8627

SOURCES: For 1639, Norris Galpin Osborn, *History of Connecticut,* III (New York, 1925), 318.

For 1680–1774, "Slaves in Waterbury" (pamphlet, Mattatuck Historical Society, Waterbury, n.d.), 2.

For 1790–1820 and 1840–1860, Steiner, *History of Slavery in Connecticut* (Johns Hopkins University Studies, XI [Baltimore, 1893]), 84.

For 1830, *Fifth Census of the United States* (Washington, 1832), 26–29.

APPENDIX 4

ANTISLAVERY SOCIETIES IN CONNECTICUT, 1837

Name	*Secretary*	*Date*	*No. of Members*
Barkhamstead	Nelson Gilbert	April, 1837	50
Brooklyn (male)	Herbert Williams	March, 1835	53
Brooklyn (female)	F. M. B. Burleigh	July, 1834	22
Canton	Lancel Foot		25
Chaplin	Deacon Jared Clark	June, 1836	
Colebrook	J. H. Rodgers	June, 1836	90
Deep River	Joseph H. Mather	July, 1835	60
East Hampton			28
Farmington (male)	Thomas Cowles	February, 1836	70
Farmington (female)			40
Greenville (male)	William H. Coit	1836	80
Greenville (female)	Miss Louisa Humphrey	January, 1836	37

Name	*Secretary*	*Date*	*No. of Members*
Hanover (Lisbon)	Deacon William Lee	April, 1837	
Hartford	S. B. Mosley	March, 1837	120
Lebanon (Goshen)	Orrin Gilbert	March, 1837	30
Mansfield	Dr. H. Skinner		300
Middle Haddam			30
Middletown	S. W. Griswold	February, 1834	
Middletown (colored)	Mrs. Clarissa Beman		
New Haven (male)	J. E. P. Dean	June, 1833	
New Haven (female)	Mrs. Leicester Sawyer	January, 1837	50
Newstead	Daniel Trowbridge		48
Norwich (male)	Alpheus Kingsley		
Norwich (female)	Miss F. M. Caulkins		
Plainfield (male)	C. C. Burleigh	August, 1835	94
Plainfield (female)			43
Pomfret			
South Cornwall	Ezekiel Birdeye	January, 1837	40

Name	*Secretary*	*Date*	*No. of Members*
South Killingly	Almond Ames	March, 1837	
Torringford (male)	Dr. Erasmus Hudson		67
Torringford (female)			36
Waterbury (male)	S. S. Deforest	July, 1836	57
Waterbury (female)			16
Warren	George P. Talmadge	May, 1836	27
West Woodstock	J. R. Guild		
Winchester	Noble J. Everett		12
Windham (Willimantic)	Thomas Gray	March, 1836	
Winsted			50
Wolcottville		January, 1837	40

SOURCE: Fourth Annual Report, American Anti-Slavery Society (1837).

APPENDIX 5

SLAVES IN CONNECTICUT, 1830

		Number
I	*Hartford County*	
	None	None
II	*New Haven County*	
	City of New Haven	4
	Cheshire	1
	Wallingford	4
III	*New London County*	
	Groton	2
IV	*Fairfield County*	
	Bridgeport	2
	Wilton	1
	New Canaan	1
	Norwalk	2
	Stamford	1
V	*Windham County*	
	None	None
VI	*Litchfield County*	
	Goshen	1
	Sharon	1
VII	*Middlesex County*	
	Saybrook	2
VIII	*Tolland County*	
	Columbia	1
TOTAL		23

Fifth Census of United States (Washington, 1832), 26–29.

NOTES

NOTES

INTRODUCTION

1. W. J. Cash, *The Mind of the South* (New York, 1941), 87.
2. Cf. Wilbur H. Siebert, *The Underground Railroad from Slavery to Freedom* (New York, 1898), 47 and *passim*. Under the Fugitive Slave Law of 1793, the aiding of fugitive slaves was a penal offense punishable by a fine of $500.
3. Henrietta Buckmaster, *Let My People Go* (New York, 1941), 59; Alexander Milton Ross, *Recollections and Experiences of an Abolitionist* (Toronto, 1876), 2–3.
4. Siebert, *op. cit.*, 33, 34, 68, 346–347.
5. Siebert, *op. cit.*, 190–191.
6. Siebert, *op. cit.*, 237, 340–342.

Chapter 1 BLAZING THE TRAIL

1. Bernard C. Steiner, *History of Slavery in Connecticut* (Johns Hopkins University Studies, IX–X [Baltimore, 1893], 9; Norris G. Osborn, *History of Connecticut* (New York, 1925), III, 318. Osborn states that the first record of a slave in Connecticut dates from 1639.
2. Henry Morris, "Slavery in the Connecticut Valley" (*Papers and Proceedings of the Connecticut Valley Historical Society* [Springfield, 1881]), 208.
3. Lewis Sprague Mills, *The Story of Connecticut* (New York, 1953), 308; James E. Coley, "Slavery in Connecticut," *Magazine of American History, XXV* (January–June 1891), 490.
4. Steiner, *op. cit.*, 18.
5. J. E. A. Smith, *The History of Pittsfield, Massachusetts, 1800–1876* (Springfield, 1876), 52; Morris, *op. cit.*, 212–213.
6. *Ibid.*, 215.

7. Steiner, *History of Slavery in Connecticut* (Johns Hopkins University Studies, XI [Baltimore, 1893]), 450.
8. Microfilm letters on the Underground Railroad in Connecticut, collection of Professor Wilbur H. Siebert, Ohio State University, 19. (This material is hereafter cited as "Letters, U.G.R.R. Conn.")
9. Dwight L. Dumond, *Antislavery: The Crusade for Freedom in America* (Ann Arbor, 1961), 17–19.
10. Frances M. Calkins, *History of Norwich, Connecticut* (Hartford, 1866), 520.
11. Steiner, *op. cit.,* 55, 68–70.
12. New London *Gazette,* December 2, 1768.
13. Lorenzo Johnston Greene, *The Negro in Colonial New England, 1620–1776* (New York, 1942), 146.
14. Steiner, *op. cit.,* 19.
15. Greene, *op. cit.,* 146.
16. F. C. Bissell, "The Reverend Samuel Peters of Hebron, Connecticut . . ." (typescript, Connecticut State Library, Hartford).
17. This account of the adventures of James Mars is based on his own book, *Life of James Mars, A Slave Born and Sold in Connecticut, Written by Himself* (Hartford, 1865). Quotations are from that source.
18. Adam C. White, *The History of the Town of Litchfield, Connecticut, 1720–1920* (Litchfield, 1920), 153.
19. Martin H. Smith, "Old Slave Days in Connecticut," *The Connecticut Magazine, X* (1906), 115ff. Quotations are from that source.
20. Anon., "Slavery in Connecticut," *Magazine of American History, XV* (January–June, 1886), 614; Coley, *op. cit.,* 492.
21. Iveagh H. Sterry and William Garrigus, *They Found a Way: Connecticut's Restless People* (Brattleboro, Vt., 1938), 262–263; Lillian E. Prudden, "A Paper . . . at the Fortnightly Club in New Haven, November 16, 1949" (typescript, Connecticut State Library), 11–12.
22. Dumond, *op. cit.,* 47, 57; Steiner, *op. cit.,* 69–70.
23. *Ibid.,* 70.
24. Wilbur H. Siebert, *Vermont's Anti-Slavery and Underground Railroad Record* (Columbus, 1937), 5.
25. Dumond, *op. cit.,* 80–81, 93.

26. Steiner, *op. cit.*, 84; Jarvis Means Morse, *A Neglected Period of Connecticut's History, 1818–1850* (New Haven, 1933), 192.
27. Robert A. Warner, *New Haven Negroes, A Social History* (New Haven, 1940), 42; Early L. Fox, *The American Colonization Society, 1817–1840* (Johns Hopkins University Studies, XXXVII [Baltimore, 1919]), 29.
28. A. Doris Banks Henries, *The Liberian Nation* (New York, 1954), 15.
29. *African Repository and Colonial Journal,* V (May, 1829), 93; Warner, *op. cit.*, 42.
30. Willbur Fisk, "Substance of an Address Delivered Before the Middletown Colonization Society at the Annual Meeting, July 4, 1835" (Middletown, 1835), 15; Fox, *op. cit.*, 29–31; Warner, *op. cit.*, 48.
31. Leonard W. Bacon, *Anti-Slavery Before Garrison* (New Haven, 1903), 9.
32. Lorenzo D. Turner, *Antislavery Sentiment in American Literature Prior to 1865* (Washington, 1929), 33.
33. William Lloyd Garrison, quoted in Bacon, *op. cit.*, 10.

Chapter 2 THORNY IS THE PATHWAY

1. William Lloyd Garrison, "A Salutation," *The Liberator,* January 1, 1831.
2. *First Annual Report of the Board of Managers of the New England Anti-Slavery Society . . .* (Boston, 1833), 13–14; W. Sherman Savage, "The Controversy over the Distribution of Abolition Literature, 1830–1860" (Washington, 1938), 9.
3. Samuel J. May, *Some Recollections of Our Antislavery Conflict* (Boston, 1869).
4. Buckmaster, *op. cit.*, 31; Dumond, *op. cit.*, 64–69.
5. *Fourth Annual Report, American Anti-Slavery Society* (New York, 1837).
6. Warner, *op. cit.;* William Jay, *An Inquiry into the Character and Tendency of the American Colonization and American Anti-Slavery Societies* (New York, 1835), 28–29; Mary H. Mitchell, "Slavery in Connecticut and Especially in New Haven," *Papers of the New Haven Colony Historical Society* (New Haven, 1951), 309.

7. Ellen D. Larned, *History of Windham County, Connecticut* (Worcester, 1880), II, 490–494; Jay, *op. cit.*, 30–39; Dumond, *op. cit.*, 211–217.
8. Morse, *op. cit.*, 196.
9. "Resolutions on the Death of William L. Garrison (Adopted by the Middletown Mental Impovement Society)," Middletown *Constitution,* June 3, 1879; cf. also Baldwin Collection, Middlesex County Historical Society, Middletown, Conn.
10. Charles H. S. Davis, *History of Wallingford, Connecticut* (Meriden, 1870), 503–504; Sanford H. Wendover, ed., *150 Years of Meriden* (Meriden, 1956), 67; E. B. Bronson, "Notes on Connecticut as a Slave State," *Journal of Negro History,* II (January 1917), 80–81.
11. *Charter Oak,* Hartford, May 1839; Charlotte Case Fairley, "A History of New Canaan, 1801–1901," *Readings in New Canaan History* (New Canaan, 1949), 223.
12. *Commemorative Biographical Record of Middlesex County, Connecticut* (Chicago, 1903), 351; James M. Bailey, *History of Danbury, Connecticut* (New York, 1896), 166–167; Clive Day, "The Rise of Manufacturing in Connecticut," (Pamphlets of the Tercentenary Commission of the State of Connecticut [New Haven, 1935]), XLIV, 12–13.
13. *Charter Oak,* May, 1839.
14. Frances A. Breckenridge, *Recollections of a New England Town* (Meriden, 1899), 168; Mary H. Mitchell, *History of New Haven County, Connecticut* (Chicago–Boston, 1930), I, 421.
15. Aella Greene, "The Underground Railroad and Those Who Managed It," Springfield *Daily Republican,* March 25, 1900.
16. Fisk, *op. cit.*, 15.
17. *The African Repository, and Colonial Journal,* XXIII (March, 1847), 92. (Hereafter cited as *African Repository.*)
18. *First Annual Report . . . New England Anti-Slavery Society,* 37.
19. Louis R. Mehlinger, "The Attitude of the Free Negro Toward African Colonization," *The Journal of Negro History, I* (1916), 286.
20. *African Repository,* XXVIII, 114–117.
21. General Assembly of Connecticut, *The Public Statute Laws of the State of Connecticut* (Hartford, 1835), 15.

22. May, *op. cit.*, 297.
23. Dumond, *op. cit.*, 249–256.
24. *Charter Oak*, May, 1839, 1; J. Eugene Smith, *One Hundred Years of Hartford's* Courant (New Haven, 1949), 199.
25. Savage, *op. cit.*, 13.
26. Theodore Weld, ed., *American Slavery As It Is* (New York, 1839), 77–82.
27. Savage, *op. cit.*, 55.
28. Steiner, *op. cit.*, 74–75.
29. Dumond, *op. cit.*, 212.
30. Steiner, *op. cit.*, 33–34.
31. *Columbian Weekly Register*, New Haven, June 23, 1838.

Chapter 3 FUGITIVES IN FLIGHT

1. This account of the adventures of William Grimes is based on his autobiography, *Life of William Grimes, the Runaway Slave, Written by Himself*, New Haven, 1855. Quotations are from that source.
2. Frederick Douglass, *Life and Times* (Hartford, 1884), 252.
3. *New Era Press*, Deep River, Conn., November 23, 1900.
4. Letters, U.G.R.R. Conn., 89.
5. Frank J. Mather, "An Address Delivered for the Benefit of the Library Association" (Deep River, 1914), 10, 21.
6. *Ibid.*, 20.
7. Mabel C. Holman, *Old Saybrook Stories* (Hartford, 1949), II, 292.
8. This narrative is adapted from *The Autobiography of James Lindsey Smith*, Norwich, Conn., 1881. Quotations are from that source.
9. J. T. Norton in *Freedom's Gift; or, Sentiments of the Free* (Hartford, 1840), 2–14.
10. C. Bancroft Gillespie and G. M. Curtiss, *A Century of Meriden* (Meriden, 1906), 253.
11. Letters, U.G.R.R. Conn., 122–123.

Chapter 4 THE CAPTIVES OF THE AMISTAD

1. The story of this affair is told in considerable detail in Simeon E. Baldwin, "The Captives of the *Amistad*," in *Papers of the New Haven Colony Historical Society*, IV

(New Haven, 1888), 331–370 (hereafter referred to as "Baldwin, *Amistad*"). The proceedings before the Supreme Court, including a statement of the basic facts and the decisions of the lower courts, are found in Stephen K. Williams, ed., *Reports of Cases Argued and Decided in the Supreme Court of the United States,* Book X (Newark, N. Y., 1883), 826–855 (hereafter referred to as "*Supreme Court Reports,* X").

2. C. L. Norton, "Cinquez—the Black Prince," *Farmington Magazine,* I, *4,* (February 1901), 3.
3. Charles Francis Adams, ed., *Memoirs of John Quincy Adams, Comprising Portions of His Diary from 1795 to 1848,* X (Philadelphia, 1876), 360. (Hereafter referred to as "Adams, *Memoirs,* X.")
4. *Supreme Court Reports,* X, 832–833.
5. Adams, *Memoirs,* X, 255.
6. Baldwin, *Amistad,* 332.
7. *Ibid.,* 332.
8. *Ibid.,* 333; *Supreme Court Reports,* X, 828.
9. Baldwin, *Amistad,* 333–334.
10. *Ibid.,* 334–335; *Supreme Court Reports,* X, 827–828.
11. Baldwin, *Amistad,* 335–336; *Supreme Court Reports,* X, 828–829.
12. Adams, *Memoirs,* X, 131–132.
13. Baldwin, *Amistad,* 337–339.
14. *Ibid.,* 338, 342; *Supreme Court Reports,* X, 828. Cf. R. Earl McClendon, "The Amistad Claims: Inconsistencies of Policy," *Political Science Quarterly,* XLVII. *3* (March 1933), 387.
15. Baldwin, *Amistad,* 339, 340.
16. *Ibid.,* 338, 341, 346–347; *Liberator,* June 12, 1840.
17. Baldwin, *Amistad,* 341.
18. *Ibid.,* 344.
19. Adams, *Memoirs,* X, 182.
20. Baldwin, *Amistad,* 345, 348.
21. *Ibid.,* 349.
22. Adams, *Memoirs,* X, 133–135.
23. Baldwin, *Amistad,* 346.
24. *Supreme Court Reports,* X, 829–833.
25. Baldwin, *Amistad,* 348.
26. *Supreme Court Reports,* X, 831.

27. *Ibid.,* 831.
28. Adams, *Memoirs,* X, 133 and *passim.*
29. *Ibid.,* 358, 360.
30. *The Emancipator,* March 25, 1841, quoted in Baldwin, *Amistad,* 354–355.
31. Adams, *Memoirs,* X, 399–401; Baldwin, *Amistad,* 355–356.
32. Adams, *Memoirs,* X, 429, 430.
33. *Ibid.,* 431, 435. (Because Adams did not deliver a transcript of his address to the reporter, *Supreme Court Reports* contains not even a summary of his argument.)
34. *Supreme Court Reports,* X, 855.
35. Baldwin, *Amistad,* 361, 365–369.
36. *Ibid.,* 362.
37. *Ibid.,* 363–364; John Hooker, *Some Reminiscences of a Long Life* (Hartford, 1899), 26.
38. Cf. Hooker, *op. cit., passim;* cf. also the account of the fugitive Charles, in Chapter 3 above.
39. Norton, *op. cit.,* 4; J. M. Brown, "The Mendi Indians Again," *Farmington Magazine,* II, *3* (July 1902), 18; anon., "Some Worthies of the Last Generation," *Farmington Magazine,* I, *10* (August 1901), 3, 4.
40. *Ibid.,* 3; Hooker, *op. cit.,* 26; Quincy Blakely, "Farmington, One of the Mother Towns of Connecticut" (Pamphlets of the Tercentenary Commission of the State of Connecticut, XXXVIII [New Haven, 1935]), 27.
41. *Ibid.,* 27–28; Norton, *op. cit.,* 4.
42. *Ibid.,* 2, 4, 5.
43. *Ibid.,* 5; Julius Gay, "Farmington Local History—The Canal" (Hartford, 1899), 17; Ellen S. Bartlett, "The Amistad Captives," *New England Magazine,* New Series, XXII (March–August, 1900), 87.
44. Brown, *op. cit.,* 18.
45. Baldwin, *Amistad,* 364; Hooker, *op. cit.,* 26.
46. Baldwin, *Amistad,* 368; Warner, *op. cit.,* 66–67, 68; Blakely, *op. cit.,* 27–28.

Chapter 5 A HOUSE DIVIDED

1. *Freedom's Gift,* 56.
2. William Goodell, *Slavery and Antislavery* (New York, 1855), 174.

3. *Ibid.,* 174–175.
4. J. G. Randall, *The Civil War and Reconstruction* (New York, 1953), 106.
5. Madeleine Rice, *American Catholic Opinion in the Slavery Controversy* (New York, 1944), 113–114.
6. Cf. Dumond, *op. cit.,* 197–203, 290–304.
7. J. H. Trumbull, *Memorial History of Hartford County,* II (Boston, 1886), 37; Carrol J. Noonan, *Nativism in Connecticut* (Washington, 1938), 138.
8. Steiner, *op. cit.,* 35.
9. Randall, *op. cit.,* 100.
10. Osborn, *op. cit.,* II, 61; *Charter Oak,* December 30, 1847.
11. Thomas P. Kettell, *Southern Wealth and Northern Profits* (New York, 1860), 110–111, 121.
12. Hooker, *op. cit.,* 342.
13. Grace P. Fuller, *An Introduction to the History of Connecticut as a Manufacturing State* (Smith College Studies in History, I [Northampton, 1915]), 42.
14. *Reminiscences of Austin P. Dunham* (Hartford, n.d.), 35.
15. Walter Hard, *The Connecticut* (New York, 1947), 226.
16. Aella Greene, *op. cit.,* March 25, 1900.
17. Lewis Ford, in *The Liberator,* March 26, 1852; Alice Stone Blackwell, *Lucy Stone: Pioneer of Woman's Rights* (Boston, 1930), 80.
18. Parker Pillsbury, in *The Liberator,* March 26, 1852.
19. Smith, *op. cit.,* 62–64.
20. T. M. D. Ward, *A Memento of the Memory of Departed Worth* (New Bedford, 1854), 22. "Proceedings of the Connecticut State Convention of Colored Men Held at New Haven on September 12th and 13th, 1849," *Yale Slavery Pamphlets, 52* (New Haven, 1849), 5–6.
21. *Middlesex Republican,* March 12, 1857.

Chapter 6 "THIS PRETENDED LAW WE CANNOT OBEY"

1. *Congressional Globe. Thirty-First Congress, First Session* (Washington, 1850), *Appendix,* 1601–1603; George W. Perkins, "Minority Report of a Committee of the General Association" (presented at Salisbury, June 1849), *Yale Slavery Pamphlets, 2* (New Haven, 1849), 9.

2. Siebert, *Underground Railroad,* 309–312; Randall, *op. cit.,* 168; Dumond, *op. cit.,* 307–308.
3. John W. Burgess, *The Middle Period, 1817–1858* (New York, 1904), 82–107, 291–294, 305; J. H. Smith, "The Mexican Recognition of Texas," *American Historical Review,* XVI (October 1910), 38.
4. Cf. John D. Hicks, *A Short History of American Democracy* (New York, 1949), 313.
5. *Ibid.,* 320.
6. Siebert, *op. cit.,* 23–24; Dumond, *op. cit.,* 308–309; Allen Johnson, "Constitutionality of the Fugitive Slave Acts," *Yale Slavery Pamphlets,* (New Haven, 1850), 166–167.
7. Burgess, *op. cit.,* 366.
8. *Ibid.,* 378–379.
9. Steiner, *op. cit.,* 35; Hicks, *op. cit.,* 218; Beman Collection (Yale University Library), 18. "The Proceeding of the Union Meeting Held at Brewster's Hall, October 24, 1850," *Yale Slavery Pamphlets, 52* (New Haven, 1851), 3–13.
10. Middletown *Constitution,* November 27, 1850.
11. J. Robert Lane, *A Political History of Connecticut During the Civil War* (Washington, 1941), 13.
12. Hartford *Courant,* October 19, 1850.
13. New Haven *Palladium,* October 26, 1850.
14. Quoted in *ibid.,* October 31, 1850.
15. *Loc. cit.*
16. New Haven *Daily Register,* November 16, 1850.
17. *Palladium,* November 6, 1850.
18. Norwich *Aurora,* October 9, 1850.
19. Elizabeth Curtis, *Letters and Journals* (Hartford, 1926), 224.
20. T. M. D. Ward, *op. cit.,* 20–21.
21. Middletown *Sentinel and Witness,* October 12, 1850.
22. George W. Perkins, "Conscience and the Constitution," *Yale Slavery Pamphlets, 2,* 8–9, 20–21.
23. Middletown *Sentinel and Witness,* October 29, 1850.
24. *Zion Herald and Wesleyan Journal,* December 11, 1850.
25. Middletown *Sentinel and Witness, loc. cit.*
26. Steiner, *op. cit.,* 35.
27. "Resolutions on Slavery," *Legislation of Connecticut* (House

Miscellaneous Documents No. 1, Thirty-first Congress, Second Session, I [Washington, 1850]).
28. Steiner, *op. cit.,* 36–37.
29. Dumond, *op. cit.,* 309.
30. Fred Landon, "The Negro Migration to Canada After the Passing of the Fugitive Slave Act," *Journal of Negro History,* V (January 1920), 22.
31. *The Liberator,* October 18, 1850.
32. *African Repository,* XXVII, *4* (April 1852), 117.
33. "Negro Population, 1790–1915," (Department of Commerce, Bureau of the Census [Washington, 1918]), 63.
34. Middletown *Constitution,* October 9, 1850.
35. Deep River *New Era Press,* November 23, 1900.
36. James Lindsey Smith, *op. cit.,* 90–91.
37. Siebert, *op. cit.,* 193–194.

Chapter 7 NEW HAVEN, GATEWAY FROM THE SEA

1. Aella Greene, *op. cit.,* March 11, 1900; cf. Chapter 2.
2. *Imprisonment of Coloured Seamen under the Law of South Carolina* (British and Foreign Antislavery Society, 1854 [?]), Yale Slavery Pamphlets, LXXIV, 3.
3. Secretary of State, State of Connecticut, *Register and Manual* (Hartford, 1960), 316–317.
4. Warner, *op. cit.,* 20–26.
5. *Ibid.,* 25.
6. *Ibid.,* 97; African Improvement Society of New Haven, *Annual Report,* III (1829), 11.
7. Letters, U.G.R.R. Conn., 1.
8. Foster W. Rice, "The Life of Nathaniel Jocelyn, 1796–1881" (publications of the Connecticut Historical Society, IV [Hartford, 1850–1881]), 219; Beman Collection, 20.
9. Letters, U.G.R.R. Conn., 95.
10. Samuel W. S. Dutton, *An Address at the Funeral of Hon. Roger Sherman Baldwin . . .* (New Haven, 1863), 8–10.
11. Amos Beman to W. S. Ward, January 13, 1851, Beman Collection, 3, 18.
12. *The Voice of the Fugitive,* May 18, 1851, Beman Collection, 19.
13. *Ibid.,* November 30, 1852, Beman Collection, 106.

14. Mary H. Mitchell, *op. cit.*, 308.
15. Aella Greene, *op. cit.*, April 1, 1900.
16. M. L. Beckwith Ewell, *One True Heart—Leaves from the Life of George Beckwith* (New Haven, 1880), 24–25.
17. Bernard Steiner, *A History of the Plantation of Menunkatuck and of the Original Town of Guilford, Connecticut* (Baltimore, 1879), 286.
18. Letters, U.G.R.R. Conn., 95.
19. *Southington News*, September 7, 1951.
20. Aella Greene, *loc. cit.*
21. *Ibid., loc. cit.*
22. *Ibid., loc. cit.*
23. Letters, U.G.R.R. Conn., 101; Mrs. Alfred H. Terry to H.T.S., March 25, 1957.
24. Letters, U.G.R.R. Conn., 67.
25. *A Memorial—Mrs. Minerva Lee Hart* (New Britain, 1885), 16–17.
26. Lillian H. Tryon, *The Story of New Britain, Connecticut* (Hartford, 1925), 72.
27. Middletown *Constitution*, November 11, 1857.

Chapter 8 WEST CONNECTICUT TRUNK LINES

1. Aella Greene, *op. cit.*, March 11, 1900; Charles W. Chesnutt, *Frederick Douglass* (Boston, 1899), 77–78.
2. Beman Collection, 73.
3. Mrs. C. A. B. Ray, *Sketch of the Life of Rev. Charles B. Ray* (New York, 1887), 33; Siebert, *Underground Railroad*, 35.
4. Ray, *op. cit.*, 46; Letters, U.G.R.R. Conn., 41; Aella Greene, *Reminiscent Sketches* (Florence, Mass., 1902), 159–160.
5. Letters, U.G.R.R. Conn., *loc. cit.*
6. Federal Writers' Project, *Connecticut* (American Guides Series [Boston, 1938]), 449; Mrs. Stowell Rounds to H.T.S., April 13, 1960.
7. Fairley, *op. cit.*, 223; *Commemorative Biographical Record of Middlesex County, Connecticut* (Chicago, 1903), 351; Letters, U.G.R.R. Conn., 35, 96; David Van Hoosear, quoted in Mrs. Stowell Rounds to H.T.S., April 13, 1960.
8. Letters, U.G.R.R. Conn., 22, 77; Mitchell, *op. cit.*, 423.

9. Cf. Eber M. Pettit, *Sketches in the History of the Underground Railroad* (New York, 1879), 34.
10. Charlotte B. Bennett, "Glimpses of Old New Milford History," *Two Centuries of New Milford, Connecticut* (New York, 1907), 20.
11. Osborn, *op. cit.*, 195–196; "Washington," *The Highways and Byways of Connecticut* (Hartford, 1947), Episode 102; Alice Stone Blackwell, *Lucy Stone: Pioneer of Women's Rights* (Boston, 1930), 32–33.
12. Louis A. Coolidge, *An Old-Fashioned Senator, Orville H. Platt of Connecticut* (New York, 1910), 5.
13. Samuel Orcutt, *History of Torrington, Connecticut* (Albany, 1878), 215.
14. Hartford *Times, Story of Connecticut, 1815–1935* (Hartford, 1936), 90.
15. Hartford *Courant,* February 6, 1962.
16. John Boyd, *Annals and Family Records of Winchester, Connecticut* (Hartford, 1871), 461.
17. *The Liberator,* March 26, 1852.
18. Mrs. Mabel A. Newell to H.T.S., April 8, 1960.
19. Theron W. Crissey, *History of Norfolk, Litchfield County* (Everett, Mass., 1900), 299.
20. Chard Powers Smith, *The Housatonic, Puritan River* (New York, 1946), 307. Cf. Siebert, *The Underground Railroad in Massachusetts* (Worcester, 1936), 4; cf. also Siebert, *Vermont's Anti-Slavery and Underground Railroad Record,* 67–89.

Chapter 9 EAST CONNECTICUT LOCALS

1. Irving H. Bartlett, *From Slave to Citizen. The Story of the Negro in Rhode Island* (Providence, 1954), 9, 18, 21, 45.
2. Elizabeth Buffum Chace, "Anti-Slavery Reminiscences" (pamphlet, Central Falls, R. I., 1891), 27–28.
3. Mary Agnes Best, *The Town that Saved a State, Westerly* (Westerly, R. I., 1943), 233.
4. Mrs. Harold S. Burr to H. T. S., July 4, 1958.
5. Mrs. Lillian L. Clarke to H. T. S., December 1958 (interview).
6. "Narrative of Mr. Nehemiah Caulkins of Waterford, Connecticut," Theodore Weld, comp., *American Slavery As It Is*

(New York, 1839), 11–17 (see Appendix). Cf. Dumond, *op. cit.*, 249–256.
7. *The Slave's Cry,* December 23, 1844.
8. Federal Writers' Project, *op. cit.*, 264.
9. Siebert, *The Underground Railroad in Massachusetts,* 11; Norwich *Aurora,* November 6, 1850.
10. Letters, U.G.R.R. Conn., 139.
11. Oliver Johnson, *William L. Garrison* (Boston, 1881), 128.
12. *Proceedings of the New England Anti-Slavery Convention, Held in Boston on the 27th, 28th and 29th of May, 1834* (Boston, 1834), 24.
13. Letters, U.G.R.R. Conn., 109, 113; Siebert. *op. cit.*, 11.
14. Letters, U.G.R.R. Conn., 113, 131, 139.
15. Cf. Chapter 2, note 22.
16. Letters, U.G.R.R. Conn., 143.
17. Federal Writers' Project, *op. cit.*, 535.
18. *Liberator,* April 4, 1851, and August 5, 1853.
19. Gilbert H. Barnes and Dwight L. Dumond, eds., *Letters of Theodore Weld and Sarah Grimke, 1822–1844* (New York, 1934), 523–524.
20. Secretary of State, State of Connecticut, *Register and Manual* (Hartford, 1960), 316.
21. Federal Writers' Project, *op. cit.*, 390.

Chapter 10 VALLEY LINE TO HARTFORD

1. "Old Lyme," *Highways and Byways,* Episode 79.
2. For details of Baldwin's activities, see Chapter 11.
3. Mrs. Harold S. Burr to H. T. S., July 4, 1958.
4. *Story of Connecticut,* 90.
5. Cedric L. Robinson to H. T. S., April 1, 1960; Mrs. Alice Weaver to H. T. S., February 10, 1962 (interview); Moodus, Conn., *Connecticut Valley Advertiser, Supplement,* September 21, 1900.
6. *The Old Chimney Stacks in East Haddam* (New York, 1887), 97–98.
7. *Liberator,* October 18, 1850; *Connecticut Valley Advertiser, loc. cit.* Among the ships built by the Goodspeeds were the schooners *Sidney C. Jones* and *Commodore,* in 1846; the schooner *Telegraph,* in 1847; and the ship *Hero,* in 1847.

8. Hannah H. Smith, "Diary, June–December, 1849" (Connecticut State Library), 80.
9. Siebert, *Underground Railroad,* 129.
10. Beaufort R. L. Newsom to H. T. S., March 30, 1960; cf. Chapters 3, 5, and 7.
11. See Chapter 11.
12. Letters, U.G.R.R. Conn., 99, 101.
13. *History of Middlesex County, Connecticut, with Biographical Sketches of Its Prominent Men* (New York, 1884), 357.
14. Henry Sill Baldwin and Mrs. Charles Perkins to H. T. S., April 3–16, 1957.
15. Baldwin, *Amistad,* 340.
16. Hooker, *op. cit., passim.*
17. Trumbull, *op. cit.,* 37; cf. *Speech of Mr. Gillette in the Senate of the United States, February 23, 1855* (Washington, 1855).
18. Trumbull, *loc. cit.*
19. Hooker, *op. cit.,* 171.
20. *Ibid., loc. cit*
21. Letters, U.G.R.R. Conn., 64–65.
22. *Liberator,* October 18, 1850; cf. Chapter 3.
23. Steiner, *History of Slavery in Connecticut,* 75–76.
24. James W. C. Pennington, *The Fugitive Blacksmith or Events in the History of J. W. C. Pennington* (London, 1849), *passim.*
25. Pennington, *op. cit., passim;* Hooker, *op. cit.,* 38–39.
26. Except as otherwise noted, this account of Pennington's manumission follows that given in Hooker, *op. cit.,* 37–41.
27. *Zion Herald and Wesleyan Journal,* October 23, 1850.

Chapter 11 MIDDLETOWN, A WAY STATION

1. *Connecticut Census, 1850* (Connecticut State Library), 214.
2. L. J. Greene, *op. cit.,* 33–34.
3. *Ibid.,* 92; *Centennial of Middletown, 1836–1936* (Middletown, 1936), 308–309.
4. L. J. Greene, *op. cit.,* 48.
5. *Ibid., loc. cit.*
6. *Ibid.,* 55.
7. *Freedom's Gift,* 58–60.

8. *Resolutions on the Death of William Lloyd Garrison; Middlesex County Gazette,* quoted in *The Liberator,* July 30, 1831.
9. Willbur Fisk, *op. cit.,* 15, 23.
10. *Fifth Census of the United States* (Washington, 1832), 28–29.
11. Louis R. Mehlinger, *op. cit.,* 286.
12. *History of Middlesex,* 143–144; Middletown *Constitution,* June 3, 1879; "Documents," *Journal of Negro History,* X (July 1925), 521.
13. Charles H. Wesley, "The Negro in the Organization of Abolition," *Phylon, the Atlanta University Review of Race and Culture,* XI (1941), 229.
14. "Thoughts on Colonization," *William Lloyd Garrison, 1805–1879; The Story of His Life Told by His Children* (Boston, 1885–1889), I, 340–341.
15. Carl F. Price, *Wesleyan's First Century* (Middletown, 1932), 50.
16. Beman Collection, 87.
17. Price, *loc. cit.*
18. *History of Middlesex,* 161; Hartford *Courant,* April 6, 1887.
19. *Ibid., loc. cit.*
20. *Resolutions on the Death of William Lloyd Garrison.*
21. Baldwin Collection.
22. Willbur Fisk to the Reverend Ignatius Few, August 1838, "Letters of Willbur Fisk," Olin Library, Wesleyan University.
23. Baldwin Collection.
24. *Ibid.*
25. Henry Sill Baldwin and Mrs. Charles Perkins to H. T. S., April 3–16, 1957; Benjamin L. Douglas to H. T. S., November 8, 1961.
26. Official records, Health Department, City of Middletown; *Dictionary of American Biography,* (New York, 1889), VI, 614.
27. George Thompson, *Prison Life and Reflections or a Narrative of the Arrest, Trial, Conviction . . .* (Oberlin, 1847), 1; Henry Wilson, *Rise and Fall of the Slave Power in America* (Boston, 1876), II, 69–73; Siebert, *Underground Railroad,* 155–156.
28. Thompson, *op. cit.,* 27.

29. Wilson, *op. cit.*, 72; Siebert, *op. cit.*, 156.
30. *Charter Oak,* June 8, 1846.
31. *History of Middlesex,* 163–164.
32. *Ibid., loc. cit.; Resolutions on the Death of William Lloyd Garrison;* Benjamin L. Douglas to H. T. S., November 8, 1961.
33. Letters, U.G.R.R. Conn., 35.

Chapter 12 FARMINGTON, THE GRAND CENTRAL STATION

1. Julius Gay, "Schools and Schoolmasters in Farmington in the Olden Time" (pamphlet, Hartford, 1892), 21.
2. Mabel S. Hurlburt, *Farmington Town Clerks and Their Times, 1645–1940* (Hartford, 1945), 192.
3. *Connecticut Census, 1790, 1800, and 1820 (Hartford County),* Connecticut State Library, Hartford.
4. Julius Gay, "Farmington Local History—the Canal" (pamphlet, Hartford, 1899), *passim.*
5. "Farmington and its Child Plainville," *Farmington Tercentenary Celebration, 1640–1940* (Farmington, 1940), 53–54.
6. Hurlburt, *op. cit.*, 192.
7. Hooker, *op. cit.*, 22.
8. *Ibid., loc. cit.*
9. *Ibid.*, 339–341.
10. *Ibid.*, 22–23, 339, 342.
11. Cf. Chapters 4, 10.
12. Blakely, *op. cit.*, 28.
13. Cf. Chapter 3.
14. C. L. Norton, *op. cit.*, 5.
15. Eleanor H. Johnson, "Farmington and the Underground Railway," *Farmington Magazine,* I, 11 (September 1901), 6–7.
16. Hooker, *op. cit.*, 339–340; Florence S. M. Crofut, *Guide to the History and Historic Sites of Connecticut* (New Haven, 1937), 207.
17. Johnson, *op. cit.*, 6.
18. Hooker, *op. cit.*, 340.
19. *Ibid., loc. cit.*
20. Johnson, *op. cit.*, 7.
21. *Ibid., loc. cit.*
22. *Ibid.*, 6–7.

23. Letters, U.G.R.R. Conn., 51, 64.
24. Aella Greene, *op. cit.*, April 1, 1900.
25. Morris, *op. cit.*, 215; Mason A. Green, *Springfield 1636–1886, History of Town and City* . . . (Springfield, 1888), 506.
26. Siebert, *Underground Railroad*, 73–75.
27. Aella Greene, *op. cit.*, August 12, 1900.
28. Joseph Marsh, "The Underground Railway," *The History of Florence, Massachusetts* (Florence, 1895), 165–167.
29. Siebert, *Vermont's Anti-Slavery and Underground Railroad Record*, 90–102.

Chapter 13 THE ROAD IN FULL SWING

1. Hicks, *op. cit.*, 204–205; Randall, *op. cit.*, 126–127.
2. *Ibid.*, 128–135; Samuel Eliot Morison and Henry Steele Commager, *The Growth of the American Republic* (New York, 1930), 491–494.
3. Ralph Volney Harlow, "The Rise and Fall of the Kansas Aid Movement," *American Historical Review*, XLI (October 1935), 1–7.
4. Mitchell, *op. cit.*, 310–311.
5. Randall, *loc. cit.;* Lane, *op. cit.*, 39–41, 43.
6. Randall, *op. cit.*, 148–156; Hartford *Courant*, March 14, 1857. For a detailed account of the case, see Vincent C. Hopkins, *Dred Scott's Case*, New York, 1951.
7. James Mars, *op. cit.*, 34–36; Helen T. Catterall, "Judicial Cases Concerning American Slavery and the Negro," *Cases from the Courts of New England, the Middle States, and the District of Columbia*, IV (Washington, 1936), 433–436.
8. *Public Acts, Passed by the General Assembly of the State of Connecticut, May Session, 1857* (Hartford, 1857), 12; Hartford *Courant*, June 13, 1857.
9. *Middlesex Republican*, March 12, 1857.
10. Middletown *Constitution*, March 18, 1857.
11. Hurlburt, *op. cit.*, 192.
12. New Haven *Journal Courier*, May 9, 1911; Edward E. Atwater, *History of the City of New Haven* (New York, 1887), 251–252.

13. "The Fugitive Slave Law and its Victims" (*Antislavery Tracts,* No. 15 [New York, 1861]), 45–46.
14. Best, *op. cit.,* 232.
15. Charles P. Bush, "The Fugitive Slave Law (A Sermon Preached in the Fourth Congregational Church, Norwich, Connecticut)" (Norwich, 1854), 1–4.
16. Leverett Griggs, "Fugitives from Slavery (A Discourse Delivered in Bristol, Connecticut, on Fast Day)" (Hartford, 1857), 3.
17. R. P. Stanton, "Slavery Viewed in the Light of the Golden Rule (A Discourse Delivered in the Fourth Congregational Church, Norwich, Connecticut)" (Norwich, 1860), 9–10.
18. *Annual Report of the American Anti-Slavery Society, May 1, 1859* (New York, 1860), 85.
19. *Middlesex Republican,* March 12, 1857.
20. New Haven *Columbian Weekly Register,* August 20, 1862.
21. Atwater, *op. cit.,* 251–252; Lane, *op. cit.,* 256; *Resolutions on the Death of William Lloyd Garrison.*
22. Bruce Catton, *America Goes to War* (Middletown, 1958), 23–25; Dumond, *op. cit.,* 370–372.
23. *Ibid., loc. cit.*
24. *Ibid., loc. cit.;* Catton, *op. cit.,* 25–27; Lane, *op. cit.,* 210.
25. Hartford *Courant,* September 24, 1862.
26. Waterbury *American,* September 26, 1862.
27. Middletown *Sentinel and Witness,* April 30, 1862.
28. Norwich *Aurora,* January 3, 1863.
29. New Haven *Columbian Weekly Register,* August 20, 1862.
30. James Lindsey Smith, *op. cit.,* 82.

BIBLIOGRAPHY

BIBLIOGRAPHY

PRIMARY SOURCES

Diaries and Personal Recollections:

Adams, John Quincy. *Memoirs of John Quincy Adams, Comprising Portions of his Diary from 1795 to 1848.* Ed. Charles Francis Adams. Philadelphia, 1876.

Breckenridge, Frances A. *Recollections of a New England Town.* Meriden, 1899.

Chace, Elizabeth Buffum. "Anti-Slavery Reminiscences." Central Falls, R. I., 1891.

Curtis, Elizabeth. *Letters and Journals.* Hartford, 1926

Douglass, Frederick. *Life and Times.* Hartford, 1884.

Dunham, Austin C. *Reminiscences of Austin C. Dunham.* Hartford, n.d.

Greene, Aella. *Reminiscent Sketches.* Florence, Mass., 1902.

Grimes, William. *The Life of the Runaway Slave, Brought Down to the Present Time, Written by Himself.* New Haven, 1855.

Hooker, John. *Some Reminiscences of a Long Life, with a Few Articles on Moral and Social Subjects of Present Interest.* Hartford, 1899.

Mars, James. *A Slave Born and Sold in Connecticut, Written by Himself.* Hartford, 1865.

May, Samuel J. *Some Recollections of Our Anti-Slavery Conflict.* Boston, 1869.

Pennington, James W. C. *The Fugitive Blacksmith or Events in the History of J. W. C. Pennington.* London, 1849.

Smith, Hannah. Diary, 1844–1850, 7 parts. Connecticut State Library, Hartford.

Smith, James Lindsey. *Autobiography of James L. Smith, Including Reminiscences of Slave Life, Recollections of the War, Education of Freedmen, Causes of the Exodus, etc.* Norwich, 1881.

Thompson, George. *Prison Life and Reflections or a Narrative of the Arrest, Trial, Conviction. . . .* Oberlin, 1847.

Weld, Theodore, and Sarah Grimke. *Letters of Theodore Weld and Sarah Grimke, 1822–1844.* Ed. Gilbert H. Barnes and Dwight Lowell Dumond. New York, 1934.

Williams, Austin. Diary, 1829–1835. Connecticut Historical Society, Hartford.

Collections:

Baldwin Collection. Letters, newspaper clippings, etc., Middlesex County Historical Society, Middletown.

Beman Collection. Letters, newspaper clippings, etc., in Johnson Wells Collection, Yale University Library.

Fisk, Willbur. Letters. Olin Library, Wesleyan University.

Siebert Collection. Microfilm letters and other materials, collected by Professor Wilbur H. Siebert, regarding the Underground Railroad in Connecticut. The originals are in the Ohio State University Library, Columbus.

Letters and Interviews:

Henry Sill Baldwin and Mrs. Charles Perkins to H.T.S., April 3–16, 1957. (Part of this letter was dictated by Mr. Baldwin on the earlier date; it was completed on the later date by Mrs. Perkins.)

Mrs. Harold S. Burr to H.T.S., April 4, 1958.

Mrs. Lillian L. Clarke to H.T.S., December 1958 (interview).

Benjamin L. Douglas to H.T.S., November 8, 1961.

Mrs. Mabel A. Newell to H.T.S., April 8, 1960.

Beaufort R. L. Newsom to H.T.S., March 30, 1960.

Cedric L. Robinson to H.T.S., April 1, 1960.

Mrs. Stowell Rounds to H.T.S., April 13, 1960.
Mrs. Alfred H. Terry to H.T.S., March 25, 1957.
Mrs. Alice Weaver to H.T.S., February 10, 1962 (interview).

Miscellaneous Unpublished Materials:

Bissell, F. C. "The Reverend Samuel Peters, of Hebron, Connecticut. . . ." Typescript, Connecticut State Library.

Holman, Mabel C. "Old Saybrook Stories." Typescript, Connecticut State Library.

Prudden, Lillian E. "A Paper . . . at the Fortnightly Club of New Haven, November 16, 1949." Typescript, Connecticut State Library.

Newspapers and Periodicals:

Deep River *New Era Press*, November 23, 1900.

Hartford *Courant*, October 19, 1850; March 14, June 13, 1857; September 24, 1862; April 6, 8, 1887; February 6, 1962.

Middletown *Constitution*, October 9, November 27, 1850; March 18, November 11, 1857; June 3, 1879.

Middletown *Sentinel and Witness*, October 12, 29, 1850; April 30, 1862.

Middlesex Republican, March 12, 1857.

Moodus *Connecticut Valley Advertiser*, Supplement, September 21, 1900.

New Haven *Columbian Weekly Register*, June 23, 1838; August 20, 1862.

New Haven *Daily Register*, November 16, 1850.

New Haven *Journal Courier*, May 9, 1911.

New Haven *Palladium*, October 26, 1850.

New London *Gazette*, December 2, 1768.

Norwich *Aurora*, October 9, November 6, 1850; January 3, 1863.

Southington *News*, September 7, 1951.

Springfield *Daily Republican*, March 11, 25, April 1, August 12, 1900.

Waterbury *American*, September 26, 1862.

Zion Herald and Wesleyan Journal, October 23, December 11, 1850.

Abolitionist Publications:

African Improvement Society of New Haven. Annual Report, III, 1829.

The African Repository, and Colonial Journal, V, XXIII, XXVIII.

American Anti-Slavery Society. Annual Reports, 1837, 1859.

Bush, Charles P. "The Fugitive Slave Law (A Sermon Preached in the Fourth Congregational Church, Norwich, Connecticut, June 25, 1854.)" Norwich, 1854.

Charter Oak, May 1839; January 9, 1845; June 8, 1846; December 30, 1847.

Freedom's Gift: or, Sentiments of the Free. Hartford, 1840.

"The Fugitive Slave Law and Its Victims." Antislavery Tracts No. 15. New York, 1861.

Gillette, Francis. "Speech of Mr. Gillette in the Senate of the United States, February 23, 1855." Washington, 1855.

Griggs, Leverett. "Fugitives from Slavery (A Discourse Delivered in Bristol, Connecticut, on Fast Day)." Hartford, 1857.

Johnson, Allen. "Constitutionality of the Fugitive Slave Acts." Yale Slavery Pamphlets. New Haven, 1850.

The Liberator, January 1, July 30, 1831; October 18, 1850; April 4, 1851; March 26, 1852; August 5, 1853.

New England Anti-Slavery Society. First Report of the Board of Managers. Boston, 1833.

Perkins, George W. "Conscience and the Constitution." Yale Slavery Pamphlets. New Haven, 1849.

———. "Minority Report of a Committee of the General Association." Yale Slavery Pamphlets. New Haven, 1849.

"Proceedings of the New England Anti-Slavery Convention, Held at Boston on the 27th, 28th and 29th of May, 1834." Boston, 1834.

The Slave's Cry, December 23, 1844.

Stanton, R. P. "Slavery Viewed in the Light of the Golden Rule (A Discourse Delivered in the Fourth Congregational Church, Norwich, Connecticut, December 19, 1860)." Norwich, 1860.

Weld, Theodore, comp. *American Slavery As It Is: Testimony of a Thousand Witnesses.* New York, 1839.

Government Publications and Sources:

Connecticut, State of. Census, 1850; Census, Hartford County, 1790, 1800, 1820. Connecticut State Library.

———. General Assembly. *The Public Laws of the State of Connecticut,* Hartford, 1835; *Public Acts . . . May Session, 1857,* Hartford, 1857.

———. Secretary of State. *Register and Manual.* Hartford, 1960.

Middletown, City of. Health Department. Official Records.

United States. Bureau of the Census. *Fifth Census of the United States,* Washington, 1832; *Negro Population, 1790–1915,* Washington, 1918.

———. *Congressional Globe,* Thirty-first Congress, First Session. Washington, 1850.

———. "Resolutions on Slavery, Legislature of Connecticut." House Miscellaneous Documents, No. 1. Thirty-first Congress, Second Session, I. Washington, 1850.

SECONDARY SOURCES

Books:

Atwater, Edward E. *History of the City of New Haven.* New York, 1887.

Bacon, Leonard W. *Anti-Slavery Before Garrison.* New Haven, 1903.

Bailey, James H. *History of Danbury, Connecticut.* New York, 1896.

Bartlett, Irving H. *From Slave to Citizen. The Story of the Negro in Rhode Island.* Providence, 1954.

Best, Mary Agnes. *The Town that Saved a State, Westerly.* Westerly, 1943.

Bissell, Richard M., Jr. *Historical Sketch of Farmington.* Hartford, n.d.

Blackwell, Alice Stone. *Lucy Stone: Pioneer of Women's Rights.* Boston, 1930.

Boyd, John. *Annals and Family Records of Winchester, Connecticut.* Hartford, 1871.

Breyfogle, William. *Make Free; The Story of the Underground Railroad.* New York, 1958.

Buckmaster, Henrietta. *Flight to Freedom; The Story of the Underground Railroad.* New York, 1958.

———. *Let My People Go; The Story of the Underground Railroad and the Growth of the Abolition Movement.* New York, 1941.

Burgess, John W. *The Middle Period, 1817–1858.* New York, 1904.

Cash, W. J. *The Mind of the South.* New York, 1941.

Catton, Bruce. *America Goes to War.* Middletown, 1958.

Caulkins, Frances N. *History of Norwich, Connecticut.* Hartford, 1866.

Centennial of Middletown, 1836–1936. Middletown, 1936.

Chesnutt, Charles W. *Frederick Douglass.* Boston, 1899.

Commemorative Biographical Record of Middlesex County, Connecticut. Chicago, 1903.

Coolidge, Louis A. *An Old-Fashioned Senator. Orville H. Platt of Connecticut.* New York, 1910.

Crissey, Theron Wilmot, comp. *History of Norfolk, Litchfield County, Connecticut.* Everett, Mass., 1900.

Crofut, Florence S. Marcy. *Guide to the History and the Historic Sites of Connecticut.* New Haven, 1937.

Davis, Charles Henry Stanley. *History of Wallingford Connecticut from its Settlement in 1670 to the Present Time, Including Meriden and Cheshire.* Meriden, 1870.

Dictionary of American Biography, VI. New York, 1889.

Dumond, Dwight Lowell. *Antislavery: The Crusade for Freedom in America.* Ann Arbor, 1961.

Ewell, M. L. Beckwith. *One True Heart—Leaves from the Life of George Beckwith.* New Haven, 1880.

Federal Writers' Project. *Connecticut.* American Guides Series. Boston, 1938.

Fowler, William Chauncey. *The Historical Status of the Negro in Connecticut.* New Haven, 1875.

Fox, Early L. *The American Colonization Society, 1817–1840.* Johns Hopkins University Studies, XXXVII. Baltimore, 1919.

Fuller, Grace P. *An Introduction to the History of Connecticut as a Manufacturing State.* Smith College Studies in History, I. Northampton, 1915.

Gillespie, C. Bancroft, and G. M. Curtiss. *A Century of Meriden.* Meriden, 1906.

Goodell, William. *Slavery and Antislavery.* New York, 1855.

Green, Mason A. *Springfield 1636–1886, History of Town and City.* Springfield, 1888.

Greene, Lorenzo Johnston. *The Negro in Colonial New England, 1620–1776.* New York, 1942.

Hard, Walter. *The Connecticut.* New York, 1947.

Henries, A. Doris Banks. *The Liberian Nation.* New York, 1954.

Hicks, John D. *A Short History of American Democracy.* New York, 1949.

The Highways and Byways of Connecticut. Hartford, 1947.

History of Middlesex County, Connecticut, with Biographical Sketches of its Prominent Men. New York, 1884.

Hopkins, Vincent C. *Dred Scott's Case.* New York, 1951.

Hurlburt, Mabel S. *Farmington Town Clerks and Their Times, 1645–1940.* Hartford, 1945.

Jay, William. *An Inquiry into the Character and Tendency of the American Colonization and American Anti-Slavery Societies.* New York, 1835.

Johnson, Oliver. *William Lloyd Garrison.* Boston, 1881.

Kettell, Thomas P. *Southern Wealth and Northern Profits.* New York, 1860.

Lane, J. Robert. *A Political History of Connecticut During the Civil War*. Washington, 1941.

Larned, Ellen D. *History of Windham County, Connecticut*. Worcester, 1880.

Macy, Jesse. *The Anti-Slavery Crusade. A Chronicle of the Gathering Storm*. New Haven, 1921.

Mills, Lewis Sprague. *The Story of Connecticut*. New York, 1953.

Mitchell, Mary H. *History of New Haven County, Connecticut*. Chicago and Boston, 1930.

Morison, Samuel Eliot, and Henry Steele Commager. *The Growth of the American Republic*. New York, 1930.

Morse, Jarvis Means. *A Neglected Period in Connecticut's History, 1818–1850*. New Haven, 1933.

Noonan, Carrol J. *Nativism in Connecticut*. Washington, 1938.

Orcutt, Samuel. *History of Torrington, Connecticut*. Albany, 1878.

Osborn, Norris Galpin, ed. *History of Connecticut in Monographic Form*, I–V. New York, 1925.

Pettit, Eber M. *Sketches in the History of the Underground Railroad, Comprising Many Thrilling Incidents of the Escape of Fugitives from Slavery, and the Perils of Those Who Aided Them*. New York, 1879.

Price, Carl F. *Wesleyan's First Century*. Middletown, 1932.

Randall, J. G. *The Civil War and Reconstruction*. New York, 1953.

Ray, Mrs. Charles A. B. *Sketch of the Life of Reverend Charles B. Ray*. New York, 1887.

Rice, Madeleine. *American Catholic Opinion in the Slavery Controversy*. New York, 1944.

Siebert, Wilbur H. *The Underground Railroad from Slavery to Freedom*. New York, 1898.

———. *The Underground Railroad in Massachusetts*. Worcester, 1936.

———. *Vermont's Anti-Slavery and Underground Railroad Record*. Columbus, 1937.

Smith, Chard Powers. *The Housatonic, Puritan River.* New York, 1946.

Smith, J. E. A. *The History of Pittsfield, Massachusetts.* Springfield, 1876.

Smith, J. Eugene. *One Hundred Years of Hartford's* Courant. New Haven, 1949.

Steiner, Bernard C. *A History of the Plantation of Menunkatuck and of the Original Town of Guilford, Connecticut.* Baltimore, 1879.

———. *History of Slavery in Connecticut.* Johns Hopkins University Studies, IX, X, XI. Baltimore, 1893.

Sterry, Iveagh H., and William H. Garrigus. *They Found a Way: Connecticut's Restless People.* Brattleboro, 1938.

Story of Connecticut. Hartford, 1936.

Trumbull, J. H. *Memorial History of Hartford County.* Boston, 1886.

Tryon, Lillian H. *The Story of New Britain, Connecticut.* Hartford, 1925.

Turner, Lorenzo D. *Antislavery Sentiment in American Literature Prior to 1865.* Washington, 1929.

Ward, T. M. D. *A Memento for the Memory of Departed Worth.* New Bedford, 1854.

Warner, Robert Austin. *New Haven Negroes; A Social Study.* New Haven, 1940.

Wendover, Samuel H., ed. *150 Years of Meriden.* Meriden, 1956.

White, Alain C. *The History of the Town of Litchfield, Connecticut, 1720–1920.* Litchfield, 1920.

William Lloyd Garrison, 1805–1879: The Story of his Life Told by his Children. Boston, 1885–1889.

Williams, Stephen K., ed. *Reports of Cases Argued and Decided in the Supreme Court of the United States,* Book X. Newark, N. Y., 1883.

Wilson, Henry. *History of the Rise and Fall of the Slave Power in America,* I, II. Boston, 1875.

Pamphlets:

Blakely, Quincy. "Farmington, One of the Mother Towns of Connecticut." Pamphlets of the Tercentenary Commission of the State of Connecticut, XXXVIII. New Haven, 1935.

Day, Clive. "The Rise of Manufacturing in Connecticut." Pamphlets of the Tercentenary Commision of the State of Connecticut, XLIV. New Haven, 1935.

Dutton, Samuel W. S. "An Address at the Funeral of the Honorable Roger Sherman Baldwin." New Haven, 1863.

Fisk, Willbur. "Substance of an Address Delivered Before the Colonization Society at the Annual Meeting, July 4, 1835." Middletown, 1835.

Gay, Julius. "Farmington Local History—the Canal." Hartford, 1899.

———. "Schools and Schoolmasters in Farmington in the Olden Time." Hartford, 1892.

Mather, Frank J. "An Address Delivered for the Benefit of the Library Association." Deep River, 1914.

"A Memorial—Mrs. Minerva Lee Hart." New Britain, 1885.

Savage, W. Sherman. "The Controversy over the Distribution of Abolitionist Literature, 1830–1860." Washington, 1938.

Articles:

Baldwin, Simeon E. "The Captives of the *Amistad.*" *Papers of the New Haven Colony Historical Society*, IV. New Haven, 1888.

Bennett, Charlotte B. "Glimpses of Old New Milford History." *Two Centuries of New Milford, Connecticut.* New York, 1907.

Bronson, E. B. "Notes on Connecticut as a Slave State." *Journal of Negro History*, II, January 1917.

Brown, J. M. "The Mendi Indians Again." *Farmington Magazine*, II, 3, July 1902.

Catterall, Helen T. "Judicial Cases Concerning American Slavery and the Negro." *Cases from the Courts of New*

England, the Middle States, and the District of Columbia, IV. Washington, 1936.

Coley, James E. "Slavery in Connecticut." *Magazine of American History*, XXV, January–June, 1891.

"Documents." *Journal of Negro History*, X, July 1925.

Fairley, Charlotte Case. "A History of New Canaan, 1801–1901." *Readings in New Canaan History*. New Canaan, 1941.

"Farmington and its Child Plainville." *Farmington Tercentenary Celebration, 1640–1940*. Farmington, 1940.

Greene, Aella. "The Underground Railroad and Those Who Managed It." Springfield *Republican*, March 11, 25, April 1, August 12, 1900.

Harlow, Ralph Volney. "The Rise and Fall of the Kansas Aid Movement." *American Historical Review*, XLI, October 1935.

Johnson, Eleanor H. "Farmington and the Underground Railway." *Farmington Magazine*, I, *11*, September 1901.

Landon, Fred. "The Negro Migration to Canada After the Passing of the Fugitive Slave Act." *Journal of Negro History*, V, January 1920.

Marsh, Joseph. "The Underground Railway." *The History of Florence, Massachusetts*. Florence, 1895.

Mehlinger, Louis R. "The Attitude of the Free Negro Toward African Colonization." *Journal of Negro History*, I, 1916.

Mitchell, Mary H. "Slavery in Connecticut and Especially in New Haven." *Papers of the New Haven Colony Historical Society*, X. New Haven, 1951.

Morris, Henry. "Slavery in the Connecticut Valley." *Papers and Proceedings of the Connecticut Valley Historical Society*. Springfield, 1881.

Norton, Charles Ledyard. "Cinquez—the Black Prince." *Farmington Magazine*, I, *4*, February 1901.

"Resolutions on the Death of William Lloyd Garrison (Adopted by the Middletown Mental Improvement Society)." Middletown *Constitution*, June 3, 1879.

Rice, Foster W. "The Life of Nathaniel Jocelyn, 1796–1881." *Publications of the Connecticut Historical Society,* IV. Hartford, 1850–1881.

"Slavery in Connecticut." *Magazine of American History,* XV, January–June, 1886.

Smith, J. H. "The Mexican Recognition of Texas." *American Historical Review,* XVI, October 1910.

Smith, Martin H. "Old Slave Days in Connecticut, Romance and Tragedy of Negro Serfdom." *Connecticut Magazine,* X, 1906.

"Some Worthies of the Last Generation." *Farmington Magazine,* II, *3,* August 1901.

Wesley, Charles H. "The Negro in the Organization of Abolition." *Phylon, the Atlanta University Review of Race and Culture,* XI, 1941.

INDEX

INDEX